AF322657

Mastering Membership

The Guide to Loyalty, Retention, and Transformational Subscription Growth

Matt Epstein

ISBN Hardback: 979-8-234-03476-2

Published by **Member Growth**
www.membergrowth.com
For information, inquiries, or permissions, please visit the publisher's website.

Note:

Company names and examples are used for illustrative purposes only and do not imply endorsement.
This book reflects the author's professional experience and perspectives. Results will vary by business, industry, and execution. The strategies discussed are for educational purposes and should be evaluated in the context of each organization's unique circumstances.

Dedication

To my kids: the reason I keep moving.

To my colleagues: the ones who showed me how.

Table of Contents

Preamble

Who is the person on the cover?

That's me… or it's you. Or it's your customer. Better yet, it's any of us walking into something bigger than ourselves.

We all serve someone: a community, a team, a family, a board, a mission. This book is about unlocking something greater—not just for your business, but for the people you serve.

I've stripped out the fluff and focused on what actually works: actionable frameworks, real-world stories, and hard-won lessons from building membership businesses at some of the world's most recognizable brands.

When you build membership the right way, you don't just grow revenue— you earn trust, change behavior, and turn customers into lifelong advocates. That's what this book is about: building something people never want to leave.

Introduction

I used to think anything could be solved with a spreadsheet.

Strategy, growth, relationships—even rest—were problems to be analyzed, mapped, and optimized. Over time, I learned the hard way that not everything can be hacked or hurried. Some things, like trust, transformation, or a good night's sleep, only arrive when you slow down and surrender to the flow.

That search for stillness led me to a wellness retreat in the desert, where my journey began by walking a labyrinth, a winding path designed not to confuse, but to calm. Step by step, it invites you to be present, to listen, and to find clarity in the quiet. As I walked that slow, deliberate path, something clicked.

I saw the connection between that meditative walk and what I do every day: build and grow membership businesses.

Membership, I realized, is its own kind of labyrinth—carefully crafted not just to engage but to lead people to something indispensable. It doesn't pull them in with force, but with meaning. At its best, it offers a journey: from curiosity to connection, from transaction to transformation.

And like a true labyrinth, no two paths are the same. One member arrives through a trial offer. Another wanders in through a referral. Some enter cautiously; others rush in and are surprised, even delighted, by what they find. But when the experience is designed with care, it can guide them all to the same place: loyalty, advocacy, and real connection.

Once inside, the journey becomes personal. Take Amazon Prime: what starts as a desire for free two-day shipping can evolve into something completely different for each person—as they discover other benefits like Prime Video, Same-Day Delivery, or Subscribe & Save. The membership adapts, becoming essential in a way that feels unique. And even cancellation doesn't have to be the end. The best programs treat it not as failure, but as another turn in the labyrinth. With the right message, a well-timed offer, or a new benefit, a former member can return more engaged than ever.

Mastering the Labyrinth Is the Key to Growth

Understanding the full member journey—how someone moves from first touchpoint to lasting loyalty—usually takes years of hard-earned experience. But it doesn't have to. The fastest path forward is learning from leaders who have already walked it, those who know how to balance acquisition and retention, attract the right members, and design experiences that turn early engagement into long-term advocacy.

That's where this book comes in. My goal is to help you navigate the complexity and opportunity of recurring revenue and membership models, showing you exactly where to focus for the greatest impact. I will guide you through the principles, patterns, and decisions that turn memberships into meaningful, lasting relationships.

But this isn't just about building better businesses. It's about mastering the craft of ongoing relationships. When you know how to guide, serve, and surprise your members at every stage, you create something rare: an experience so compelling that leaving feels unthinkable, and each step forward unlocks something new.

Whether you are a C-suite executive rethinking a mature service, a product leader scaling a membership program, or a founder building a brand rooted in connection, this book is your roadmap from potential to performance.

You are not just navigating the labyrinth. You are designing it.

How Membership Builds Closer Relationships

For most of modern commerce, relationships ended at checkout. You bought a book, a flight, a pair of shoes—and that was it. Every year started at zero, with businesses scrambling to bring back the same customers they'd already earned.

Membership *flips* that model.

Instead of chasing repeat purchases, businesses build enduring relationships that generate predictable revenue and deliver continuous value. The result isn't just convenience—it's a fundamentally different way to grow.

At its best, membership taps into something deeper than perks or discounts. It speaks to human psychology—the need for belonging, identity, and transformation. A fitness membership isn't about access to a gym; it's about becoming stronger, healthier, and more confident. A professional association isn't just about networking; it's about accelerating a career and feeling part of something bigger.

And for businesses, the impact is just as profound: recurring revenue, richer data, higher lifetime value, and alignment around long-term customer success. *Put simply, membership doesn't just make consumption easier for customers—it makes companies better businesses.*

The Change is Already Happening

Recurring revenue models—once reserved for essentials like cable TV, mobile phone plans, or even health insurance premiums and home mortgages—now shape everything from AI to fitness, media to artisanal coffee. Companies aren't just selling products anymore; they're building relationships.

What's most striking isn't just how many industries are embracing membership—it's how each one is experimenting with new ways to create and sustain value over time. Software has shifted from one-time purchases to ongoing relationships. Media is increasingly built around bundles and tiers. Nonprofits are prioritizing membership over ticket sales. Even physical products are being reimagined with recurring plans and premium feature subscriptions.

This shift from transactions to membership is one of the most significant changes in how value is created and sustained. And yet, for something so central to the future of business, there's still no widely accepted playbook for how to do it well. Too often, companies rely on trial and error or chase silver-bullet solutions that promise overnight success. I've seen this firsthand, even at companies you'd expect to have mastered the model.

The companies that succeed understand this: it's not about any one feature, benefit, or campaign. It's about a system, a set of interactions that work together to earn trust, deepen engagement, and sustain value over time. Membership is not a marketing tactic or a pricing scheme. It's an operating model that demands structure, discipline, and continuous improvement.

Every touchpoint matters: the ease of signup, the clarity of communication, the emotional impact of the first experience, the rhythm of new features, the tone of customer support. When all of it works together, the result is more than just retention—it's transformation.

There's no shortcut to building a great membership business.

But there *is* a way through the labyrinth.

And when you learn to navigate it with intention, you create something powerful: a journey that turns initial interest into deep, enduring loyalty— guiding members forward, again and again.

The Goal of This Book

This book is your guide to building a membership business that's not just profitable, it's built to endure. Whether you're launching from scratch or scaling an established program, you'll learn how to design a membership that attracts, engages, and retains for the long run.

Introduction: A New Lens for Membership

See the model differently—and understand why that mindset shift unlocks new opportunities for sustainable growth.

Part 1: Mastering the Member Journey—Attracting Members

Design irresistible benefits, tell the right story, and convert interest into signups with a strategy rooted in real customer insight.

Part 2: Mastering the Member Journey—Building the Growth Foundation

Create a complete retention engine: onboarding, engagement, churn prevention, winback[1], referrals, gifting, and monetization—everything you need to keep members for life.

Part 3: Structure, Accountability, and Action

Build the team, systems, and habits that make growth not just possible—but repeatable and scalable.

---

[1] **Winback:** The process of re-engaging former members who have canceled or lapsed, typically through targeted outreach, improved offers, or reminders of new value. Effective winback strategies focus on understanding why a member left and addressing that reason directly—turning past customers into future loyalists.

While every business will apply these principles in its own way, the frameworks in this book are designed to give you a real head start. Mastering a journey where each step deepens the relationship, rather than ending it, is what separates transactional businesses from transformational ones.

When experiences evolve with your members, growth becomes more durable than any single tactic or trend.

Think of this book as both a guide and a toolkit, but more than that, as a challenge to see membership differently. When you master the art of turning customers into members, you don't just grow revenue. You build community, loyalty, and impact that lasts.

Before we dive in, I want to offer a bit of context about who is guiding you through this. Not just the frameworks or philosophies—but the real, lived path that led me here...

Finding My Path:
The Winding Road to Membership Expertise

Author's Note: Before we talk frameworks and flywheels, let me start with the human story. This book wasn't written in a straight line—it was learned.

Learned in the late nights when the strategy that worked last quarter suddenly didn't. Learned in experiments that failed loudly, and in others that failed so quietly I almost missed the lesson. Learned in the long work of unlearning and rebuilding what I thought I knew.

This isn't a hero story. It's a field report from the messy middle—the place where theory meets reality and comes back changed. It's about detours that didn't feel like progress at the time, but shaped everything about how I think about growth. It's about the lesson I had to earn over years—that great systems aren't installed overnight.

They're built the way trust is built—inch by inch. Step by step. Relationship by relationship. One turn of the flywheel at a time. If you're looking for the highlight reel, you're in the wrong place. But if you want to know what it actually takes—the real work behind the frameworks—then let's begin.

I grew up a classic underachiever—smart enough for advanced classes, too unfocused to follow through. I coasted on quick thinking and charm—until it stopped working. That wake-up call came my freshman year at the University of Wisconsin–Madison, when I failed out after just two semesters.

Getting Lost, Then Finding a Way Out

Hitting bottom forced a reset. A blunt conversation with a dean made it clear: there were no shortcuts this time. Shame and determination fueled me forward. After a year at community college, I returned to Wisconsin with discipline instead of excuses and earned my degree the hard way, with no shortcuts. That early lesson in accountability became a throughline in my life—and later shaped how I saw membership businesses, which thrive not on grand promises but on consistent value and continuous improvement.

With my economics degree in hand, I followed instinct more than a plan and moved to New York City. No job lined up—just an apartment with four strangers in Brooklyn and a determination to figure it out. My career began at NERA Economic Consulting, where I turned a mind-numbing data-entry temp gig into a full-time research role. The analytical work sharpened my thinking, but I wanted something that blended business with my passions and put me closer to music and growth.

That search led me to SiriusXM, where I found my first professional home. Working in corporate finance gave me a front-row seat to how a subscription business operated: analyzing content deals, modeling new initiatives, and creating budgets for marketing and programming. It was my first exposure to a true subscription business and the mechanics of recurring revenue. While I felt I was positioned to climb, I realized I didn't just want to support growth—I wanted to drive it.

Pivoting Through Business School

When I set my sights on business school, I assumed experience would make up for my 2.8 GPA. It didn't. Despite strong test scores and recommendations, I was waitlisted by four schools. So, I kept pushing. Less than two months before classes began, the Darden School of Business at the University of Virginia welcomed me.

Those two years rewired how I thought about business and myself. Surrounded by brilliant, driven peers, I began to see patterns in how great companies scaled and evolved. An internship at Red Light Management reconnected me with my love of music. What began as labeling posters and answering phones turned into analyzing data for artists like Phish and Dave Matthews Band. By linking ticket sales, email signups, and social media, I learned that even art thrives on understanding audiences. Still, I wanted to build at scale. That's when Amazon called.

The Amazon Era: From Intimidation to Impact

When I joined Amazon in 2011, it wasn't yet the behemoth it is today, but you could feel it coming. The company was fast-moving, relentless, and infamous for its intensity. My coworkers weren't theorists discussing business ideas—they were builders. At first, I was intimidated. Then I realized what an extraordinary opportunity it was to learn and grow alongside them.

Knowing I'd eventually return to the East Coast, I set out to learn everything I could about how Amazon created innovation. I started on the Amazon Music team as a product manager, then moved into vendor management, negotiating with record labels, and finally into business development and strategy, helping launch Prime Music. Each role taught me a different piece of the membership puzzle: how technology, partnerships, and member economics intertwine to create loyalty.

Amazon Prime, Global Strategy, and New Challenges

The real turning point came when I joined the Amazon Prime team—the beating heart of Amazon's retail engine. My mission was deceptively simple: figure out what made Prime members spend more. Leading a small cross-functional team, we dug into years of behavioral data, searching for the patterns that separated high-value members from everyone else. What we found changed how I think about growth entirely.

When we presented those findings to Amazon's senior leadership, the stakes were real. But what stuck with me wasn't the pressure—it was the clarity of what the data revealed. Customer behavior isn't random. The right behaviors, cultivated deliberately over time, compound into outsized lifetime value. That insight became the foundation for everything that followed.

Later, as marketing lead for the first-ever Prime Day, I learned the thrill and exhaustion of scaling something globally. It showed me that great membership programs require both precision and endurance. My final role— as GM of the Mid-Atlantic region for Prime Now, Amazon's now-defunct two-hour delivery program—taught me the other half of the equation: every membership business eventually faces the reckoning between growth and profitability. I'd spend years learning to navigate that tension.

Returning to My Roots: Leadership at SiriusXM

After seven years at Amazon, I was ready for a new challenge. I wanted to apply everything I'd learned about scaling membership businesses somewhere familiar. When I saw an opportunity at SiriusXM—a company that still felt like home—I knew it was time to return.

As VP and GM of the Streaming Business, I was no longer behind the scenes. I was in the hot seat, responsible for transforming SiriusXM's digital presence from a secondary focus into a standalone growth engine. Armed with lessons from Amazon, I dove in headfirst—reshaping brand positioning, pricing, marketing strategy, and member experience.

We made big changes. We moved away from SiriusXM's traditional high-low pricing model, which offers deep discounts at acquisition and deeper ones when subscribers threaten to cancel, and toward consistent, non-discounted pricing. We overhauled the brand's market positioning, working with an external agency to create separation from the mature satellite radio business. We invested heavily in performance media and leveraged exclusive content to drive conversion.

Some bets paid off. Others didn't. But every experiment reinforced a core belief: membership success is a system, not a slogan.

After four years, I found myself at a crossroads. My passion for music, which had once been my fuel, was starting to feel like work. Subscriber growth was slowing, and I could see why: SiriusXM's streaming business had hit a ceiling that only a fundamental shift could break. Without moving to fully interactive music—the experience Spotify and Apple Music offered—the service would stay profitable, but growth would plateau.

It was a humbling realization: even the best strategy can't outrun a value proposition that no longer fits the market.

A Familiar Model, A New Challenge

Then came an unexpected email from Walmart that I almost ignored. I was a devoted Prime member who'd spent years inside Amazon's culture. I hadn't set foot in a Walmart in years, and I wasn't sure I could work for a brand I barely knew. But something made me read the message again. I got curious about how they were thinking about membership.

I started digging into Sam Walton's story and the early Walmart playbook, and it hit me that there was so much more innovation there than I realized. A lot of what people credit Amazon for—relentless focus on value, operational excellence, long-term thinking—Walmart had been doing for decades. When I learned they were serious about scaling Walmart+, I saw a rare kind of challenge: the chance to build membership at massive scale, with the leverage of the world's largest retailer behind it.

I joined as VP of Member Experience and Value Proposition. Being a corporate officer gave me a backstage pass to how Walmart really works. What struck me most wasn't the scale—I'd seen scale at Amazon. It was something harder to replicate: Walmart's ability to elevate the in-store experience through relentless attention to detail.

I'd watch leaders walk a store, spot a problem in seconds—a misplaced display, a gap in inventory, a bottleneck at checkout—and set change in motion before we left the aisle. Their clarity of observation and bias for action was humbling. Amazon had taught me how to optimize digital experiences. Walmart taught me that physical retail, done right, is just as sophisticated.

Walmart's discipline sparked a question that's guided me ever since: *If great retail leaders can instantly see what's working in a store, why can't membership leaders develop the same instincts for their programs?* That question became the seed of the framework that would eventually grow into this book.

During my time at Walmart, we launched initiatives that reshaped Walmart+: Walmart Cash, new onboarding flows, discounted memberships for students and low-income households, partnerships with Paramount+ and Expedia, Walmart+ Week, and more. Each project taught me more about scale, value creation, and the nuances of serving millions of members.

But despite the impact, something was missing. Working out of Hoboken, I was far from Walmart's cultural center in Bentonville—and I felt it. Unlike Amazon, where I could live the company's heartbeat every day, here I was a few beats removed. It became clear: to keep growing, I needed a different path.

Stepping Back, Moving Forward

By mid-2024, I was ready for my next chapter. Burnt out on corporate politics, I asked myself a simple question: *What do I actually want to do?*

The answer wasn't another big title. It was impact, variety, and flexibility; the chance to shape multiple businesses instead of one. So, I stepped back, started consulting, and began helping companies across industries grow their membership businesses—while finally putting my frameworks and lessons into writing.

Why This Book—and Why Now

Despite the explosion of membership models, there is still no clear, practical guide for building and scaling them, especially now that AI can be your execution partner. There are books on subscriptions and retention, but few that connect strategy with execution. And fewer still written by people who've actually built these systems at scale.

This book fills that gap. It distills what I've learned across three industries into a framework you can adapt to any business. The companies may look different, but the mechanics of how you attract, engage, and retain members are universal once you know how to see them.

Whether you're launching your first program or scaling a mature one, this is your roadmap for building something that lasts. In a world built on recurring relationships, mastering membership isn't just an advantage—it's the foundation of long-term growth.

From Strategy to Execution: How to Use This Book

I love nonfiction books that spark debate: the kind that challenge me with bold perspectives and fresh ideas. But too often, I'm hooked for the first few chapters only to drift away as the book slides into page after page of feel-good stories that just restate the same point. My Kindle is a graveyard of half-finished titles, books that start strong then keep circling the same idea with endless anecdotes. I promised myself this wouldn't be one of them.

This isn't a theory-heavy manifesto or a highlight reel of someone else's success. It's a playbook, practical from start to finish. Each chapter builds on the last, introducing key concepts and immediately translating them into strategies you can apply inside your own company.

Membership businesses are complex. There's no one-size-fits-all blueprint. That's why this book is meant to fuel discussion. These ideas gain power when teams debate, challenge, and adapt them together. Whether you're a junior analyst eager to make an impact or a CEO setting long-term vision, these frameworks will resonate differently depending on your perspective. That's the point.

So don't just read this book. Use it. Pull out sections for your next team meeting. Challenge your assumptions. Challenge my suggestions—I'm sure I got some things wrong. Map your blind spots. Try the frameworks, test them, break them, and rebuild them stronger. The more people across your organization understand the engines of membership growth, the more unstoppable your business becomes.

Now, let's get to work.

Fundamental Concepts That Will Shape This Book

Before we dive deeper, it's worth aligning on the core principles that will guide this entire approach. These are the threads that run through every chapter of this book; the ideas that separate average membership programs from enduring ones:

1. **The Power of Membership Over Subscription:** Understanding the difference between a "subscriber" and a "member" shifts how a company builds loyalty, engagement, and long-term value.

2. **Competitor Insights as a Growth Accelerator:** Studying competitors is not just about establishing a benchmark for comparison. It is the fastest way to identify opportunities, avoid pitfalls, and sharpen your own strategic positioning.

3. **Retention as the True Growth Engine:** Acquisition opens the door, but retention drives sustainable growth. The real value of a membership model lies in keeping members engaged over time, not just getting them to join.

4. **Data as the Foundation of Accountability:** Growth doesn't happen by accident. It requires clear metrics, assigned ownership, and a cadence of measurement that holds teams accountable. Driving customer action, not just focusing on the desired outcomes, must become part of the operating rhythm.

5. **AI as the Membership Multiplier:** Artificial intelligence is changing what's possible. From personalized experiences to predictive retention strategies, AI empowers even lean teams to operate like scaled enterprises. If they know how to harness it.

Let's unpack each of these foundational ideas in more detail.

1: The Power of Membership Over Subscription

Words shape perception, and in the world of recurring revenue, the difference between a subscriber and a member is more than semantics. It's a mindset shift that changes how companies engage, retain, and grow their customer base.

A subscriber pays for access. It's transactional. They sign up, get the product or service, and can cancel at any time. The relationship is functional in the exchange of money for utility. And once the need fades, so does the relationship.

A member is something more. Membership implies belonging, identity, and ongoing value beyond just the core service. It's not just about access—it's about experience, perks, recognition, and emotional connection. A strong membership creates a sense of community and signals, "This is for me."

Of course, not every company that uses the term "member" truly delivers on that promise. The key is to build a foundation that offers a compelling value proposition, fair pricing, and a commitment to continuous improvement. When done right, being a member is more than a transaction; it's the beginning of a relationship that grows over time.

From Transactional to Relational: The Strategic Shift

For decades, companies have referred to their customers as subscribers, reinforcing a pay-to-access mindset. Consider traditional magazines. You pay, you get a monthly issue, and that's the end of it.

There's no deeper connection, no sense of belonging, and no added value beyond the product itself. The same pattern emerges with "Subscribe and Save" models for recurring product deliveries.

The New York Times recognized this limitation and evolved its offering from a simple digital subscription to NYT All Access, which includes extras like word games, cooking guides, podcasts, and more. They deliberately moved away from a pure subscription model toward a membership experience where users feel part of a community of informed readers.

The streaming industry is following suit. While companies like Hulu, Disney+, and Apple Music long used "subscriber" language, Netflix and Spotify increasingly use "member" language. They use personalization to emphasize recommendations just for you. They're reinforcing a feeling of belonging, one that shapes how customers engage and how long they stay. And that connection allows additional benefits to be introduced over time, which creates a growth flywheel.

This shift creates a powerful psychological transformation:

- Instead of "I pay for Spotify," it becomes "I'm part of Spotify and the service increases my connection to the artist."
- Instead of comparing price to content, members consider the overall experience.
- Instead of a one-time exchange, membership creates an ongoing relationship.

That shift opens the door to more. Add-ons, perks, and partner benefits all feel more natural in a membership model because the relationship is already deeper than just content-for-cash.

Beyond Transactions: Community as the Differentiator

Membership isn't just about access; it's about belonging. The strongest programs aren't built on a list of benefits, but on the feeling of being part of something bigger. F45 isn't just a gym—it's life-changing team training. Udemy isn't just online courses—it's a bridge between learners and experts. The future of membership won't be defined by perks alone, but by the emotional connection that keeps people coming back.

What's emerging is membership as social infrastructure. Members won't just consume content or products; they'll co-create them. We're already seeing this with Patreon creators, Discord communities, and collaborative playlists. The most successful future memberships will be those where members feel genuine ownership in the community's direction and growth.

Memberships will also blur into the background of everyday routines. We do not "decide" to use Netflix or HBO Max anymore. They are simply part of life. The best memberships become invisible and indispensable, woven into habits, devices, and defaults.

The goal is not just satisfaction. It is making members feel understood, supported, and better off over time.

Membership Creates a Relationship; Subscription Is Just Access

Switching to member language is about more than tone; it's about loyalty. Members are less likely to churn as they feel invested. They associate your service with their identities. They're more forgiving of hiccups, more responsive to engagement, and more likely to advocate for your brand.

That's why this book talks about members, not subscribers. Building a successful recurring revenue business isn't about charging for access; it's about creating a relationship that lasts, where all members feel connected to the service, and potentially, depending on the type of service, other members.

Think of the difference like this: being a subscriber is like renting a space for a party. Being a member is like belonging to the club itself. That distinction changes everything, from how you position your offer, to how you build products, to how you earn long-term connection. Just remember, it's easy to slap 'member' on your pricing page—harder to deliver a genuine sense of belonging.

And throughout this book, we'll explore exactly how to make that transition, and why the companies that do it well don't just grow. They thrive.

2: Competitor Insights as a Growth Accelerator

During my time at Walmart, we conducted countless store visits. We'd talk with store associates, observe how customers shopped, and identify areas of opportunity. But we didn't stop there. We'd also visit competitors like Target, Dollar General, Kroger, and more. This practice originated with Walmart's founder, Sam Walton, who famously spent more time in Kmart stores than Kmart's own management.

Walton's focus was on learning what the competition was doing well and adapting the best ideas. This relentless curiosity wasn't just productive; it was revolutionary. Walmart's growth as the world's largest retailer came from perfecting existing concepts, not inventing entirely new ones. When Walton spotted a better approach in a competitor's store, he didn't just copy it; he adapted and improved it until it became uniquely Walmart's own.

This fundamental mindset—learning from competitors to accelerate your own growth—remains just as powerful today. It's a reminder that the best ideas often come from outside your four walls, if you're willing to look, listen, and refine.

The Wisdom of Being Second

Being first isn't always the advantage we assume it to be; sometimes, the view from second place offers the clearest path to market leadership.

Consider Netflix: it didn't invent streaming, but it watched the early experiments—YouTube's breakout momentum and Amazon's first serious push with Unbox—and then did what great competitors do: it refined the model. Netflix paired a curated library with premium programming, invested heavily in recommendation algorithms that made discovery effortless, and delivered a seamless experience across devices. The result was simple: they learned from others' missteps without paying the full price of making every mistake themselves.

Similarly, Apple was not the first to launch smartphones, tablets, or smartwatches. Instead, Steve Jobs and his team meticulously studied existing products, identified their shortcomings, and created superior alternatives that defined entire categories. As Jobs famously said, "Good artists copy, great artists steal," acknowledging that innovation often comes from improving upon existing ideas rather than creating entirely new ones.

This approach works because larger, rapidly growing services have typically refined their layouts and offerings through extensive A/B testing and customer feedback loops. Their success represents thousands of hours of optimization and millions of dollars in research, lessons available for observation at no cost. Why create something new when you can learn from what already works well?

Digital Store Visits: The Modern Competitive Analysis

In today's digital landscape, conducting "store visits" is more accessible than ever. Just as Sam Walton traveled with his notepad observing competitors, businesses can now analyze competitors' experiences using only a smartphone and screen recording tools, making competitive intelligence gathering more accessible than ever before. At Amazon, we called this practice "Walking the Store"—and it wasn't optional. Every employee was expected to do it and report back with problems spotted or opportunities for improvement.

These digital reconnaissance missions offer unprecedented access to competitors' thinking. By following the complete member journey, from clicking an ad through signing up, experiencing the product, and even canceling, you can uncover invaluable insights:

- How do they articulate their value proposition in ads and landing pages?
- What does their signup flow prioritize? What friction points do they eliminate?
- How do they handle onboarding and early engagement?
- What retention tactics do they employ when you attempt to cancel?

Each of these elements represents countless hours of strategic thinking and optimization that are instructive. By documenting these journeys systematically, you create a playbook of industry best practices and see pitfalls to avoid.

> **Resource Connection**: To support your competitive analysis efforts, I have compiled an extensive gallery of screenshots covering membership flows across different industries. See www.membergrowth.com/screenshots. These examples provide a starting point for your own competitive intelligence gathering.

Beyond Direct Competitors

The most valuable insights often come from the edges of your category. Focus only on direct rivals and you'll echo their limitations. Innovation happens at the intersections, where ideas travel and evolve. Study membership models across industries to surface the principles—and discover applications your competitors overlook.

Take Southwest Airlines, which modeled its rapid plane turnaround times on NASCAR pit crews rather than other airlines. Borrowing this playbook gave them efficiency levels the industry had never seen. Or consider Toyota, which transformed auto manufacturing by applying lessons from American supermarkets. By mirroring how stores restocked shelves as items sold, Toyota pioneered the "just-in-time" system—an approach that reshaped global manufacturing.

This approach requires asking broader questions: Who excels at solving similar problems in different contexts? What can a restaurant's approach to customer service teach a software company? How might a luxury hotel's onboarding experience inform consistent delivery of vitamins and supplements? By casting a wider net, you discover solutions that your direct competitors may not yet have considered.

Competitive Intelligence as a Continuous Practice

Let's be honest: it's tempting to check out your competitors once, take some notes, and call it a day. But treating competitive analysis like a one-and-done task is a mistake. It's critical to treat it like a muscle and work it constantly. If you stop paying attention to how your competitors are evolving, you'll wake up one day and realize they've passed you.

Here's how to stay a step ahead:

- **Play the role of a new member regularly**: every few months, sign up, onboard, cancel, rejoin. Take screenshots. Jot down what's changed. This kind of reconnaissance reveals patterns and innovations before they become obvious to everyone else.
- **Watch for strategy pivots**: A subtle change in pricing, benefits, or how a brand talks about itself can be a big signal. What your competitors emphasize today might become table stakes tomorrow.

- **Dig where members vent**: scroll through reviews, Reddit threads, App Store comments, and social media. You'll find out what's annoying their members and what's delighting them. That's your roadmap for differentiation.
- **Follow who they're hiring**: Job postings are one of the best early signals. If they're suddenly bringing on retention marketers or data scientists, that tells you exactly where they're heading. Talent reveals strategy.

By making this process routine, you shift competitive intelligence from reactive to proactive. The insights gained become a continuous source of innovation, helping you stay ahead of market trends rather than merely responding to them.

The Ethics of Competitive Learning

While studying competitors provides invaluable insights, it is essential to maintain ethical boundaries. The goal is not to copy but to learn and improve. Amazon's Jeff Bezos embodied this philosophy when he said, "We watch our competitors, learn from them, see the things that they were doing for customers and copy those things as much as we can."

Ethical competitive analysis means:

- Respecting intellectual property and not infringing on patents, trademarks or copyrights.
- Using only publicly available information or services open to any customer.
- Learning concepts rather than copying execution.
- Giving credit where credit is due.
- Adding your own innovation rather than merely duplicating what others are doing.

The most successful adaptations do not just mimic competitors; they transform good ideas into great ones by adding unique value and perspective.

"If you know the enemy and know yourself, you need not fear
the result of a hundred battles."—Sun Tzu, The Art of War

In today's market, the "enemy" isn't your competition—it's stagnation. The businesses that win don't just watch rivals; they learn from them, evolve faster, and move further.

By treating competitors as teachers, not threats, you build what every membership business needs most: a flywheel of continuous learning and improvement.

3: Acquisition vs. Retention: Seeing the Full Picture

People usually view retention as a post-signup concern: how do you keep someone after they join? But here's the truth: retention isn't a step in the member journey. It's a thread that runs through every stage of it.

From the first time someone hears your value proposition to when they consider the offer, subscribe, and engage with the service—each of these moments shapes whether they'll stick around. That means retention is something you build into every touchpoint. In fact, how you acquire members plays a huge role in how long they'll stay.

Let's take an extreme example. Imagine a website landing page that says, "Get $100 free for signing up!" It would likely drive a surge in signups, but also a wave of immediate cancellations. Most people wouldn't care about the actual value of the service as they'd join for the $100 and cancel as soon as they could. It sounds absurd, but I have seen versions of this work. At SiriusXM, we tested an offer that gave away a device to new members, and even after filtering fraud, the economics pleasantly surprised us.

Now picture the opposite: a landing page designed like a long-form article, complete with a detailed quiz that ensures every prospective member fully understands the benefits before joining. Far fewer people would make it through, but those who did would be far more likely to stay. Sounds extreme, right? Yet fashion boxes like Stitch Fix and meal kits like HelloFresh ask dozens of questions up front—partly for personalization, but also to filter out deal seekers.

The truth is, neither extreme works. The magic happens when acquisition and retention strategies align—when your message is clear, your offer compelling, and the experience delivers on the promise. The tighter the alignment between what you say and what members experience, the stronger your retention will be.

The key to retention is simple: *provide something people genuinely want and value.* Your goal is to make the membership feel indispensable and to make it a true "no-brainer." So how do you get there? You ask.

It sounds obvious, and it is. Ask what they want. Ask if they got what they expected. Ask how their last interaction went. Ask why they're leaving. Ask what would bring them back. And most importantly, act on what you learn.

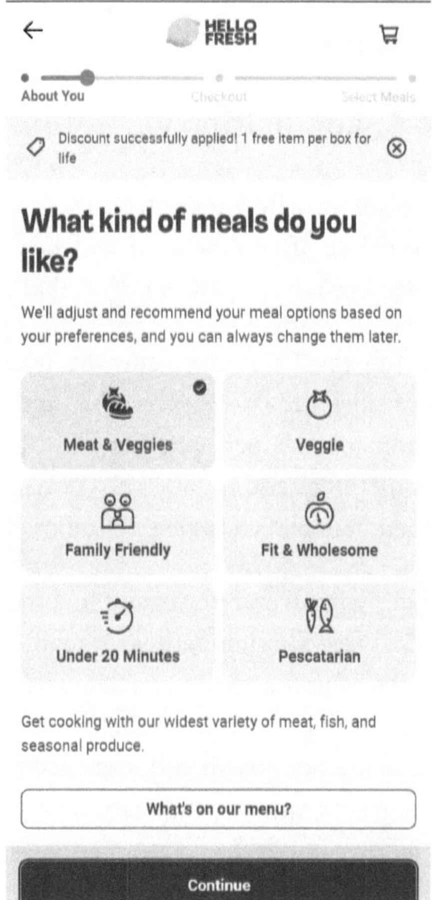

To make this concrete, think about a restaurant. How do they know if you enjoyed the meal? You might leave a tip, but that mostly reflects service. A manager might ask, but most people just say "great," even when it wasn't.

Now imagine quick thumbs-up/thumbs-down buttons at key moments—when you sit down, order, or get your appetizer (like the airport bathroom smiley-face buttons). Crude, but effective. They capture real-time sentiment fast. But that would be tough to execute at a world-class restaurant.

That's one of the biggest advantages of digital membership: you can build seamless feedback loops. Quick surveys, star ratings, post-interaction prompts, or direct outreach can all surface what's working and what isn't.

But the best feedback is behavioral—because you don't have to ask at all. If someone comes back to the same restaurant a week later, that's a strong signal. Membership programs can read similar signals through repeat logins, ongoing engagement, and benefit usage. When you listen to what members do—not just what they say—you get a deeper, more reliable read.

Gathering feedback is only step one. What matters is what you do with it. Spot patterns. Prioritize problems. Rally a team to fix them. Great retention depends on a feedback-action loop that never stops turning.

But don't wait too long. Early adopters are often your most loyal and vocal members—and if you don't give them a reason to stay from day one, you'll lose them. Bringing them back later is far harder than keeping them engaged from the start.

Balancing Acquisition and Retention

Balancing acquisition and retention takes more than good intentions. It takes discipline, measurement, and a relentless focus on data and member experience.

Which brings us to the next critical foundation of membership growth.

4: Data as the Foundation of Accountability

Messy data is the enemy of growth

When your marketing team thinks you have 100,000 active members but billing shows 90,000, you're flying blind. Misalignment like this leads to bad decisions, missed targets, and fractured trust. From day one, your systems must provide a single source of truth for member behavior—one that's accessible across the entire organization. When every team speaks the same data language, you move faster, test smarter, and scale without chaos.

A single source of truth doesn't happen by accident—it's built. That means a clear data pipeline that defines where member data originates, how it's validated, and where it ultimately lives. Your acquisition events, product usage, support interactions, and billing system all need to flow into a shared foundation with consistent identifiers, agreed-upon definitions (like "active member"), and automated checks that flag discrepancies before they spread. When the pipeline is clear, the numbers stop being negotiable—and the organization can finally debate strategy instead of arguing over spreadsheets.

What's tracked is what's actioned

Membership businesses are complex ecosystems with countless moving parts. To understand what's really happening, you need more than surface-level reporting—you need the right data and a constant focus on variances, both positive and negative.

Most companies understand this at a basic level. They create dashboards that track lagging indicators of business health: marketing spend, signups, member count, total revenue, and similar metrics. These are helpful for understanding the overall situation, but they show success after it happens.

For example, knowing your paid member count decreased last month tells you there is a problem, but it does not tell you what caused the problem or how to fix it. Without a deeper understanding, teams end up scrambling, creating output and action without a true eye toward outcome and impact.

The key is to identify and track input metrics—the specific, controllable actions that drive your desired outcomes. These are the leading indicators that predict future success and give you clear levers to improve your business. What behaviors do your most valuable members exhibit in their first week? Which features correlate with long-term retention? How quickly do members need to experience their first "win" to become engaged? Put simply, input metrics are the behaviors that cause the outcomes you care about.

But simply defining input metrics isn't enough. Companies also need to create robust reporting packages and develop accountability systems to consistently track and improve these metrics. Each metric needs a dedicated owner, clear targets, and regular reviews. Without this accountability structure, even the best metrics will fail to drive meaningful change.

By shifting focus from reacting to output metrics to improving input metrics, companies unlock long-term, scalable membership growth. Whether streaming services optimizing first-week engagement, fitness apps tracking early workout completion, or subscription boxes monitoring month-two retention, the takeaway is clear: small, measurable actions drive big results. And input metrics should be visible to everyone—not hidden in a spreadsheet. The more people who can see and interpret the signals, the more insight you unlock.

The data foundation you build becomes the shared language that aligns the organization. When everyone knows which metrics matter and who is responsible for moving them, execution gets faster—and results follow.

5: AI as the Membership Multiplier

There has never been a better time to launch, scale, and optimize a membership service, because AI is your ultimate copilot. Whether refining acquisition strategy, enhancing member retention, or crafting hyper-personalized experiences, AI can amplify your efforts and help you scale faster than ever before. Here are ways that AI can drive improvement in your member experience:

- **Understanding Member Needs Through AI:** One of the biggest challenges in membership businesses is understanding what members truly want. AI can help analyze member behavior, predict churn risks, and identify which benefits drive the highest engagement.
- **Survey Optimization & Feedback Analysis**: Instead of manually sorting through survey responses, AI tools can generate smart survey questions and even analyze results at scale to surface key insights. Want to know which new benefit will resonate most? AI can analyze open-ended feedback and quantify common themes.
- **Personalized Member Journeys**: AI can help automate onboarding sequences, create dynamic email campaigns, and tailor in-app experiences based on real-time engagement. If a member is not using a core feature, AI can trigger a targeted email or push notification nudging them back into the experience.
- **Predictive Churn Modeling**: The best membership businesses are proactive, not reactive. AI-driven churn models can flag at-risk members before they cancel, allowing your team to intervene with personalized retention strategies, whether this is a special discount, a targeted upsell, or an engagement email.
- **Smarter Customer Service:** AI can handle the first touchpoint with members through chatbots or listen to care agent calls to summarize required actions. This frees up your human team to focus on high-value interactions that build trust and loyalty.

- **Optimizing Communications and Conversions:** AI can take the lead in crafting copy and content for both subject lines and emails and even test unique tones of voice to find what resonates most with your audience. It can generate multiple variations of landing pages and run real-time experiments to determine which drives the highest conversions. Imagine an algorithm that dynamically adjusts text based on the visitor's past behavior—this is where we're heading and it is happening at warp speed.

Used well, AI improves relevance. Used poorly, it becomes spam at scale.

AI-Powered Personalization

For years, personalization has meant "people who bought this also bought that." That won't cut it anymore. With AI, businesses can predict needs before members even articulate them—curating offers, content, or experiences tailored to each individual. Think of Spotify's Discover Weekly: it feels magical because it knows you better than you know yourself. Soon, every membership business—from fitness apps to grocery delivery—will be expected to deliver that level of "felt intimacy" at scale.

This is not just about recommendations. It is about adapting the journey in real time, so the experience stays relevant as a member's needs change.

The Human-AI Partnership

While AI can optimize and automate many aspects of a membership business, it is important to remember that we are not fully at the stage of complete automation—at least not yet. AI suggests content strategies, but human creativity is still needed to craft a compelling membership experience. AI can flag members at risk of churn, but a well-trained customer service team knows how to turn that insight into action. AI can create new button copy, but a strategic marketer understands how to align messaging with long-term brand positioning.

The best membership businesses aren't waiting for AI to fully mature; they are using it today to get a competitive edge. Start using AI now to enhance personalization and narrative creation, from surveys to onboarding to retention. AI can make every touchpoint feel customized and relevant to each individual member.

Just remember: AI thrives on data. The more you experiment, the better it gets. Clean, structured data is the fuel that turns AI from a shiny toy into a growth engine.

Quick Wins to Try Now

- Use AI surveys to pinpoint which benefits members want most.
- Test AI-generated onboarding emails and push notifications.
- Use AI to analyze your churn data and flag at-risk segments.

The companies that embrace AI today—and pair it with smart, human-led strategy—will define the next decade of the membership economy. Yes, AI can be complex to implement, which is why bringing in experts, whether as full-time leaders or trusted consultants, can accelerate your path. But the real key is mindset: start small, test fast, and fuel your systems with clean data. Do that, and you'll unlock not just incremental improvements, but entirely new ways to acquire, engage, and retain members.

The future of membership will belong to the businesses that don't just use AI as a tool but master it as a growth engine.

Jim Lecinski - Professor of Marketing at Northwestern-Kellogg and co-author of 'The AI Marketing Canvas: A Five-Step AI Plan for Marketers'

I've spent a lot of time thinking about how artificial intelligence is changing membership businesses, and the short answer is this: AI lets us move beyond blunt segmentation into genuine 1:1 connection. What excites me is the shift from static personas to living systems. With the right signals—behavioral, contextual, even emotional—models can adapt in real time, so every touchpoint feels uniquely relevant to the person on the other end. I call that "adaptive intimacy at scale," and when you get it right, the experience feels paradoxically more human, not less.

The biggest near-term opportunity isn't a clever campaign or a shinier app; it's predictive engagement. We've all built churn saves. What AI enables now is sensing when interest is fading before a member raises their hand—or worse, disappears. Blend behavior, sentiment, and usage, and you can intervene with the right nudge at the right moment. That's a mindset shift from "saving members" to "sensing members," and it turns retention from a firefight into a continuous relationship system.

Pricing, churn, and lifetime value are where this really compounds. AI uncovers micro-patterns humans miss—minute usage shifts, unmet needs hiding in the noise, small willingness-to-pay differences that add up at scale. Those insights power dynamic offers and genuinely personalized experiences, which in turn improve retention. Over time, the data feeds a flywheel: better modeling informs better pricing, which improves engagement, which boosts LTV, which funds the next round of member value. That's how an AI-powered membership keeps getting smarter without getting creepier.

Will AI replace community? I don't believe it can—or should. The best membership programs are built on trust and shared purpose. Technology can strengthen that foundation: summarize feedback, match people with common interests, and handle the repetitive personalization so humans can invest in the conversations that matter. Used well, AI becomes the invisible infrastructure that supports connection rather than overshadowing it.

Content is another lever. When a member feels like the next article, course, or feature was created just for them, perceived value skyrockets. Imagine a membership that evolves with your life—curating exactly what you need at each moment, then adjusting as your goals change. The risk is letting the machine drive taste. The answer is editorial judgment on top of algorithmic intelligence: automation for scale, human curation for soul.

That balance leads naturally to ethics. The line gets crossed when personalization stops helping and starts manipulating. Members should understand what data you use and why, and they should have real choices. The goal isn't to watch people; it's to understand them well enough to serve them. The most competitive programs in the next decade won't just be the smartest—they'll be the most principled. Integrity is the differentiator.

If you put all of this together, a modern membership organization looks like this: a sensing system that spots risk early; an adaptive layer that tunes price, messaging, and experience for the individual; and a human core— community, support, editorial—that deepens trust. Done right, the technology disappears into the background, and the member just feels known. That's the bar I'm pushing for.

Final Thoughts: Building a Membership Business That Lasts

As recurring revenue becomes central to both top-line and bottom-line growth, the last two decades have proved membership works. The next decade will be about refining, improving, and earning that growth—every day. The companies that thrive won't treat membership as a billing mechanic, but as an evolving relationship stitched into how people live, work, and connect. The operating rhythm is simple and relentless: listen → strategize → test → iterate → improve → repeat.

Flexibility is now a feature, not a flaw. Members expect personalization—not just in the benefits and experience, but also in how they pay, so the service fits their lives, not the other way around. Trust, not terms, is the glue that keeps members engaged and coming back.

Think of this shift as the rise of the relationship economy. The transaction economy sold products; the membership economy builds connections. And connections can compound in value—not just for the company, but for the people they serve.

The test is straightforward: Are we making members' lives better over time? The companies that can answer "yes" with real evidence—measurable outcomes, leading indicators, visible improvement—stand apart.

What separates exceptional programs isn't checking boxes; it's the discipline of continuous improvement. The strength of this approach is its practicality. Whether you're launching new or revitalizing old, start where you are. Prioritize the few moments that matter now, run focused tests, measure what changes, then expand what works.

Ideas are cheap. Actions compound. Design for retention from day one, learn aggressively from competitors, and steer with leading indicators—not lagging excuses. That's how you unlock a durable flywheel.

Do that, and you won't just run a membership—you'll create something people never want to live without.

Part 1:

Attracting Members

Chapter 1

The Membership Flywheel™: Navigating the Path to Sustainable Growth

In 2018, MoviePass looked unstoppable.

Millions of people paying $9.95 a month for unlimited movies. A simple idea. A viral brand. A line out the door.

And then—collapse. Within two years, it was gone. Not because the idea was bad, but because the model was broken. MoviePass mastered acquisition but ignored everything that came after. They could get members in the door but not keep them there. The demand was real. The system wasn't.

That story isn't an anomaly. It's a warning.

Across industries, the same pattern repeats: explosive growth followed by painful decline. Subscription boxes rise fast and vanish faster. Streaming services spike after hit shows, then bleed cancellations. Fitness apps celebrate record January signups, only to lose half their users by March.

The graveyard of failed membership businesses isn't filled with bad products—it's filled with good ones that never mastered the complete member journey.

Because membership success isn't about signing people up. It's about earning the right to keep them.

Jeff Bezos once said, "We see our customers as invited guests to a party, and we are the hosts. It's our job every day to make every important aspect of the customer experience a little bit better."

That's the essence of great membership businesses: a daily, deliberate commitment to creating value that compounds. But knowing that isn't the challenge. Operationalizing it is.

Membership businesses are uniquely complex. They stretch across marketing, product, operations, finance, and service. Teams obsess over acquisition metrics while neglecting onboarding. They chase engagement but forget renewal. Each department owns a fragment of the experience, but no one owns the system. When no one owns the system, churn becomes everyone's problem and no one's job.

That's why I built the **Membership Flywheel™**—a framework designed to bring order to that chaos. It breaks the member journey into nine interconnected stages, showing how growth emerges not from isolated wins but from harmony between them.

Think of it as a production system for loyalty. Each stage feeds the next. Flow matters. Feedback matters. Break one link and the whole system stalls. But when you align them—acquisition, onboarding, engagement, retention, and beyond—the momentum becomes unstoppable.

The Flywheel isn't just a model; it's a mindset. A way to turn membership from a marketing tactic into an operating system for sustainable growth.

And once it starts spinning, it doesn't just move your business forward—it keeps it moving.

Part 1: Why Systems Matter More Than Features

Picture yourself touring two factories that produce the same product. From the outside, they appear identical, both housed in state-of-the-art buildings, using the same raw materials and with machinery humming inside.

In the first factory, chaos reigns. Raw materials of exceptional quality sit untouched in one corner while workers at the initial assembly station scramble to process a sudden influx. Further down the line, employees stand idle, checking their watches as they wait for components to arrive. In the finishing department, workers frantically try to fix defects that the earlier stations should have caught. The loading dock fluctuates between overflowing with finished products and sitting idle with impatient distributors.

The second factory presents a stark contrast. Materials flow seamlessly from one station to the next. Workers move with practiced efficiency, each understanding how their role contributes to the final product. Quality checks occur throughout the process, not just at the end. The pace is steady, predictable, and sustainable. When a machine begins performing below standard, sensors alert maintenance before production is affected. The loading dock operates like clockwork, with distributors receiving shipments exactly when promised.

That's the difference between struggling and thriving membership businesses. Your benefits are your raw materials. Your technology is your machinery. Your marketing campaigns, onboarding sequences, engagement initiatives, and renewal processes are your assembly stations. And your member experience is the final product.

When membership businesses fail to implement a systematic framework, the momentum breaks down just like in our dysfunctional factory.

A company might excel at attention-grabbing marketing campaigns that bring potential members flooding in but then lose them with a confusing onboarding process. Or perhaps members make it through onboarding only to encounter inconsistent engagement opportunities or conflicting renewal messaging.

The most successful membership businesses operate more like Toyota's legendary production system, where every station is carefully designed, continuously measured, and constantly improved. That's what the **Membership Flywheel™** delivers: a system that turns chaos into consistency, waste into momentum, and scattered efforts into a synchronized engine for growth.

Why Frameworks Matter in Practice, Not Just Theory

Most leaders roll their eyes at the word framework. They've seen too many that live on whiteboards, not in the real world. The kind that sound smart in meetings but vanish the moment things get messy.

That skepticism isn't wrong. Most frameworks are built for simplicity, not systems. They freeze what should flow. But membership doesn't work that way. It's not a straight line or a funnel—it's a living, breathing ecosystem that changes every time a member does.

That's why a good framework doesn't add rigidity; it adds rhythm. It gives shape to chaos. It translates complexity into clarity and helps teams move from reacting to repeating what works.

Most membership businesses rely on oversimplified models that split the journey into two buckets: acquisition and retention. But anyone who's operated one knows that's fantasy. Between those poles live dozens of crucial inflection points—onboarding, activation, engagement, renewal, reactivation—where the real battles for growth are won or lost.

Without structure, companies spin in reactive cycles. One quarter is all about acquisition. The next, churn reduction. The next, a shiny new partnership. Each feels urgent, but none connect. Teams celebrate isolated wins while systemic problems persist. It's not incompetence—it's fragmentation.

A well-designed framework changes that. It gives teams a shared language and a shared map. It turns "who owns this?" into "how does this connect?" It replaces opinions with operating rhythm. Marketing, product, finance, and service stop pulling in different directions and start turning the same wheel.

That's what the **Membership Flywheel™** is built for—not to simplify your business, but to synchronize it.

Part 2: What's Ahead - Your Roadmap to Membership Excellence

In the chapters ahead, we'll unpack every stage of the Membership Flywheel™—from how great companies design value propositions that truly resonate, to how they price, distribute, and deliver ongoing engagement that compounds over time.

This isn't theory. It's the operating manual I wish I'd had earlier in my career—the one built not from case studies, but from the patterns I've seen repeat across hundreds of membership businesses.

Each chapter blends strategy and execution: what to do, why it works, and how to make it stick. You'll learn how world-class teams think about acquisition, onboarding, engagement, renewal, and winback—and how the best align those pieces into one seamless system. You'll see the pitfalls that quietly erode retention, the playbooks that reverse them, and the metrics that prove they work.

The goal is simple: to turn your membership into a growth engine that runs on rhythm, not reaction.

The Nine Stages of Membership Growth

The Flywheel is a living system. The diagram below shows how its nine stages connect. Each stage builds on the last and strengthens the next. Together, they create the continuous motion that separates one-time success from sustainable growth.

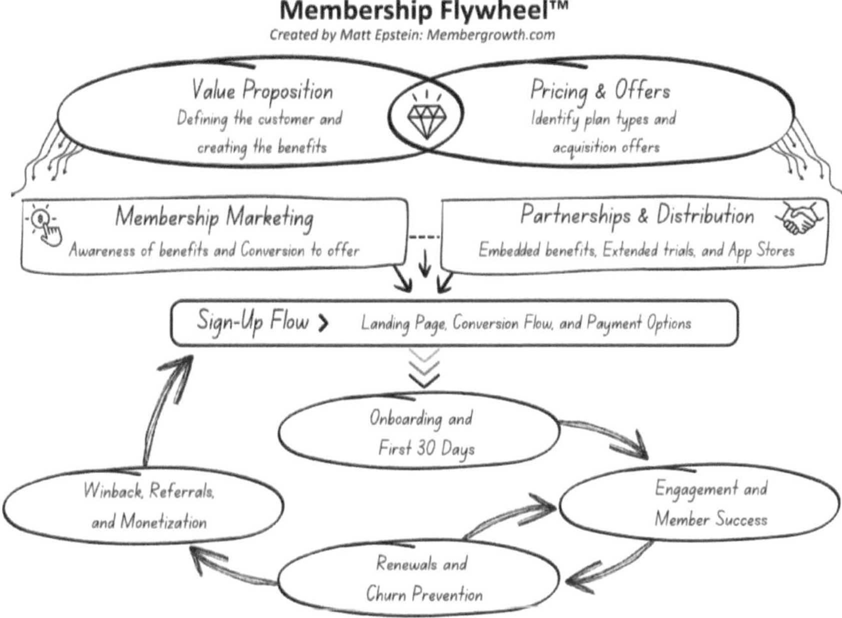

How the Flywheel Works: A Deep Dive into the Membership Journey

1. Value Proposition & Member Benefits

Every successful membership starts with a clearly defined value proposition. This isn't just a service tagline—it's a strategic articulation of the outcomes your members will achieve. Strong programs differentiate between **primary benefits** (e.g., free delivery, access to exclusive content, enhanced service levels) and **secondary benefits** (e.g., community access, surprise-and-delight moments, member-only content) to create emotional and functional resonance.

Your value proposition should evolve with your audience. What resonates in your early growth phase may shift as you expand into new segments or geographies. Best-in-class companies use research, behavior signals, and customer feedback loops to continuously refine the benefits that matter most.

2. Pricing & Offer Strategy

Pricing is more than a revenue decision—it's a behavioral design tool. Whether you use tiered plans, usage-based models, or all-you-can-eat access, your structure should align with how your members perceive value. Trial structures like "first month free" lower barriers, while discounting longer-term plans can increase perceived value without cutting margins.

Importantly, pricing may differ by acquisition channel. Digital ads might benefit from aggressive free trial offers, while organic traffic may support locking members into longer-term plans. Testing these combinations allows you to optimize not just for conversion, but for retention and long-term yield.

3. Awareness & Conversion Marketing

Membership marketing is different because you're not selling a one-time purchase—you're selling an ongoing relationship. Your brand narrative should anchor on two things: (1) transformation—who someone becomes or what gets easier once they join—and (2) value discovery—how you consistently build awareness and excitement for the benefits included with membership.

Balance performance marketing (e.g., SEM, paid social, affiliate) with brand storytelling through content, video, and influencers. Early-stage companies may lean heavier into performance media, but over time, sustained growth comes from emotional connection and repeat engagement—especially as you saturate core segments.

4. Distribution & Partnerships

Acquisition doesn't have to be limited to your paid or owned channels. Strategic partnerships—especially those with aligned audiences—can create efficient, scalable growth for both companies.

When designed well, partnerships do more than lower acquisition costs—they can lend credibility, enhance targeting precision, and shorten the education curve by tapping into pre-existing trust. Choose partners whose audiences align with your value proposition and who are willing to co-own performance outcomes.

5. Signup Flow Optimization

The signup experience is your conversion bottleneck. Every added field or second of delay creates drop-off. Great programs simplify this process with a clear value proposition upfront, limiting form fields, including trust signals (e.g., testimonials, secure checkout), and focusing on optimizing for mobile. They also use A/B testing to refine landing pages, optimize offer messaging, and ensure consistent design. Your best signal is not signup rate alone. It is whether the members you acquire go on to activate, engage, and retain. Conversion quality matters more than volume.

6. Onboarding & First 30 Days

This is your retention inflection point. Members who don't see value quickly are unlikely to stay. Use onboarding to orient, activate, and personalize. That might include guided tutorials, welcome emails, product tours, or early engagement challenges.

Design the experience to surface your strongest benefits fast. Use behavioral cues (e.g., what content they clicked, what features they explored) to personalize touchpoints. The goal is to create the "aha moment" that turns a prospect into a retained member within the first week.

7. Ongoing Engagement & Customer Service

Memberships must earn relevance every day. Personalization engines (e.g., recommendations, nudges, gamification) keep members moving along their journey. It's crucial to highlight under-used features, recommend additional benefits, and prompt return visits during lulls in activity.

Customer support should be proactive, not reactive. Use data to detect when members hit friction (e.g., failed logins, inactivity) and intervene early. At scale, service should become a retention tool, not just a cost center.

8. Churn Management & Renewals

Churn is not a binary "leave or stay" moment—it's a process. Members often signal exit intent weeks in advance through usage drop-off, failed renewals, or negative feedback. Predictive models can surface these signals so your team can act early with targeted saves, including discounts, alternative plans, personalized messages, and more.

For renewals, test various tactics: reminder emails, value recap summaries, surprise-and-delight benefits, or exclusive member upgrade offers. If someone does cancel, ensure the exit experience is graceful—because you're setting up the potential for getting them to come back later. Cancellation is not the end of the relationship. It is a moment to protect trust.

9. Winback, Referrals & Monetization (Member Growth Loops)

Former members are a goldmine—if you re-engage them correctly. Winback campaigns that reference prior usage or improvements made since they left tend to perform best. Time your outreach to coincide with seasonal interest or known behavioral patterns.

Referrals scale when they feel native and easy. Offer dual-sided rewards and integrate sharing prompts at natural moments, such as after positive service experiences, milestones, or achievements. For monetization, think about upsells to additional products or tiers, but also which complementary services or partner offers increase value and deepen retention.

The Interconnected System

Each of these stages doesn't operate in isolation. They reinforce each other. Your onboarding lays the foundation for engagement, which drives retention, and ultimately determines whether winback is worth pursuing. Your pricing strategy informs acquisition tactics, which determine the kind of members you attract—and how likely they are to renew.

That's the quiet power of a system: it compounds. Small improvements, stacked across multiple touchpoints, create exponential results. The membership businesses that win don't rely on hero moments—they rely on harmony. They refine every stage, every quarter, every cycle, turning feedback into fuel and alignment into advantage.

Most companies still chase the wrong prize. They celebrate new signups but ignore the members quietly slipping out the back door. Yet the math has always been clear: keeping a member is far more profitable than finding a new one. Retention isn't the back half of growth—it's the backbone of it.

The **Membership Flywheel™** solves that imbalance. It forces equal attention across the entire journey, making sure the energy you spend at the top doesn't leak out the sides. It's not about adding complexity; it's about creating continuity.

From Diagram to Operating System

Membership growth isn't a mystery—it's a system. Once you start seeing your business as a connected flow, you stop chasing spikes and start compounding momentum. That's the promise of the **Membership Flywheel™**: not a marketing campaign, but a durable operating model that makes tomorrow's growth easier than today's.

If there's one truth to carry forward, it's this: design the journey, earn the renewal.

Acquire with intent.

Onboard with purpose.

Engage with empathy.

Retain with rigor.

Do that consistently, and every metric that matters—LTV, margin, referrals, renewal rate—starts to bend in your favor.

Membership is more than a product strategy; it's a business philosophy. You don't need a dozen different playbooks—you need one you can tune to your model with precision and discipline.

That's what comes next. In the following section, we'll see how the Flywheel flexes across industries—from SaaS to streaming, retail to fitness, fintech to nonprofits—revealing where the pressure points shift and how the same system can power wildly different businesses.

This is the turning point where the Flywheel stops being a diagram and becomes your engine.

Let's align it to your world—and put it to work.

Part 3: Adapting the Membership Flywheel™ Framework to Your Business

Over the years, I've had hundreds of conversations with leaders trying to grow recurring revenue businesses. And while the industries, customers, and price points vary widely, one pattern has always held true: the same principles apply, but the pressure points change.

Every membership business runs on the same flywheel, yet each must decide where to push hardest. A streaming platform lives and dies by engagement frequency. A SaaS company obsesses over workflow integration.

A fitness brand focuses on habit formation, while a nonprofit membership relies on emotional connection and purpose. The framework remains constant—the choreography shifts.

This chapter explores how the **Membership Flywheel™** plays out in practice—not by replacing it, but by tuning it to your business. Each model pushes on different stages, depending on where value and momentum come from. Let's see how that works in the real world, starting with one of the most common approaches: freemium.

Freemium Models: Turning Free into Fuel

Few membership models have reshaped modern growth strategy more than freemium. At its core, it's simple: offer something valuable for free to attract users at scale, then convert a portion into paying members who want more. It's a gateway model built on reciprocity—give enough value upfront that users feel compelled to deepen the relationship.

Spotify is perhaps the gold standard. Its free tier isn't a cheap sample—it's a fully usable experience, good enough to create daily habit. Once that habit forms, the friction of ads or the desire for offline listening makes upgrading feel inevitable. The same dynamic plays out in SaaS tools like Zoom, Canva, or Notion. Free users become emotionally and operationally dependent on the product before they ever reach for their wallets. That dependency isn't accidental; it's engineered.

The freemium model works because it flips the funnel. Instead of paying for every lead, you invest in a product experience that markets itself. But the tradeoff is complexity. You're now managing two member journeys instead of one—each with different motivations, metrics, and value equations. The free user's currency is attention and engagement; the paying member's is commitment and cash. They live side by side, but they don't behave the same.

The companies that master freemium design for this duality. Free is a habit engine. Paid is a depth engine.

Most failures in freemium come from losing balance between the two. Make the free tier too generous and you risk training users never to pay. Make it too restrictive and they'll never form the habits that lead to conversion. The art lies in knowing where to draw that line—generous enough to build trust, scarce enough to make "more" feel worth it.

When executed well, freemium can be one of the most powerful growth engines in the world of membership. It turns marketing spend into product experience, uses behavior to segment and qualify your most likely converters, and builds an always-on audience for winback and referral campaigns. But it's not for the faint of heart. Running a freemium model means running two operating systems simultaneously—each requiring constant optimization, feedback loops, and careful choreography between product, marketing, and data teams.

Major Shifts in the Flywheel

Freemium doesn't replace the Flywheel—it stretches it. The first version runs on attention, not revenue. "Pricing" becomes the cost of time, data, or tolerance for ads. "Retention" means daily usage, not renewals. Then, at the point of conversion, the second Flywheel begins. Now the currency changes to dollars, and the focus shifts to deepening perceived value so members continue paying long after the novelty wears off.

Freemium is deceptively complex because you're running two engines that must feed each other seamlessly.

Hardware-Driven Memberships:
Turning Purchase into Commitment

Some of the most durable membership businesses start with a physical product. Companies like Peloton, Oura Ring, and Starlink all blend an upfront investment in hardware with an ongoing subscription that gives that hardware purpose.

When someone spends real money on a device, they're not just making a purchase—they're joining an ecosystem. They've literally bought in.

That initial transaction changes the psychology of membership. The purchase itself becomes a form of pre-commitment, filtering out casual users and attracting those already motivated to engage. These members are more qualified, more active, and more loyal. But the magic doesn't come from the hardware—it comes from what happens *after* the box opens.

The hardware is the doorway; the membership is the experience that lives inside it. Without ongoing value such as fresh content, real-time insights, connected features, the physical product eventually becomes a relic. The companies that get this right treat the subscription not as a bolt-on, but as the heartbeat of the product. The data, updates, and services layered on top of the device keep it alive.

That's why hardware-based memberships can command premium pricing. Once someone is embedded, the subscription feels less like a fee and more like upkeep—if you keep delivering evolving value.

Major Shifts in the Flywheel

Hardware-based memberships expand the Flywheel from a single funnel into a *two-stage commitment engine*. The first sale is transactional—convincing customers to invest in the hardware itself. The second is relational—convincing them to stay through the ongoing membership experience.

To make this work, onboarding must begin at physical unboxing. The first week with the product should script the "aha moment" that defines the long-term habit—connecting device setup directly to subscription engagement. Some companies require the membership from the start, while others use free trials to prove its worth before billing begins. Both can work, but the differentiator is how seamlessly the physical and digital experiences connect.

This model can be highly defensible, but it raises the bar: when members buy in physically, disappointment cuts deeper.

Nonprofit Memberships: Leading with Mission, Not Perks

Membership isn't just for commerce—it's equally powerful in purpose-driven organizations. Nonprofits use memberships to generate recurring support and deepen connection to their mission. I see it firsthand on the board of my local performing arts center, where our funnel moves from first-time attendee, to repeat visitor, to member, and ultimately to donor. Museums, zoos, and cultural institutions follow a similar pattern, blending access and altruism into a model that sustains both community and operations.

What makes nonprofit membership unique is that emotional value often outweighs functional value. Members don't join for discounts or free parking—they join because they believe in something bigger than themselves. Their sense of belonging is rooted in purpose, not perks. The most successful organizations know this and design their programs accordingly: memberships that feel less like transactions and more like acts of participation.

That doesn't mean benefits don't matter. Recognition, exclusive previews, and behind-the-scenes access help members feel closer to the work they're supporting. But those benefits should amplify the mission, not replace it. If the experience ever starts to feel like buying privilege instead of fueling purpose, the emotional contract breaks.

Major Shifts in the Flywheel

For nonprofits, the Flywheel revolves around storytelling, recognition, and renewal timing. The "value proposition" stage is no longer about features or access—it's about *impact*. The most important communication isn't what members get, but what their contribution makes possible. Engagement means participation—events, volunteering, advocacy—not just usage.

Renewals depend less on utility and more on reinforcement. Impact stories shared before renewal windows remind members why they joined in the first place. Recognition moments—naming donors, featuring members, inviting them to special gatherings—turn passive supporters into active ambassadors.

The nuance, however, is balance. Membership should complement, not cannibalize, broader fundraising. Set pricing too high and you risk crowding out larger gifts; overload the program with perks and you risk eroding the spirit of giving. The strongest nonprofit memberships find harmony between generosity and gratitude—creating a relationship built not on benefits, but on shared belief.

Social Memberships: Where Belonging Becomes the Product

Some memberships sell access. Others sell identity. Social clubs and creator-led communities both win when belonging becomes the product—whether the "host" is a brand, a space, or a person.

At their best, these memberships sell identity. You're not just joining a gym or a workspace—you're joining a world. Every event, every space, every email reinforces that membership isn't about amenities, it's about alignment: *people like me belong here.* When that emotional signal is clear, retention follows naturally. When it wavers, churn can spike overnight.

The tricky part is that this dynamic cuts both ways. Because belonging is so central, even subtle shifts in tone or culture can ripple through the community. Growth that outpaces curation, inconsistent programming, or poorly handled member feedback can fracture trust fast. At the price points many of these memberships command, tolerance for mediocrity is nonexistent.

The strongest social memberships act like great hosts. They build feedback loops into the community, protect the vibe, and make members feel seen. When done right, members don't just stay—they recruit.

Major Shifts in the Flywheel

In social memberships, *curation is acquisition.* The "Value Proposition" stage isn't about discounts or perks—it's about selectivity and alignment. Who gets in defines what the brand stands for, making referrals critical. The "Engagement" stage depends on ritual and rhythm: must-attend events, member-only milestones, and a consistent "vibe" that makes participation feel essential. And "Customer Service" becomes "Member Success," with urgency and empathy baked into every interaction.

The biggest risk is identity erosion—growth outpacing curation, programming losing spark, or perks multiplying without purpose.

Creator-Led Communities: When the Product Is the Person

Creator-led communities run on the same psychology. Members pay for proximity to a voice they trust—often through platforms like Substack, Patreon, and YouTube.

These memberships thrive on authenticity. Members aren't buying access to a library of content—they're buying proximity to someone they feel knows them. The creator's personality, tone, and worldview are the differentiators. That intimacy is powerful, but it's also fragile. If a creator burns out, shifts direction, or loses consistency, the emotional connection can break quickly. And because creators often rely on third-party platforms, their businesses are vulnerable to forces outside their control—algorithm changes, policy shifts, even sudden de-platforming.

The best creator-led memberships recognize that their most precious asset— the creator's voice—is also their most finite resource. They protect it. They systematize without sterilizing, building repeatable structures that preserve authenticity while reducing burnout. Many use a freemium model to widen their funnel: free posts, limited-access podcasts, or short video clips that allow fans to sample before subscribing. But what converts and retains members isn't the tease—it's the trust.

For platforms, the job is simple: reduce friction for creators and keep the relationship feeling direct.

Major Shifts in the Flywheel

In creator communities, the Flywheel's center of gravity shifts from company to individual. The "Value Proposition" stage lives and dies on the strength of the creator's personal brand.

"Acquisition" happens through content discovery and reputation, not paid media. "Engagement" depends on cadence and consistency—the rhythm that keeps members feeling connected. And "Retention" is rooted in authenticity: as long as the creator keeps showing up with honesty and purpose, the community stays intact.

For platforms, retention starts with creators: if creators churn, members follow.

Enterprise / B2B Memberships: Building Renewal Through Results

Membership isn't just a consumer play—some of the most powerful programs operate quietly in the business-to-business world. These are memberships built not around entertainment or convenience, but around access, insight, collaboration, and growth. Think of companies like Slack, HubSpot, Zoom, and GitHub. What they sell isn't a product—it's impact.

B2B memberships thrive on delivering measurable outcomes. A business customer doesn't renew because they "feel loyal"; they renew because they can prove ROI. That makes these models both uniquely durable and uniquely demanding. Every touchpoint—from onboarding to engagement to renewal—must show value in hard numbers: time saved, revenue generated, productivity gained, risk reduced.

What makes these memberships so compelling is that they embed the client deeper into the ecosystem with every use.

The more teams adopt the tools, data, or community, the harder it becomes to imagine operating without them. Just like consumer subscriptions build habit, enterprise memberships build *dependency*—the good kind. They institutionalize value, making renewal not just likely but logical.

Enterprise loyalty is built on trust and results: you earn a place in workflows, strategy, and success metrics.

Major Shifts in the Flywheel

The B2B Flywheel turns on proof. "Acquisition" involves education and credibility—convincing multiple stakeholders that your membership delivers quantifiable business outcomes. "Onboarding" becomes implementation—ensuring value is realized quickly and visible across departments.

"Engagement" centers on adoption depth: how many people are using it, how often, and with what results. "Renewal" depends on documentation—the ability to demonstrate that staying is cheaper, easier, and smarter than switching.

In the B2B world, the sale is just the start. What matters most is what happens between renewals—the everyday reinforcement of impact that makes renewal feel like a no-brainer. When you get that rhythm right, retention stops being a target and becomes a reflex.

Seasonal and Temporary Memberships: When Churn Signals Success

Not every membership is built to last forever—and that's not necessarily a flaw. Some models are designed for life stages, milestones, or short bursts of intense utility. Think of dating apps like Tinder, Hinge, or Bumble, where success literally means you no longer need the product. Or platforms for new parents like Care.com, which solve urgent, temporary needs during a specific season of life.

These businesses face a fascinating paradox: when they work perfectly, members leave. The mission is to help people achieve an outcome, not to hold them hostage. For that reason, the definition of success looks different. The goal is not infinite retention—it's maximizing value *while the member is active* and finding creative ways to extend or re-engage when the next need arises.

The best of these programs embrace impermanence: they front-load value, capture revenue smartly, and design winback for the next life moment.

Major Shifts in the Flywheel

For seasonal or temporary memberships, the Flywheel accelerates quickly—and intentionally winds down. The "Value Proposition" must deliver immediate payoff, not promise it down the road. "Retention" becomes less about longevity and more about intensity—how frequently and effectively members use the service during their active window. "Winback" plays a central role, because members often return when life repeats a need: a new relationship, another child, or a new career stage.

Success depends on outcomes: help members win, even if they outgrow you. They leave as advocates—and often return when the next chapter begins.

Recurring Revenue Businesses:
Turning Obligation into Relationship

Some of the world's largest recurring-revenue businesses don't think of themselves as membership organizations at all. Health insurers, mortgage lenders, phone carriers, and utilities all operate on the same basic principle: customers pay them every month, often for years, sometimes decades. They already have what most companies crave—recurring revenue. What they often lack is recurring *affection*.

In these industries, the customer relationship tends to be defined by obligation, not choice. People pay their premiums, their mortgages, or their utility bills because they must, not because they want to. The experience is transactional and bureaucratic. Engagement usually happens only when something goes wrong. It's a model that sustains revenue but rarely builds loyalty.

But it doesn't have to be that way. These companies have a massive, often untapped opportunity to borrow from membership thinking—to treat their customers not as accounts to be managed, but as people to be retained, educated, and emotionally connected. When they do, the shift can be transformative.

Imagine a health insurer that operates less like a claims processor and more like a wellness partner—proactively helping members stay healthy, save money, and navigate the system. Or a mortgage lender that builds an ongoing relationship beyond the closing date, offering guidance, home equity tools, and rewards for longevity. Even utility providers are beginning to personalize experiences with usage insights, sustainability milestones, and community programs that give customers a reason to feel invested.

The key is to move from *collection* to *connection*. When customers feel like their recurring payments lead to progress—better health, smarter homes, greater financial security—the emotional equation changes. Suddenly, the payment becomes a symbol of partnership rather than penalty.

Major Shifts in the Flywheel

For recurring-revenue industries, the Flywheel doesn't need to be invented—it needs to be *re-humanized*. "Acquisition" is often baked in through necessity, so the opportunity lies in "Engagement" and "Retention." Companies must reimagine onboarding not as paperwork but as orientation: helping customers understand what they've joined and how to make the most of it.

Engagement becomes education—consistent, helpful, proactive communication that builds competence and trust. And renewal isn't about extracting another payment—it's about reinforcing progress and shared goals.

When companies in these sectors adopt a membership mindset, they move from passive revenue to active loyalty. The difference between a bill and a bond is simple: one you pay, the other you believe in.

Transactional Businesses: Using Membership Principles to Build Habit Without Subscriptions

Not every business charges a recurring fee—but every business can benefit from recurring behavior. The same mechanics that make membership models powerful, such as clear value, consistent engagement, emotional connection, and a sense of progress, can transform even transactional industries into engines of predictable growth.

Retailers, restaurants, and financial institutions have all begun to borrow from the membership playbook. The smartest ones don't simply chase transactions; they design systems of return. Whether it's a shopper coming back for a weekly grocery run or a customer repeatedly using a financial app, the goal is the same: build patterns of trust and habit that make repeat usage feel natural, not forced.

Fintech makes this obvious: products like Cash App, Chime, and Robinhood drive repeat behavior through rewards, early access, gamified progress, and personalized insights. Every earned benefit reinforces participation.

The same principles apply in retail and service industries. Starbucks uses gamification and tiers to make every purchase feel like a step toward something bigger. Sephora's Beauty Insider program turns spending into status, guiding customers through a journey of discovery and recognition.

Airlines, hotels, and even automotive brands are layering similar mechanics—progress tracking, community, exclusivity—to convert transactions into relationships.

The key shift for transactional businesses is recognizing that membership doesn't have to mean "monthly billing." It can mean *predictable behavior*. The value exchange moves from subscription revenue to recurring participation. That means measuring engagement not by renewals, but by repeat usage, frequency, and share of wallet.

Major Shifts in the Flywheel

For transactional models, the Flywheel's focus moves from retention to repetition. "Pricing" remains per-use, but "renewals" are replaced by the act of coming back. "Engagement" is the heartbeat—every purchase, tap, or login is both a transaction and a touchpoint that strengthens the relationship.

Design reasons to return: show progress, recognize loyalty, and celebrate milestones—so repeat behavior feels natural.

When done right, transactional businesses can capture the best parts of membership—habit, advocacy, predictability—without the friction of recurring payments. In other words: you don't have to charge like a membership business to grow like one.

Loyalty Services: Turning Engagement into a Gateway

Before we wrap up, it's worth clearing up one of the biggest points of confusion in membership strategy: loyalty programs are not memberships. They share DNA, but they operate on different physics. Programs like Starbucks Rewards, Delta SkyMiles, and Nordstrom's Nordy Club are powerful tools for engagement—but they don't ask customers to commit financially. The "price of entry" is usually an app download or an email address, not a recurring fee.

That difference—paid vs. free—changes everything. Loyalty programs are typically marketing tactics; paid memberships are business models. Loyalty builds reach and data. Membership builds revenue and predictability. Loyalty is about earning points; membership is about earning trust. That said, the best companies don't treat the two as rivals—they treat loyalty as a *feeder system*.

A free loyalty program widens the funnel, helping customers experience early wins, gather benefits, and build familiarity with the brand. A subset of those engaged users will naturally be open to paying for deeper access, exclusivity, or elevated experiences. In this sense, loyalty programs, like freemium models, can become powerful acquisition engines for paid membership when they're structured with intent.

Loyalty programs can also serve as early indicators for who's worth inviting into a paid tier. When you can identify your most active, highest-value participants through behavioral data, you can graduate them into programs that offer more status and more tangible perks, creating a ladder of engagement that feels earned, not sold.

Major Shifts in the Flywheel

The Flywheel for loyalty services runs on awareness and engagement, not subscription revenue. "Pricing" isn't measured in dollars but in data, attention, and participation. "Retention" hinges on consistent interaction—earning and redeeming points, checking balances, visiting stores—not on renewal billing.

When paired with a paid membership, loyalty becomes the upstream engine that fills your acquisition funnel with qualified prospects. The key is to design connective tissue between the two experiences: benefits that preview what "paid" feels like, messaging that clarifies the step up in value, and data systems that make the transition seamless.

If the goal is predictable revenue and higher lifetime value, loyalty should never be a substitute for membership. It should be the spark that lights the fire.

One Flywheel, Many Paths

Every membership business runs on the same Flywheel, but no two spin quite the same way. A streaming platform lives and dies by content discovery and engagement frequency. A B2B network measures its value in relationships and learning. A hardware-driven program blends physical product and digital experience, while a creator-led community is built on trust and personality. Different shapes, same physics.

That's the beauty of this framework—it bends to fit you. You don't need to reinvent your model to make it work. You need to identify *where your momentum comes from* and apply force there. The Flywheel gives you a shared language for understanding that flow: how value becomes habit, how habit becomes loyalty, and how loyalty compounds into growth.

When you know your model, you know your leverage points. A freemium app might obsess over onboarding and upgrade prompts. A social club might refine the culture of belonging. A fintech startup might optimize daily engagement, while a nonprofit might focus on storytelling before renewal. The details differ, but the system holds.

Membership mastery isn't about doing everything—it's about doing the right things in sync. When each stage reinforces the next, the result is compounding strength. Over time, the Flywheel stops feeling like a framework and starts feeling inevitable.

And when you get it right, something powerful happens: staying becomes easier than leaving. That's how you build not just growth, but resilience.

Adapting to Your Stage of Maturity

The same Flywheel can look entirely different depending on where you are in your journey. A new membership needs clarity. A scaling one needs focus. A legacy business shifting toward membership needs transformation. Just as no two industries share the same emphasis, no two companies share the same starting point. Your Flywheel priorities will shift based on where you are in your growth journey.

- **New Programs** should start with the foundation: a compelling value proposition, the right pricing and offer strategy, and a clean signup flow. Without those, no amount of retention work will matter. Once people are joining, shift quickly to onboarding—showing new members value fast enough that they never second-guess the decision.
- **Established Programs** often find their biggest wins in engagement and renewals. Dig into why people leave. What moments predict churn? Often, the fix isn't adding more—it's *refining what already works* and making it more visible, consistent, and easy to love.
- **Businesses Transitioning to Membership** face a different challenge entirely: redefining value. You're not just selling products anymore— you're selling a relationship. That means reframing messaging, realigning incentives, and designing distribution that attracts recurring customers instead of one-time buyers. The transition is rarely simple, but it's worth it.

Final Thoughts: Building Your Growth Engine

The **Membership Flywheel™** isn't a theory—it's an operating system for sustainable growth. Each stage builds on the next, turning small, consistent improvements into exponential impact. When you refine one stage, you strengthen them all.

In the chapters that follow, we'll break down each stage of the Flywheel, exploring how world-class membership businesses design, measure, and optimize them in practice. You'll see how leading programs engineer ecosystems where every interaction reinforces value—and how you can do the same.

You'll learn what to measure, what usually breaks, and how to fix it.

The goal isn't just to grow faster. It's to grow *stronger*. To build a system that compounds loyalty, revenue, and impact—quarter after quarter, year after year.

So, as we move ahead, map your Flywheel. Test it. Refine it. Strengthen it. Because once it starts spinning, it becomes more than a framework. It becomes your growth engine—and every turn makes the next one easier.

Let's get to work—and start building momentum that never stops.

Chapter 2

Crafting Your Irresistible Member Offer

The Moment That Changed How I Think About the Customer

A few years ago, I sat in a high-stakes business review at SiriusXM, facing the CEO across the conference table. Like every month, we dissected our numbers—what was working, what wasn't, and which initiatives could move the needle. But this time was different. Our numbers were down because we'd stretched beyond our core superfans and were trying to convert a broader audience that didn't yet "get" the value. I understood every data point and came prepared to explain why things had shifted and how we planned to fix it.

Then the CEO cut through all of it with a simple question: "Matt, who is your customer, and what problem are you solving?"

I hesitated. I fumbled through demographic insights and engagement trends, but deep down, I knew I wasn't truly answering the question. I had been so focused on specific tactics that I had lost sight of the foundation of the business. That moment was a wake-up call, and it permanently changed how I think about membership growth.

Learn from my mistake: if you can't answer that question clearly, your offer will drift, your marketing will get louder, and your retention will quietly get worse. This chapter will help you build a value proposition that makes joining—and staying—feel like the obvious choice.

Part 1: Who's Your Customer—Really?

Here's where every great membership business begins—not with what *you* want to offer, but with what *they* need.

The problem is that too many companies jump straight into execution. They start building before they've taken the time to pause—to discuss, debate, and research what their customers truly want. Even more importantly, they skip over understanding who their customer really is.

And no, it's rarely "everyone." The tighter your customer definition, the sharper your offer becomes.

This is when you need to slow things down. Make sure the next few questions are being asked, debated, and answered. It doesn't matter whether your membership is still being built, fully mature, or somewhere in between—it's always the right time to dive into this work.

Because here's what I've seen, time and again, in every company I've worked with—from Amazon and Walmart to the startups I advise: these questions rarely get answered clearly. And when they do, they're not aligned, operationalized, or top of mind when strategic decisions are made.

So, let's fix that—right here, right now. Let's stop building for ourselves and start creating clear solutions to real, persistent problems.

Start Here: Understand Your Customer and Their Problem

Before you build (or rebuild) your membership offering, get crystal clear on three things:

1 - Who is your ideal customer?

Describe them in vivid detail. Who are they? What do they care about? What stage of life or business are they in? What does a great day—or a bad day—look like for them? The more specific you get, the more real they'll feel.

Empathize deeply. Step into their world. Imagine their daily routine—their frustrations, goals, and tradeoffs. Tools like AI can even help you craft realistic personas that make these customers come to life.

2 - What specific problem are they facing?

What's keeping them up at night? What pain point does your membership solve? You're not selling a list of benefits—you're solving a problem that matters.

3 - What outcome are they hoping for?

Paint a vivid picture of transformation. How will their life or work be better because of your membership? What's easier, faster, or less stressful?

Here's the magic: When you understand your customer at a human level— what drives them, frustrates them, excites them—everything else gets easier. Pricing. Positioning. Retention. All of it.

A Framework for Defining Your Customer's Problem

Now that you've started thinking about who your customer really is, let's get specific about the problem they need you to solve.

Many companies struggle at this step because they define the problem too vaguely ("people want to be healthier") or too broadly ("we want to help everyone improve their wellness"). The goal here isn't to be clever; it's to be crystal clear.

A strong problem statement connects the customer, the cause, and the consequence—and then highlights the transformation they're craving.

You can think of it like this:

[Customer Segment] → *struggles with* → *[Challenge]*

↓ *Because of* → *[Root Cause]*

↓ *Which leads to* → *[Pain Point]*

↓ *When they really want* → *[Ideal Solution]*

For example, let's say you're creating a fictional health and wellness membership. Here's a focused problem statement:

"A busy urban millennial professional struggles with maintaining a healthy lifestyle because they lack the time to research the best supplements, exercise routines, and meal suggestions. This leads to frustration, wasted money trying out different miracle pills, unrealistic exercise routines, and inconsistent eating habits, when what they really want is a simple, expert-guided plan that tells them how to be healthier, personalized for their body type, budget, and interests."

See how that works? That one statement does a lot: it identifies *who* the customer is, *what's* causing the problem, and *what* outcome they want. From here, you can immediately see what a high-value membership might include:

- Personalized health assessments with clear recommendations
- Expert-curated supplement kits, delivered monthly
- Quick, realistic workouts tailored to tight schedules
- Meal planning tools with optional grocery delivery

Notice how a clear problem naturally guides you toward relevant, compelling solutions—unlike generic "benefits" that sound nice but don't meet a real need.

Common Pitfalls and Practical Solutions

At this stage, you've defined your customer and their problem—the foundation of any strong membership business.

Before moving on to design your value proposition, it's worth pausing to understand a few common pitfalls that can quietly derail your strategy.

Each one is fixable with the right approach, as long as you catch it early.

Mistake #1: Problem Statements That Are Too Vague

The Issue: Many companies define member needs with broad statements like "People want to save money on groceries." This lacks the specificity needed to develop truly compelling solutions.

The Solution: Create detailed problem statements that identify:

- Who experiences the problem (demographics, psychographics, behaviors)
- What specific pain they feel (emotional, financial, practical)
- Why it matters to them (impact on their life or goals)
- When and how often they encounter it (frequency, triggering situations)

Before: "People want convenient meal options."

After: "Working parents with children under 12 struggle to prepare nutritious weeknight dinners because they're exhausted after work and have limited time. This leads to repetitive meals, unhealthy takeout choices, and guilt about not providing better options for their families. What they really want is a solution that minimizes planning and preparation time while still delivering wholesome meals their children will actually eat."

Mistake #2: Solution-First Thinking

The Issue: Companies often define problems in terms of their solution: "People need a better meal-planning app." This approach obscures the actual customer need.

The Solution: Separate the problem definition from your solution. Describe what frustrates customers without reference to how you will solve it.

1. Start by reviewing your marketing materials and product documentation

2. Highlight any instances where you define customer needs in terms of your product features

3. Rewrite these statements to focus exclusively on customer challenges

Before: "Customers need a more intuitive grocery delivery interface."

After: "Customers get frustrated when grocery shopping online because they can't easily find the specific items they want, leading to incomplete orders or substitutions they don't like."

Mistake #3: Assuming Without Validating

The Issue: Companies make educated guesses about customer problems rather than confirming them through research.

The Solution: Validate your problem statements through:

- Customer interviews (aim for at least 15-20 conversations)
- Behavioral analysis (what do usage patterns reveal about pain points?)
- Quantifying the impact (how much time/money/effort does this problem cost?)

If you can't check those boxes, you're taking a gamble on your value proposition rather than building from real, actionable insight. Validation can be as simple as well-structured interviews, user tests with recorded feedback, or asking friends and family for brutally honest reactions—as long as you treat it like research, not reassurance.

Part 2: Study Competitors and Ask Your Customers

Don't reinvent the wheel. Chances are, other companies are already trying to solve a similar problem for your audience—even if they don't look like direct competitors.

For example, a service offering nutrition counseling covered by insurance could offer valuable lessons for a care management platform focused on Medicare patients. I recently worked with a client on exactly that. The industries were different, but the member pain points—trust, access, cost—were almost identical.

The key is to look broadly and listen deeply. Study competitors across adjacent categories and talk directly to your prospective and current customers. Both groups are treasure troves of insight—if you ask the right questions and summarize their responses in a way your team can use.

The secret is discipline: following a clear playbook for studying the competition, testing ideas, and refining your value proposition with precision.

Learn from Your Competitors (But Don't Copy Them)

Take a deep dive into what's already working and failing in the market. The best way to do this is to become a customer of your competitors.

When we were building out Walmart+, my team and I did something simple but revealing: we signed up for Amazon Prime, Instacart+, FreshDirect, and other grocery delivery services just to see how they worked. We wanted to experience firsthand:

- What was the first-day experience like? Did I immediately understand the value? Was the onboarding clear?
- Which benefits did I actually use? Were there benefits I thought would be valuable but ignored in practice?

- Did anything make me second-guess my membership?
- What unexpectedly delighted me? Were there benefits I didn't expect to like but became compelling?

High-performing membership businesses systematically evaluate competitors, summarizing their strengths and weaknesses in a format that the entire team can analyze. This ensures that strategic gaps and opportunities don't go unnoticed.

As you're evaluating the Value Prop for your service, work with your team to identify 8-12 relevant competitors across three categories:

- Direct competitors (3-4 companies offering similar services)
- Adjacent competitors (2-3 companies serving the same needs but doing so differently)
- Inspiration companies (3-5 companies in other industries with similar business models)

For each, evaluate the specific benefits each offers, their likely target customer, and how those benefits stack up against your customer's needs. Then ask: what's missing—and what could we do better?

Once you've mapped the landscape, the next step is to test those insights with the people who matter most: your customers.

Ask Your Customers What Actually Matters

While working on this book, I started re-watching Mad Men and remembered why Don Draper, the enigmatic creative director, excels at persuasion. His genius wasn't just in crafting the perfect slogan; it was in the way he asked questions. Don Draper asked sharper questions than anyone in the room. You should too. Use both data and human stories to understand *why* your benefits matter, not just *what* they are.

So how do you supercharge Don Draper's strategy and bring it to your membership business? The most effective approach combines quantitative validation (what do large numbers of customers say they want?) with qualitative depth (why do these benefits matter to this specific person?).

Quantitative Benefit Testing Examples

Survey at least 200-300 potential members from your target demographic with these critical questions:

1. **"Rank these potential benefits from most to least valuable."**
   This tells you what truly matters vs. what benefits are just nice to have.

2. **"How likely would you be to use this benefit? (1-5 scale)"**
   Some benefits sound great in theory but get ignored in practice.

3. **"What's missing that would make this membership a no-brainer for you?"**
   This highlights gaps you hadn't even considered.

4. **"Would you pay for these benefits at this price point?"**
   Use discrete choice testing to evaluate different combinations of benefits and price points. This gives you more reliable insight into perceived value and willingness to pay than asking, "How much would you pay?" in the abstract.

Qualitative Benefit Exploration

While surveys tell you *what* people value, interviews and focus groups tell you *why* they value things. With 15-20 participants from your target market, dig deeper with open-ended questions:

1. **"Walk me through your current experience with [problem area]."**
   Listen for emotional touchpoints, frustrations, and workarounds.

2. **"If you had a magic wand to address [problem area], what would you do?"**
   Understand their ideal outcome, not just the absence of problems.

3. **"Of these potential benefits, which would make the biggest difference in your life, and why?"**
   Look for stories and specific use cases, not just general preferences.

4. **"Describe a situation where you would use this benefit."**
   Concrete scenarios reveal how benefits fit into customers' lives.

Bringing It Together

Combining quantitative prioritization (what matters most) with qualitative depth (why it matters) creates a powerful foundation for your value proposition.

You'll know not just which benefits to offer, but how to position and communicate them so they resonate emotionally with your audience—while uncovering any potential barriers to joining before they become costly mistakes.

Part 3: Map Your Benefits

You've defined your customer, pinpointed their problem, and identified the benefits that truly excite them. That work gives you the foundation—now it's time to turn it into something tangible: a membership offering that serves their needs and drives action.

The goal here is clarity. Great memberships don't just pile on features; they organize them around what members value most. This is where structure turns insight into strategy.

Primary vs. Secondary Benefits: Creating a Strategic Framework

At the heart of every great membership program are the Primary or Hero Benefits—the undeniable, must-have features that convince people to sign up. These are immediate, undeniable, and easy to explain—the things that make someone say, "I'd pay for that." Think of:

- Amazon Prime's free two-day shipping
- Costco's wholesale pricing
- AAA's roadside assistance
- HBO Max's exclusive content
- Spotify's ad-free music streaming

Each of these benefits solves a clear, pressing problem—the kind that makes joining feel like a no-brainer.

For some services, one primary benefit is enough, but for many, it is not sufficient to keep members engaged long-term. This is where secondary benefits come in. These benefits enhance the experience, making the membership feel richer over time.

While they may not drive the initial signup, they add layers of value that increase engagement and reduce churn. For instance:

- Amazon Prime Video (secondary to shipping)
- Costco's travel and insurance discounts (secondary to wholesale pricing)
- AAA's lockout service (secondary to roadside assistance)
- Content downloads for HBO Max (secondary to exclusive content)
- Spotify's curated playlists (secondary to ad-free listening)

These secondary benefits create reasons for members to continue engaging with the service well beyond their initial reason for joining.

The Strategic Purpose of Different Benefit Types

You've done the hard part—defining your customer, their pain points, and the benefits that matter most.

Now it's time to connect the dots. Every great membership program balances its benefits across three goals: acquisition, engagement, and retention. Get that balance right, and you'll create a system that attracts members, keeps them active, and makes them stay.

→ Acquisition: Hook with Tangible, Immediate Value

Primary benefits are usually the reason people sign up in the first place. These should be clear, tangible, and easy to explain. If potential members can't quickly grasp why your membership is worth paying for, they'll move on. The hook must feel both valuable *and* believable.

→ Engagement: Keep Members Interested and Delighted

Secondary benefits come into play after signup. These are the "surprise and delight" moments that deepen engagement over time. While they may not drive the initial purchase, they help members feel like they're getting ongoing value—and discovering new perks as they go.

→ Retention: Build an Ecosystem of Value

Retention happens when the membership becomes a habit. If your offer is too one-dimensional—useful only for a single purpose—members will eventually churn. The best programs create a well-rounded benefit ecosystem that integrates into a member's daily life and feels hard to give up.›

A word of caution: stick to one or two primary benefits and no more than three to five secondary ones. Beyond that, you risk "feature overload," where members get confused or overwhelmed. It's fine to offer more behind the scenes, but keep your core offer focused.

Take Amazon Prime, for example: the service includes dozens of perks, but it consistently promotes just a few. That clarity is a big part of what makes Prime feel so accessible—and indispensable.

Case Study: Costco's Executive Membership

Costco's Executive Membership is a textbook example of a no-brainer value proposition. Instead of overwhelming customers with vague perks, Costco delivers clear, tangible benefits that are easy to understand and justify. The result? One of the most successful membership models in retail.

Simplicity in Structure

Costco offers only two tiers: Gold Star and Executive. The Executive Membership, priced at $120/year, gives 2% cash back on eligible purchases. For frequent shoppers, this math makes it easy: spend $6,000 annually and the membership pays for itself. No mental gymnastics—just clear value.

Store Design Reinforces the Value Message

Costco's warehouse-style stores are intentionally no-frills. The layout, lighting, and shelving all send the same message: "We invest in low prices, not fancy displays." This physical environment reinforces the core membership promise—value above all.

The "Treasure Hunt" Keeps Members Coming Back

A secondary benefit that fuels engagement is Costco's ever-changing inventory. Limited-time products and rotating deals create a "treasure hunt" experience, encouraging return visits even when customers don't have a shopping list. It's both functional and emotionally engaging.

Fewer Choices, More Confidence

Costco strategically limits its product selection—around 4,000 SKUs compared to over 50,000 in a typical supermarket. This curated assortment simplifies decisions and reinforces trust: "We've already found the best value for you." That clarity is a benefit in itself.

The Result? An Industry-Leading Renewal Rate

Costco boasts a renewal rate of about 90%—far above the norm. Why? Because their membership program aligns price, experience, and benefits into a clear, compelling promise. It's not just about discounts; it's about trust, consistency, and simplicity done exceptionally well.

Benefit Mapping Exercise: Aligning Benefits with Strategic Goals

To structure your own membership benefits effectively, use this benefit mapping exercise with your team:

1. List all potential benefits you could offer.

2. For each benefit, score (1-5) its potential impact on:

- Acquisition (driving initial signups)
- Engagement (increasing regular usage)
- Retention (preventing cancellations).

3. Identify the 1 or 2 benefits with the highest acquisition scores as your Primary Benefits.

4. Select 3 to 5 benefits with the highest engagement and retention scores as your Secondary Benefits.

This exercise forces prioritization and ensures your membership structure has a clear strategic focus rather than a scattershot collection of unrelated benefits.

Potential Benefit	Acquisition Impact (1-5)	Engagement Impact (1-5)	Retention Impact (1-5)	Total Score	Type
Free 2-day shipping	5	4	4	13	Primary
Video streaming	2	5	4	11	Secondary
Music streaming	1	4	3	8	Secondary
Early access to sales	3	3	2	8	Secondary

A great membership isn't about stacking more benefits—it's about structuring them to deliver value at every stage of the journey. Too many benefits, and you confuse the message. Too few, and you fail to meet the needs of different member types.

Primary benefits should make signing up irresistible, while secondary benefits deepen engagement and give members reasons to stay. But here's the most interesting part: what's considered "primary" vs. "secondary" can vary dramatically by member.

When I was on the Amazon Prime team, most members joined for the retail benefits like free same-day delivery and shipping with no minimum. Digital perks like Prime Video and Prime Music were secondary for many. But for some new members, that started to shift. As Prime Video launched more exclusive content, some members came in because of video content—and only later came to appreciate the shipping benefits. Their engagement and retention patterns, as well as the amount they spent at Amazon before and after joining, were completely different, but both groups remained loyal.

The best membership programs recognize that value isn't one-size-fits-all. Instead, they build layered experiences that not only attract members but keep them coming back. So, the real question is: *Do your membership benefits make both joining and staying feel like an obvious choice?*

Part 4: Evolve or Die—How to Refresh Your Value Prop

A great value proposition isn't static. What works today might lose its appeal over time. You need to develop a system for refreshing the benefits as member needs evolve. This is especially true if you see declining conversion rates or usage patterns, or when competitors offer new benefits to their members.

When to Reassess Your Value Proposition

You don't need to test constantly, but you do need discipline around when and why to revisit your offer. Key moments include:

- **Before Launch**: Validate core assumptions before investing in full development.
- **When Growth Plateaus**: Identify if your value proposition no longer resonates.
- **When Competition Increases**: Ensure your differentiation remains meaningful.
- **When Usage Patterns Change**: Adapt to evolving customer needs and behaviors.
- **When Considering Price Increases:** Tie a price increase to an enhanced benefit launch to make the price increase feel like a positive rather than a negative. This topic is discussed in more detail in Ch 10: The Levers Behind Continuous Growth

How to Test and Evolve Your Value Proposition

Surveys tell you what people say they want. Tests show you what they actually do. That's why Amazon prioritized experimentation over opinion. Use these approaches to test new value proposition elements:

1. **A/B Testing[2] Landing Pages**: Create new pages testing different benefits or messaging to measure impact on conversion rates.

2. **Limited-Release Benefits**: Roll out new benefits to a small segment of members to gauge usage and satisfaction before full deployment.

---

[2] **A/B Testing** – A method of experimentation where two or more variations are shown to different segments of members to determine which performs better based on a key metric.

3. **Competitive Response Testing**: When competitors launch new features, survey your members to understand the appeal and whether similar benefits would enhance your offering.

4. **Benefit Sunsetting Analysis**: Before removing underutilized features, test with a small member segment to measure impact on retention.

At Amazon Prime, we tested every new benefit concept against a simple framework:

Would it drive new memberships? Increase engagement? Reduce churn?

Just as importantly, we asked whether it reinforced our core promise—making members' lives easier and more convenient. That discipline kept the team focused and the membership evolving with customer needs.

Mike Amsel - Former Weight Watchers CMO and former SVP, Growth for SiriusXM

I had the privilege of meeting Matt through work, back when I was running growth at Pandora. Pandora, the music company, is a classic freemium business with three tiers of service/value for the listener: an ad-supported free experience, a paid ad-free radio tier, and a fully interactive premium offering, all built on best-in-class personalization services to provide the best possible song recommendations to the listener.

My job was to drive high-quality listeners to the platform, at profitable costs, and then figure out how to pull every single lever possible to help them stay, engage, upgrade, and retain on platform, including the tens of millions of listeners already active on the service.

After about a year in the role, SiriusXM acquired Pandora, and Matt was my counterpart leading the streaming business at SiriusXM. Almost immediately, we found ourselves shoulder to shoulder trying to answer the same question: how do you leverage multiple platforms to create a better customer experience and a better business outcome? More specifically, how do you position different services so they feel additive across a listener's journey, rather than competitive in the customer's mind?

That work, the late nights, the healthy debate, the investments in strategy, the execution and insights became the foundation of our relationship that would fuel many lively discussions over the years, even as both of us moved on to other organizations. We continue to push each other on our convictions and complement each other's thinking in ways only a therapist would truly appreciate. I'm proud to call Matt a friend, and I'm glad he's putting his hard-earned wisdom and mastery on paper to share with others.

I've found Matt to be a rare breed in business, an operator who's deeply systems-minded but always grounded in the human question that matters most—why would a real person care enough to do this again tomorrow? He's able to move from 10,000 feet to 10 seamlessly and has a vision and foresight that avoids the short-term pitfalls that many marketers fall into.

One of the most durable lessons I learned from our time working together and apply in my daily practice: **great membership businesses require teams to master both the science and the soul of the experience.**

The science is table stakes. You need strong data discipline—the math, the measurement, clean holdouts, target reach and frequency, structured split testing. You need a clear view of the consumer journey, with an understanding of how people move through the funnel and which interventions will actually change behavior. You need defined cohorts of customers that allow you to predict outcomes accurately…and you need an alignment between engineering, analytics, product, and marketing teams to maintain a clean data layer despite constant releases and test iterations. If you're reading this book, I assume you already know you need the ground truth and operational rigor to manage the business for growth; without it, you're just telling yourself stories, and there's already enough pseudoscience in this industry.

But science alone doesn't build habit, loyalty, or love. And it certainly doesn't create breakout growth.

It's the soul of the experience that is the catalyst for great companies and what separates enduring membership businesses from just another newsletter/loyalty program.

The soul of a service isn't just found in the consistency of its brand platform—its voice, fonts, logos, or colors. Those matter, but they're only the surface. The soul lives in the promise you make when someone signs up; it's in the clarity of the value your service provides and in the discipline with which you deliver on that promise. It's the confidence to serve a specific audience relentlessly on their journey, speaking to them in compelling ways and knowing all too well the goal they have in mind. Over time, that consistency turns a service/subscription into a relationship—one where your social channels stop functioning as customer support and start functioning as consumer advocacy.

It's a slippery slope, but Matt and I would always joke it's a sign of success when you find a small minority of members using your service in unique and innovative ways beyond its original intent (think of all those blogs dedicated to gaming airline points, front running features from new Apple feature releases, or finding the best discounts at Walmart/Costco).

When it's done well and a trusted relationship is established, your business starts to feel alive. In my eyes, membership companies evolve in three stages: from a purely transactional service, to a utility that meaningfully improves daily life, and finally to a trusted platform with a relationship people rely on. When this change happens, retention stops being something you optimize towards and becomes something you've already earned. Those three stages—transactional, utilitarian, and trusted relationship—are the progressions I've consistently seen separate high-churn subscriptions from products people stay with for years, and it's because they've established a soul that transcends the category.

When describing a membership's soul, I can think of three practical examples I've seen in my life, both as a consumer and as a marketer, that have showcased the clarity of understanding an audience and successfully built a trusted relationship that transcends the category.

1. **Duolingo is the first example that comes to mind**. Years ago, if you told me that push notifications about the emotional health of a cartoon owl would help me learn Italian, I would have asked to have you institutionalized. And yet, here we are.

    Duolingo didn't just compete with incumbent language-learning products; it redefined the category and materially expanded the TAM (total addressable market). Sure, they used smart gamification—breaking learning into manageable steps, rewarding progress, and reinforcing habits through repetition. But those mechanics alone don't explain their success.

    What set Duolingo apart was personality. The voice. The tone. The animations. The way the product speaks to you as you move through a lesson: encouraging, playful, occasionally guilt-inducing, but always supportive. These weren't surface-level branding choices; they were expressions of a clear promise: learning a language can be interactive, rewarding, and even fun.

    That consistency in personality gave Duolingo a soul. And with it came trust. Over time, the app stopped feeling like a chore or a tool you used; it started feeling like a trusted companion you returned to. That's how Duolingo didn't just steal share—it won the category.

2. **Peloton is the next example that stands out.** They didn't just transform at-home exercise; they reshaped how people experience fitness altogether. What could have easily resembled the transactional workout programs of the past—think P90X, where content is delivered and motivation is left to the user—instead became something far more trusted and deeply embedded in millions of people's lives.

Peloton invested heavily in community, personalization, and coaching, weaving each into every moment of the experience. The result was a connection that went well beyond an exercise class. I know Peloton members who would be more excited to run into their favorite Peloton instructor on the street than most A-list celebrities.

That loyalty wasn't accidental. The product was designed to encourage consistent use through streaks and progress tracking. The community reinforced behavior through simple but powerful gestures—high fives, shout-outs, shared milestones. Coaches weren't just instructors; they were ever-present guides, pushing mental toughness, celebrating wins big and small. Coaches started showing up not just in classes but across social media and live activations, making them feel more like a friend than a talking head on TV telling you to bike/run/row faster.

Over time, something subtle but powerful happened. People didn't just work out more—they had more fun, felt connected to others, and stayed committed to the habit, all from the isolation of their own homes. Peloton built a soul into its service, both inside the product and outside in the real world, that made the experience feel alive. And that soul is what turned a piece of equipment into a category-defining relationship.

3. **The final example is a lived experience from my time at Pandora.** Early in my tenure, a major A-list pop star was releasing a highly anticipated album. Pandora had a massive user base, and we were focused on activating listeners to drive more listening hours. We decided to send an email campaign promoting the release to everyone who listened to pop music.

   It sounded harmless at the time.

   Instead, the campaign produced a measurable drop in engagement, depressed activation for that cohort for weeks, and delivered the highest unsubscribe rate I saw during my time in the role.

Why? Because the soul of Pandora was built on a simple promise: it knew your music taste better than you did. Pandora wasn't just a radio service; it was the trusted friend who always played the right next song. And when that friend suddenly started promoting an artist outside of your personal taste zone—no matter how popular the release—it broke that trust. We violated the very soul of the service we had worked so hard to build.

That moment became a lasting lesson for me. Once trust is established, it must be protected relentlessly. Understanding the emotional connection your customers have with your product isn't a nice-to-have—it's foundational. Break it, and the data will let you know immediately.

These trusted relationships aren't reserved for the world's largest entertainment apps. In my experience, most membership missteps happen early—when companies rush to launch without clearly articulating where value is created or how the service earns a meaningful place in a customer's life. One recent experience made this especially clear.

Several months ago, I stayed at a boutique hotel in New York City. The stay itself was exceptional. From the doorman to the concierge to the waiter at dinner, everyone knew our names, remembered our preferences, and made the experience feel personal. It didn't feel transactional; it felt thoughtful. It felt like a home away from home.

After the stay, the hotel followed up with an offer to join a new membership tier they were launching for frequent guests. Given my interest in establishing a consistent NYC base, I was intrigued and asked what value the membership would provide. The answer was straightforward: early access to room reservations, small discounts on rates, and priority bookings at their restaurant.

On paper, those benefits sounded reasonable. In reality, they missed the point entirely. The value I experienced during my stay wasn't about booking mechanics or discounts—it was trust, familiarity, and a sense of belonging. The hotel had already earned emotional equity by making me feel known and taken care of. But instead of building on that relationship, the membership framed value as a list of transactional perks.

Had the membership been positioned around the job I was actually hiring it to do—creating a true home base in New York—the value would have been obvious. Access to shared spaces between stays. Support for hosting meetings or events. The ability to receive packages, extend benefits to family and friends, or participate in curated experiences led by the hotel's team, all likely perks included but featured nowhere in the value proposition of the membership. In other words, the value wasn't aligned to the customer's real needs; it was built to the business's operational levers.

What went wrong wasn't pricing or execution; it was misalignment. The business misunderstood where value was truly created and, as a result, struggled to convert interest into commitment. When I later spoke with the hotel's manager, they acknowledged the membership had been difficult to sustain and was likely to be discontinued—ending the program before it ever really started.

The lesson is simple, but often ignored: membership is not a pricing tactic or an add-on feature. It is a product in its own right. And like any product, it requires a clear understanding of customer needs, a disciplined definition of value, and the commitment to deliver that value consistently over time. Get this wrong, and you'll be fighting an uphill battle to even get started.

The last piece of advice I'll offer builds on everything that comes before it. Once you've established a membership base and begun to see traction, it's critical you study your outliers. Focus on your most engaged customers, the small group of "super loyals" who show up consistently and extract the most value from your service.

Go beyond demographics and dashboards. Talk to them. Understand how they think about your product, the role it plays in their lives, and the relationship they believe they have with your brand. Pay close attention to the moments of magic—the experiences that moved them from trying your service, to forming a utility-based habit, to ultimately trusting it enough to stick around. When do they think to use your service, what triggers that demand, and how does your service show up as the solution in their minds?

There is an extraordinary amount of insight locked inside your most loyal customers, and most companies never take the time to ask for it. Those learnings become the blueprint for growth: not by chasing new features or promotions, but by understanding how to move less engaged users up the same value curve your best customers have already climbed.

While these anecdotes are fun, the outcomes of these companies speak for themselves in the data and performance observed. I've spent way too much time looking at retention trends across subscription service verticals, leveraging competitive tools like Antenna to track trends. (You'll see much of their coverage in the WSJ/business press covering the streaming wars, and some is available for free on their website.)

In each major category—music, video streaming, fitness, language, grocery shopping, etc.—there's always one service that outperforms its peers by anywhere from 15% to 50% on retention, and in each scenario, it's a service that has established a strong and recognizable soul that wins the category.

If you've worked in subscription marketing, you know how hard it is to unlock one, two, or five points of churn improvement—and how celebrated those wins are. But the businesses that truly outperform don't get there by mastering the science alone; they get there by pairing it with soul. They grow it responsibly over time, starting with their best customers and moving it to the masses.

So as you read this book and think about the mechanics of building membership—acquisition, onboarding, engagement, retention—don't stop at the science. Ask yourself: what is the soul of your product, platform, or service? And just as importantly, how are you deliberately unleashing that soul back to your customers?

Because membership isn't a pricing model or a label. It's a promise you keep in small, consistent ways—until habit turns into identity, and identity hardens into loyalty.

That's the work.

And when you get it right, that's the win.

Final Thoughts: Make Membership an Easy "Yes"

At its core, every great membership comes down to one thing: making the decision to join feel effortless.

If you haven't clearly defined your core customer and the benefits you offer, your membership will struggle to gain traction. But once you identify a specific problem and design benefits that make joining a no-brainer, everything else becomes easier.

Here's your playbook for turning "maybe" into "yes":

- **Define your target customer**
  Get specific—demographics, psychographics, behaviors. Who are they really?
- **Write a focused problem statement**
  Use this format: *"A [customer] struggles with [challenge] because [root cause]…"*
- **Validate it through real conversations**
  Talk to 15–20 actual customers. Run a survey with 200–300 potential members. Listen first, then refine.
- **Benchmark against competitors**
  Analyze 8–12 relevant offerings: direct competitors, adjacent services, and inspiration brands in other industries.
- **Map your benefits with strategic clarity**
  Identify your primary (hook) and secondary (engagement) benefits. Score each in terms of how they support acquisition, engagement, and retention.
- **Test, iterate, evolve**
  Launch landing page tests, pilot benefits with small groups, and refresh your offer when growth plateaus.

The goal is not to be everything to everyone. It's to be the *obvious choice* for the right customer. When your offer is clear, relevant, and well-validated, saying yes becomes easy—and staying becomes automatic.

The best membership businesses don't just market aggressively or add random perks. They deeply understand their members' needs and build solutions that make membership feel like a must-have. When a customer looks at your membership offering, the value should be so obvious that the decision to join requires almost no deliberation. Once someone becomes a member, they should be continuously reminded of the value they're receiving—a theme we'll dig deeper into in Ch 9: Reinforcing Value and Reducing Churn.

That simple question—"Who is your customer, and what problem are you solving?"—should guide every decision you make about your membership.

Get that right, and everything else follows: growth, retention, and long-term success.

Chapter 3

Pricing for Growth and Loyalty

Pricing & Offer Strategies – The Art and Science of Setting the Right Price

Few decisions shape a membership business more profoundly than pricing. Get it right, and you create a foundation for sustainable growth. Get it wrong, and even the best product can struggle to find its audience.

This chapter explores the art and science of pricing membership services—blending lessons from multi-billion-dollar subscription models with hard-earned insights from pricing missteps along the way. Just remember: if people don't value your membership, no price is low enough.

Part 1: Pricing a Membership Service

Pricing a membership service is fundamentally different from pricing a retail product. With a traditional product, the pricing equation is relatively straightforward: you set a price, customers decide whether to buy, and the transaction concludes. The relationship between price and value is immediate and contained within that single purchase decision.

Membership businesses operate in an entirely different paradigm. Your pricing strategy isn't just about facilitating the initial sale, it's about creating a sustainable relationship that encourages members to stay subscribed month after month, year after year.

This ongoing commitment transforms pricing from a tactical decision into a strategic cornerstone that shapes everything from acquisition costs to retention rates to lifetime value.

Unlike e-commerce businesses that can A/B test prices and measure results within days, membership companies must play the long game. A pricing structure that drives impressive signup numbers might reveal its flaws only months later when retention data emerges. Price too high and you create friction at every stage, from acquisition to retention, especially after promotional periods end. Price too low, and you risk not only undervaluing your service but potentially making your entire business model financially unsustainable.

I have witnessed the profound impact of pricing decisions firsthand at SiriusXM, Amazon, and Walmart. At each company, pricing was not treated merely as a revenue lever but as a strategic foundation that influenced every aspect of the business. SiriusXM's approach offers a particularly instructive case study in membership pricing strategy. The company employed what we called "high/low" pricing—maintaining a premium MSRP of $25-$30+ per month while discreetly offering members who contacted customer service threatening to cancel dramatically reduced rates as low as $3/month.

We complemented this core strategy with a portfolio of specialized options: discounted student plans to capture younger demographics, add-on plans for additional streaming logins, premium-priced tiers that few people purchased but that made standard offerings seem more reasonably priced by comparison, and years ago, lifetime memberships for high-commitment customers. Each pricing adjustment created ripple effects throughout the business that weren't always immediately apparent.

Was this the optimal pricing approach for SiriusXM? The answer isn't straightforward. As the service has matured and growth has plateaued, certain aspects of this model have created challenges.

Yet during the company's expansion phase, this pricing strategy helped build a subscriber base exceeding 30 million subscribers with remarkably low monthly churn rates[3] of 1.6%. In that context, it worked.

Perhaps the most valuable lesson from SiriusXM's experience is the extraordinary persistence of pricing decisions. Nearly 25 years after the company's launch, the advantages and limitations of its original pricing model continue to shape the business's strategic options. This underscores a critical truth: pricing choices can outlive the market conditions that initially justified them, creating a legacy that future leadership teams must navigate.

For this reason, developing a membership pricing strategy requires a deliberate blend of market research, consumer psychology, financial modeling, and systematic testing. Rushing pricing decisions to market can create constraints that limit your strategic flexibility for years to come. The chapters that follow will provide a framework for developing a pricing approach that not only drives initial conversion but sets the foundation for sustainable membership growth and retention.

The Three Core Approaches to Membership Pricing

The most successful membership businesses take one of three approaches to pricing: market positioning, perceived value or cost to serve, and, in practice, they usually blend them. Each has its advantages, risks, and real-world examples that illustrate why pricing is more than just math; it's psychology, branding, and economics combined.

---

[3] **Churn Rate** – The percentage of members who cancel or stop using a service within a given period, typically monthly. Churn rate is a critical retention metric because it directly impacts long-term growth. Churn Rate = (Customers Lost During Period ÷ Total Customers at Start of Period) × 100

Approach 1 - Market Positioning: Pricing to Compete

One of the most common membership pricing strategies is benchmarking against competitors to define your market position. But pricing is more than just a number; it's a signal of your brand's identity and value proposition.

Are you positioning as the premium choice with exclusive benefits, the affordable alternative expanding access, or the mass-market leader setting industry standards? Your pricing instantly communicates where you fit.

Price too low and you risk skepticism rather than excitement. If competitors charge around $100 per year and you introduce a $50 membership, potential members may assume something is missing. Without strong brand equity, a price that seems "too good to be true" can backfire.

Price too high and the burden shifts to proving your worth. A $150 membership in a $100 category must clearly articulate and deliver superior value. Every interaction—marketing, onboarding, and service—must reinforce why your business is worth the premium membership fee.

At its core, pricing must align with perceived value. Underpricing can erode brand perception and leave money on the table. Overpricing demands continuous justification and exceptional execution. Either way, your price is more than a revenue lever; it is one of the strongest expressions of your brand in the market.

I witnessed this positioning dynamic firsthand during the launch of Walmart+. Our pricing strategy wasn't determined in isolation but in direct relationship to Amazon Prime's established position. We deliberately priced Walmart+ below Prime—$98 per year versus Prime's $119 at the time—to reinforce Walmart's core brand promise of everyday low prices. This pricing decision wasn't just about affordability, it was a strategic extension of Walmart's fundamental value proposition, carrying that promise from product pricing into the membership itself. The price differential created an immediate and intuitive communication of value.

Implementing Competitive Price Positioning

To apply this approach effectively, begin by developing a comprehensive competitive pricing analysis. This requires understanding not only the headline prices of your competitors but also the complete pricing architecture: monthly rates, annual discounts, introductory offers, family plans, and special promotions.

Create a structured analysis that allows you to compare benefits across multiple dimensions. For example, if you're launching a meditation app, your competitive analysis might include both traditional meditation competitors and related wellness services that compete for the same discretionary spending. Your analysis might look something like this:

Service	Monthly	Annual (Monthly Equivalent)	Annual Savings	Free Trial	Family Plan	Key Differentiator
Headspace	$12.99	$69.99 ($5.83)	55%	14 days	Yes	Sleep & focus content
Calm	$14.99	$69.99 ($5.83)	61%	7 days	No	Celebrity narrators
Insight Timer	Free/ $9.99	$59.99 ($5.00)	50%	Free tier	No	User-generated guided meditations
BetterSleep	$9.99	$59.99 ($5.00)	50%	7 days	Yes	Sleep-first angle
Apple Fitness+	$9.99	$79.99 ($6.67)	33%	1 month	Yes	Apple integration
Peloton App	$12.99	$129 ($10.75)	17%	30 days	No	Live fitness and meditation classes
YouTube Premium	$11.99	$119.99 ($10.00)	17%	1 month	Yes	Ad-free videos including meditation
Spotify Premium	$10.99	$109.99 ($9.17)	17%	30 days	Yes	Music streaming, incl. Meditation content

Notice that this includes services beyond traditional meditation apps and fitness platforms, music services and broader content subscriptions. This broader perspective helps you understand:

1. Where price sensitivity thresholds exist across related categories.

2. How competitors structure the relationship between monthly and annual plans.

3. The prevailing standard for trial periods in your market segment.

4. Family plan pricing strategies and potential revenue multipliers.

5. How various competitors articulate their key differentiators.

This comprehensive view allows you to make pricing decisions with full awareness of both direct competition and adjacent alternatives competing for the same customer wallet share[4]. When a potential member evaluates your offering, they aren't just comparing you to identical services, they are weighing your membership against all the other subscription commitments they have made to date.

Armed with this competitive landscape analysis, you can then overlay your own value proposition and strategic objectives. If your meditation app offers unique features, such as proprietary technology, exclusive content, or innovative social components, its premium prices might be justified. If you're entering a crowded market and need to build scale quickly, you might price slightly below established competitors and additionally, emphasize specific advantages of your program.

---

[4] **Share of Wallet** measures the percentage of a customer's total spending in each category that goes to your business. It's useful because most customers won't dramatically increase their overall spending without an income change—so the real opportunity is capturing a larger share of what they're already spending.

Remember that your initial pricing position establishes expectations that can be difficult to adjust later. Price increases require careful communication and clear value justification. We'll come back to how to raise prices without breaking trust later in this chapter. Starting with a deliberately low acquisition price might drive initial growth but it might create challenges when your business needs to raise rates in the future to achieve profitability.

The most sophisticated membership businesses take this competitive analysis further by segmenting it along customer personas or use cases. Different customer segments may have varying price sensitivity and competitive alternatives. Understanding these nuances allows you to develop tiered offerings or specialized plans that maximize both market coverage and revenue potential.

Approach 2 - Perceived Value: Pricing Based on What Members Are Willing to Pay

While competitive benchmarking provides an external context for your pricing strategy, a member-centric approach focuses on perceived value, that is, what your target members believe your service is worth to them. This method recognizes that the ultimate arbiter of pricing power isn't your competitors but your members' subjective assessment of the value you deliver.

The Psychology of Perceived Value

Perceived value exists at the intersection of benefits received and price paid. Members don't evaluate your offering in absolute terms but relative to their perception of what they're getting in return. This perception varies dramatically across different member segments and contexts. A busy professional might value a time-saving service entirely differently than a cost-conscious student, even when the offering is identical.

What makes perceived value particularly powerful for membership businesses is that it accounts for both tangible and intangible benefits. While retail products are often evaluated on objective specifications, memberships blend practical benefits with emotional and identity-based value.

Peloton members, for example, aren't just paying for on-demand fitness classes; they're buying into a lifestyle. It is the convenience, the community, and the accountability of seeing their username on the leaderboard that create stickiness. These psychological drivers often become more powerful retention tools than the core product itself.

Implementing the Price Sensitivity Meter

One of the most effective methodologies for capturing perceived value is the Van Westendorp Price Sensitivity Meter (PSM). This approach goes beyond simplistic "what would you pay?" questions by measuring price perceptions across multiple dimensions. Here's how to implement it effectively:

First, identify a representative sample from your target market. Include both current members (if you have them) and prospective members who fit your ideal customer profile. Aim for at least 200-300 responses to ensure statistical reliability, with proportional representation across key demographic segments.

Next, after introducing your service concept clearly (with visual aids if possible), ask the following four questions:

1. **Too Expensive**: "At what price would you consider this membership to be so expensive that you would not consider purchasing it?" (This establishes your upper price boundary)

2. **Expensive But Worth It**: "At what price would you consider this membership to be expensive, but still worth considering?" (This helps identify the premium price threshold)

3. **Bargain**: "At what price would you consider this membership to be a bargain—a great deal for the money?" (This identifies perception of exceptional value)

4. **Too Cheap**: "At what price would you consider this membership to be so inexpensive that you would question its quality or credibility?" (This establishes your lower price boundary)

These questions deliberately avoid suggesting specific price points that might anchor respondents' thinking. Instead, allow respondents to input any price they believe appropriate. The resulting data create four distinct curves when plotted on a graph, with price on the horizontal axis and percentage of respondents on the vertical axis.

The analysis of these curves reveals several crucial insights:

- **Point of Marginal Cheapness**: Where the "too cheap" and "bargain" curves intersect, indicating the lowest viable price
- **Point of Marginal Expensiveness**: Where the "too expensive" and "expensive but worth it" curves intersect, indicating the highest viable price
- **Optimal Price Point**: Where the "too cheap" and "too expensive" curves intersect, indicating the price with minimal resistance
- **Indifference Price Point**: Where the "bargain" and "expensive but worth it" curves intersect, indicating the price with maximum consumer acceptance

These four points define your "acceptable price range" and help identify the optimal positioning within it.

Segment-Based Analysis

The true power of this approach emerges when you analyze price sensitivity across different member segments. By filtering responses based on demographic factors, usage patterns, or other segmentation criteria, you can uncover significant variations in perceived value. This segmentation might reveal that some segments have higher willingness to pay than others and that certain benefits drive perceived value more strongly for specific segments.

Implementation Recommendations

To effectively implement a perceived value pricing approach for your membership business:

1. **Invest in proper research**: Don't rely on informal polling or small samples. Proper price sensitivity research requires methodological rigor and adequate sample sizes.

2. **Segment your analysis**: Don't treat all potential members as a monolithic group. Segment responses to identify opportunities for tiered pricing or targeted promotions.

3. **Test actual behavior**: Whenever possible, validate survey findings against actual purchase behavior. People sometimes respond differently with real money at stake.

4. **Revisit regularly**: Perceived value isn't static. As your membership evolves and market conditions change, what members value will shift as well.

5. **Align with acquisition strategy**: Ensure your pricing strategy aligns with how you plan to acquire members. Higher-priced tiers may require different acquisition channels and messaging.

By understanding not just what competitors charge but what your specific members truly value, you can develop a pricing strategy that maximizes both conversion and revenue while reinforcing your unique value proposition in the market.

Approach 3 - Cost-to-Serve: Pricing for Sustainable Profitability

The third essential pricing strategy shifts focus from external considerations to internal economics. Cost-to-serve pricing ensures your membership fee adequately covers the expenses of delivering your promised benefits while generating healthy margins for growth and innovation. This approach provides a crucial reality check on pricing strategies derived from competitive positioning or perceived value research.

The membership business model can create an illusion of infinite scalability and margin expansion. After all, once you've built the core service, adding another member seems virtually costless. This misconception has led numerous membership businesses to price below sustainable levels, creating an appearance of rapid growth that masks fundamental economic flaws. When these businesses eventually need to raise prices to achieve profitability, they often face substantial member backlash and churn. Conducting a thorough cost-to-serve analysis requires collaboration with your finance team to capture all expense categories associated with membership delivery. From there, create a per-member financial analysis that understands how much of the membership fee you collect goes to your bottom line now, and how much you forecast that number to change two to three years in the future.

This analysis often reveals surprising insights. For example, Netflix initially grew on the back of a massive content library created by licensing content from production studios, but as members began consuming more original, high-cost content, the economics shifted, which increased content spend per user. This led to a gradual evolution in pricing strategy and the introduction of tiered plans, including an ad-supported tier to balance profitability and accessibility.

Strategic Pricing Guardrails

Cost-based analysis establishes critical guardrails for your pricing decisions rather than dictating a specific price point. These guardrails include:

- **Floor Price**: The absolute minimum sustainable price that covers direct costs and contributes to fixed expenses.
- **Break-Even Timeline**: The period required to recoup acquisition costs at different price points.
- **Margin Requirements**: The pricing needed to achieve target profit margins as the business scales.
- **Investment Capacity**: How pricing affects your ability to fund ongoing product development and growth initiatives.

When integrated with competitive and perceived value approaches, these guardrails help you avoid pricing decisions that might look strategically sound but prove financially unsustainable. The goal is not necessarily to maximize short-term profits but to ensure your pricing supports the long-term health of the business.

All 3 Approaches - Finding the Optimal Balance

Ultimately, sustainable membership pricing emerges from the intersection of these three approaches:

- **Competitive Positioning**: Where you want to sit in the market.
- **Perceived Value**: What members believe your service is worth.
- **Cost-to-Serve**: What you need to charge for long-term viability.

The sweet spot lies where your price is positioned appropriately against competitors, perceived as fair or better by members, and delivers the financial performance needed to support ongoing investment in the service. When these three factors align, you've discovered a pricing strategy that can drive both growth and profitability.

Remember that pricing isn't just a financial decision; it's a positioning tool that shapes how members perceive your membership and influences their decision to join and stay. The ultimate question isn't simply "What can we charge?" but "Does our pricing make joining and staying an obvious choice while building a sustainable business?"

Part 2: Choosing the Right Plan and Pricing Model

Once you've set the right price for your membership, the next big decision is how to charge for it. Should you prioritize monthly plans, which lower the barrier to entry but often come with higher churn since members are reminded each month of the charge on their credit card? Or should you focus on annual plans, which increase commitment, improve cash flow, and reinforce long-term retention, but require large upfront payments that may turn away some prospective members?

The Case for Annual Subscriptions: Retention & Long-Term Commitment

If retention is your top priority, an annual membership model is one of the best strategies available. When Amazon launched Prime in 2005, they only offered an annual plan and waited more than 10 years to launch a monthly plan. This wasn't an accident; Amazon knew that once members committed for a full year, they would naturally shift over more of their shopping because the more they used their membership, the more valuable it felt. This is what psychologists call sunk-cost bias: when people prepay for something, they are more likely to continue using it to "get their money's worth."

Another company that thrives on annual memberships is Costco. Unlike Amazon, Costco has never offered a monthly membership. This structure forces customers to make an investment in the service, which keeps them coming back to justify the cost.

Annual plans work well because they offer three key advantages: lower churn rates as members are locked in for a longer commitment period, stronger cash flow as businesses can reinvest revenue upfront rather than waiting for incremental monthly payments, and more "skin in the game" to drive engagement.

The Case for Monthly Subscriptions: Lowering the Barrier to Entry

While annual plans improve retention, they also create more friction at signup. This is why streaming services such as Netflix, Spotify, and Disney+ have always included a monthly option. In fact, many streaming video services, such as Disney+ and Hulu, have removed the annual option entirely. For these services, their priority is acquisition at scale. By offering low-cost, no-commitment plans, they make the signup decision frictionless. Typically, services offer a discount for annual plans. So, if the churn rates between monthly and annual are similar, a company will make more money from a monthly member.

Similarly, Peloton and Tonal use a monthly pricing model for their content subscriptions, even though their hardware requires a significant upfront investment. This keeps the subscription cost seemingly low and allows them to reach a wider audience. Monthly plans work well for certain memberships because they drive more acquisition through lower upfront cost and lack of commitment.

The Best of Both Worlds: A Hybrid Pricing Model

Most membership services offer both monthly and annual plans simply because it's hard to predict which option will resonate best with a given customer. But it's important to remember: every additional choice creates friction—and friction kills conversion. That's why I encourage clients to test plan structures across marketing sources. What works for one audience or channel may underperform in another.

A common approach is the "two months free" model, where the annual plan is priced at the equivalent of 10 monthly payments (a ~17% discount). It's usually the sweet spot: a compelling nudge toward commitment without overly devaluing the monthly plan. For example, a $9.99/month offer becomes $99/year.

That said, I'm seeing more companies push harder—offering 50%+ discounts on annual plans—to shift behavior toward longer-term value. These tactics can work, but they need to be tested carefully and monitored against customer retention and margin impact.

There's no one-size-fits-all model, but here's a general framework I recommend as a starting point:

- **$69/year or less** → *Annual plan only* (the price is already low; prioritize commitment)
- **$70–$149/year** → *Offer both monthly and annual* (balance flexibility and value)
- **$150/year or more** → *Monthly plan only* (optimize for cash flow and upfront conversion)

As always: test, measure, and iterate. Pricing is strategy, and strategy is contextual.

Part 3: Additional Plan Types and Tiering

Beyond the fundamental choice of monthly vs. annual pricing, many membership services deploy special pricing strategies to accelerate growth, increase accessibility, and improve retention.

The Double-Edged Sword of Lifetime Memberships

In the early 2000s, SiriusXM was in financial trouble. To generate fast cash, we introduced a lifetime subscription. For a one-time fee of $399 to $599, members could get unlimited access to SiriusXM… forever. At first, it looked like a brilliant move. The company pulled in a flood of immediate revenue, and members were thrilled to lock in a price. But over time, those lifetime members became a major financial liability. Unlike traditional subscribers, who paid monthly or annually, these customers required ongoing service without generating any new revenue.

SiriusXM quickly realized they had made a deal with the devil—each year, more lifetime members kept using the service, but no additional money was coming in. Eventually, SiriusXM had to impose transfer fees and limits on how often a subscription could be moved to a new device.

They aren't alone. Language learning platforms such as Rosetta Stone and Babbel have offered lifetime plans. While immediate revenue is attractive, many companies later realize they traded long-term sustainability for short-term cash. In contrast, Tesla's early free lifetime Supercharging drove demand, but once scale arrived, it was phased out. Lifetime offers can work—but only with explicit constraints, clear economics, and a plan to stop.

Cohort-Based Discounts: Expanding to Underserved Audiences

Not all members have the same willingness or ability to pay full price. This is where cohort-based discounts come in—offering targeted price reductions to specific customer groups without devaluing the broader membership. One of the most successful examples of this is Amazon Prime, which provides discounted membership for members receiving government assistance or who are full-time students.

Their goal is to expand Prime's reach while still maintaining the premium perception of the service. At Walmart+, we took a similar approach, launching a discounted plan for low-income individuals. To prevent fraud and misuse, we partnered with a third-party company to verify eligibility for government assistance programs. This ensured that only eligible customers received the discount, preserving the value of the full-price membership. This launch resulted in a large influx of new members into the program.

Keep in mind that not all discount programs work. At SiriusXM, we introduced a $4/month student plan. This was a massive discount from the standard $10.99/month pricing. The expectation was that college students would love the deal and flock to the service. They didn't. After running the program for months, we realized that demand wasn't the issue, relevance was. Unlike Spotify, which dominates the student

Meet Walmart+ Assist

Walmart+ membership for half the price

Qualify for government assistance of SNAP, WIC, Medicaid & more? You can save big on Walmart+. Join now for just $6.47/month or $49/year!*

Start your free 30-day trial

market, SiriusXM's content (curated radio, talk shows, and news) just wasn't compelling enough for most college students. *A discount doesn't create demand; it only converts existing demand.* Before offering a lower price to a cohort, make sure that the audience wants what you're selling.

Part 4: Onboarding Offers

Once you determine the right price, you need a strong call to action to join now. That's where offer strategy comes in: free trials and discounted membership are two of the most powerful tools for acquisition.

So, which do you use? I've seen this debate play out repeatedly. Some teams swore by free trials, believing they reduced friction and got people in the door. Others championed discounted memberships, arguing that upfront commitment led to higher long-term retention. While typically a membership business chooses one path as its primary onboarding offer, the most successful services use both, strategically.

Free Trials: A Powerful Tool with Hidden Risks

Streaming video services are a good example of the power of free trials and how that strategy changes over time. When Netflix launched its streaming service, they focused on a 30-day free trial to get people to discover and engage with content. The strategy worked because it gave members a chance to get hooked, especially when their primary competition was cable TV and DVDs. New members would start binge watching a show, get halfway through a season, and by the time their trial ended, the idea of canceling felt painful. But here's the twist. In 2020, Netflix eliminated free trials entirely, since Netflix had built such a dominant brand that new members did not need to "try before they buy" anymore and Netflix shifted its acquisition strategy to rely on its brand reputation and its content library to lure new signups.

This highlights the fundamental tension with free trials. While free trials lower the barrier to entry, they also tend to attract members who aren't serious about staying. This isn't to say that free trials don't work because they absolutely do, but work best when the service is habit-forming, such as streaming content, grocery and meal kit delivery and fitness services. In addition, if your brand is new or unfamiliar, a free trial lets new members experience the value before making a purchase decision. Keep in mind that free trials are not a magic bullet. They need to be carefully structured to prevent abuse and ensure they lead to conversions. Ultimately, it's not about whether free trials work, it's about whether they work for your business.

I often get asked how long free trials should last? The truth is there's no one-size-fits-all answer. At the time of writing, here is a snapshot of what is common across industries:

- **Streaming Video**: Netflix currently offers *no free trial*; many others have scaled back. Paramount+ and Apple TV+ still offer 7-day trials. Hulu stands out with a 30-day trial for new/eligible users.
- **Streaming Music**: Spotify, Apple Music, Amazon Music Unlimited, and Tidal commonly offer 30-day free trials (occasionally 3 months during promotions).
- **Retail & Grocery Delivery**: Amazon Prime and Walmart+ often offer 30 days free. Instacart+ and Target Circle 360 commonly offer 14 days free (region and promo dependent).
- **Ride & Food Delivery**: Uber One, DashPass, and Lyft Pink sometimes offer 30-day trials, expanding to 60–90 days in special campaigns.
- **News & Media**: Outlets like The New York Times, Washington Post, and Wall Street Journal typically leverage trial or introductory offers around 30 days, though terms vary by region or subscription status.

So, while most trials fall between 7 and 30 days, some extend longer during promotional periods.

What really matters, though, isn't the length, it's the percentage of trial members who convert to paid members (called the trial-to-paid conversion rate). In my past roles, I've seen this number vary wildly—from 20% to 80%—depending on factors like your product value, brand strength, and signup experience.

Here's a simple rule of thumb:

- If your trial-to-paid conversion rate is **above 50%**, free trials are likely working well.
- If your trial-to-paid conversion rate is **below 50%**, consider experimenting with discounted memberships instead, as they attract more committed users and can reduce churn.

The Power and Pitfalls of Discounted Memberships

If free trials attract users with nothing to lose, discounted memberships bring in people who are curious and committed. Whether it's 50% off the first year, three months free with an annual plan, or a free gift for joining, discounted offers create strong incentives while still requiring a financial commitment that signals actual intent. Here are some common examples across industries:

- **Streaming Video:** Disney+, Hulu, and HBO Max sometimes use aggressive introductory pricing (e.g. deeply discounted first-month or first-few-month rates) rather than standard free trials.
- **Retail Memberships:** AARP offers 25% off some memberships; Walmart+ sometimes provides $40 off annual plans through partners; Sam's Club occasionally promotes large discounts on initial memberships (though offers vary by region).
- **Language Learning:** Duolingo, Babbel, and Rosetta Stone periodically run discounts of up to 60% off for first-year members to encourage early conversions.
- **News & Media:** The New York Times, Washington Post, and Wall Street Journal frequently offer steep introductory rates (e.g. $1/week or deeply discounted first year) to attract new readers.

Discounted memberships lower the barrier to entry without removing it. This small financial stake means users are more likely to take the service seriously, making it easier to turn early interest into long-term retention.

When used strategically, discounted memberships drive conversions without undermining your value. Unlike free trials, they create buy-in from the start. But they must be carefully structured to balance short-term growth with long-term retention. Discounts should reward signups, not train members to expect perpetual deals. Think of them as an acquisition lever, not a retention crutch. If members only stay because of recurring discounts, they're not truly committed.

Limited-time promotions like "Get 3 free months if you sign up by Sunday" or "Upgrade to annual and get a free gift" work well because they combine urgency with value. The most effective approach is a hybrid strategy:

- Use targeted discounts in specific channels or for defined segments.
- Run broad discounts sparingly, ideally tied to major events or marketing pushes (e.g., a product launch or annual campaign).

But be careful: you don't want to create a culture where people wait for certain annual events to join. One way to avoid this is limiting discount eligibility to first-time members only, and another is to change when the discounts are offered.

The bottom line is that discounted memberships are a powerful tool, but only when used with intention. They should attract the right kind of member; one who sees your service as worth the price even after the promotion ends.

The Art of the Offer: Getting the First Yes

In the end, the goal of an offer strategy is simple; make it easy for prospective members to say yes. That doesn't mean giving away too much or constantly giving discounts. Instead, it means lowering the barrier just enough to get people in the door while ensuring they stick around. If you're designing a membership offer, ask yourself:

- **Do I need to reduce friction?** → Offer a free trial.
- **Do I need to increase commitment?** → Use a discounted membership.
- **Am I targeting an underserved audience?** → Try a cohort-based discount.
- **Am I keeping my offers fresh?** → Rotate strategies to avoid offer fatigue.

The best membership businesses don't just throw deals at the wall to see what sticks. They design offer strategies that bring in the right members, at the right time, with the right incentives. That's how you turn first-time users into long-term members.

Part 5: A Framework for Testing Offers

The lesson from the best membership companies is simple: **treat pricing as an ongoing experiment, not a one-time decision.** This framework outlines how to systematically test offers, evaluate results, and implement price changes in a way that minimizes risk and builds long-term value.

1. Segment and Hypothesize

Start by identifying *who* you want to test with. New members, high-value members, or deal-seekers may respond very differently to the same offer. From there, develop clear hypotheses to test:

- "Will a $1 trial outperform a free trial?"
- "Does showing the monthly equivalent of an annual plan increase conversions?"
- "Do high-value members prefer added perks over a price discount?"

A good test starts with a good question.

2. Design Clean Tests

The gold standard is the **A/B test** (test group vs. control group). But if your audience is large enough, you can expand to A/B/C testing to measure multiple variations at once.

- **Group A (Control):** Current pricing and offer structure
- **Group B (Price Test):** New price with same value proposition
- **Group C (Value Test):** Same price with an enhanced or modified value proposition

Keep it simple: change one element at a time (trial length, discount depth, bundle design, or tier positioning). If you test too many variables at once, you won't know which one made the difference.

3. Measure Conversion *and* Retention

Low prices almost always boost signups, but they can destroy long-term value. Don't just measure acquisition—track customer acquisition cost (CAC) against lifetime value (LTV). Look at 90-day and 180-day retention, not just day-one conversion. When long-term data isn't available, use engagement metrics as an early proxy: logins, purchases, or usage patterns that predict retention.

4. Balance Hard vs. Soft Benefits

Not every test needs to be about dollars off. Framing matters just as much. "Founder's Circle," "Early Access," or "Member-Exclusive Pricing" can perform better than a straight discount, while also reinforcing brand and community value.

5. Match Test Design to Scale

Big companies can test dozens of variations at once. Smaller organizations need to focus. As a rule of thumb, aim for at least 100 participants per test group to ensure statistically meaningful results. If your base is small, test fewer variables but keep testing regularly.

6. Iterate Relentlessly

Think of testing as a muscle. Small shifts in language, anchoring, or tier descriptions can create meaningful lifts in conversion or retention. The point isn't to "find the answer" once—it's to build a culture of continuous learning.

Optimizing offers isn't about squeezing members. It's about aligning price with value in a way that drives both growth and loyalty. By combining systematic testing with transparent, empathetic communication, you can strengthen your pricing power while reinforcing member relationships. In the end, sustainable pricing isn't a trick. It's a strategy that makes the business healthier *and* members more successful.

Chris Rupp – Start-up Advisor and Former Chief Customer Officer at Victoria's Secret

I first met Matt at Amazon. I was serving as Vice President of Amazon Prime, accountable for the full P&L, global growth, and the benefits portfolio across countries. Matt owned a critical slice of the Prime experience through Prime Video, so we collaborated often—aligning content and benefits, negotiating what would be most valuable to members, and ensuring the offer hung together as a single promise rather than a bag of parts.

Those years gave me a front-row seat to how he thinks: customer-obsessed, systems-minded, and relentlessly empirical about what actually changes behavior. When he told me he was writing a book on membership, it made immediate sense. He's done the reps across categories and companies; turning that experience into a playbook is the natural next step.

My view on membership is simple: people are busy, and they're not shopping for "transactions," they're shopping for *relationships* that reduce friction and improve life on repeat. A good subscription says, "Let me know you, learn your preferences, and keep upgrading the experience without you having to start over every time." That's why the model has spread. Once a service truly understands you—music, movies, groceries, travel, food delivery—it can anticipate and curate. The more you use it, the better it gets; the better it gets, the more you use it. That's the flywheel.

You see it clearly in media. My kids love Spotify; they swear it understands them better than I do. I've tried other services, but at a certain point the specific way *you* consume music—your saved playlists, your replayed tracks, the artists you discover through friends—becomes the product. The social layer is part of the value. When your listening history turns into shareable lists, you're not just streaming; you're connecting through taste. That's modern membership: personalized utility plus community signal.

Ownership versus access is another fault line. My instinct, like many Gen Xers, is to buy the condo after a great trip—to plant a physical flag. But I've learned that ownership can become obligation. Gen Z intuits this. Renting an Airbnb instead of buying a place leaves them flexible. They can change their mind without dragging a mortgage behind them. The same logic powers subscriptions in mobility and food: I can pay ride by ride with Uber or pay for a membership that lowers my cost per trip and boosts my priority. If I'm using it a lot, the membership is cheaper and better. The economics reinforce the behavior, and the behavior justifies the economics.

CLEAR at the airport is one of my favorite examples because the value is visceral. In Seattle last weekend, the regular security line stretched 100–150 people deep. TSA PreCheck was maybe 30 people. CLEAR for PreCheck? Five. I walked right through. Is it always like that? No—smaller airports like Columbus won't deliver the same time savings. But the larger the airport, the more pronounced the benefit. That's the membership test in miniature: does it save me time or stress *right now*? If yes, I'll pay. If it does so predictably, I'll stay.

There's a misconception about membership that it's primarily a marketing lever. In my experience, it's an *operating model*. It touches inventory, logistics, last-mile, payments, customer service, pricing, and product design. The promise you make in the app has to be something your teams can keep at 5:30 p.m. on a Tuesday when a family is trying to eat dinner and the bar for friction is zero. If your organization isn't wired to deliver the benefit easily, cheaply, and reliably, no amount of promotion will save the churn that follows.

What I appreciate about Matt's approach is the focus on *fit*. Not every benefit belongs in every program, and not every program needs to be everything. The goal isn't to build a museum of perks; it's to assemble a short list of high-frequency wins that matter to your core customer and then make those wins effortless. Get the renewal math right. Push toward annual plans when they are truly better for the member, because they stabilize retention and give you room to invest in long-horizon improvements. And resist the temptation to launch new shiny benefits just to have something to announce—improve the benefits you have until they sing.

If you're building from scratch, don't start with advertising; start with usage. Remove friction for customers who already have intent: simple trials, clear explanations, and a value story that's instantly legible. Then keep your end of the bargain. If you say, "priority support," answer the message faster. If you say, "free delivery," mean it—no death by fees in the fine print. The moment a member senses that your promises are conditional or riddled with exceptions, trust evaporates.

Membership is a long game. The compounding comes from frequency and habit, not stunts. Make it easier to get what people already want from you. Tailor and anticipate. Recognize that a subscription isn't just a payment plan; it's a relationship contract. When you honor that, the economics tend to work because the member keeps coming back—and keeps telling other people why.

I've spent a lot of time around programs that changed how people live their day—Prime, CLEAR, the media platforms that curate our evenings—and I come back to the same test. Does this membership reduce the mental load? Does it turn a hassle into a habit *in my favor*? When the answer is "yes" repeatedly, you don't need to convince me with ads. You've already convinced me with my life. That's the bar Matt sets in his thinking, and that's why I'm excited to see this book out in the world. It's not about adding another subscription to the pile—it's about designing the few that deserve to be there.

Final Thoughts: Pricing Is More Than a Number, It's a Strategy

Pricing a membership service isn't just about setting a number. Instead, it's about building a long-term strategy that balances acquisition, retention, brand perception, and profitability. The best membership businesses treat pricing as a living system that evolves with their product, market, and members. At its core, strong pricing balances market positioning, perceived value, and cost-to-serve. Your offer strategy—whether it's free trials, discounts, or annual plans—should attract the *right* members, not just more of them. When pricing aligns with your brand and business model, it becomes a true engine for growth. Before locking in your strategy, ask:

- Does this reflect what we want to be known for?
- Are we attracting the right members?
- Are we balancing short-term growth with long-term health?

In the end, your price should make joining feel like a no-brainer—and staying feel like money well spent

Chapter 4

Designing Frictionless Signups

The Moment of Truth—How Landing Pages and Signup Flows Make or Break Your Membership

You've spent months, maybe even years, building the perfect membership program. The benefits are crystal clear, the pricing is competitive, and your marketing machine is humming, driving potential members straight to your site.

And then... nothing.

Despite clicking your ad, searching for your brand, or landing on your homepage, those interested prospects don't convert. They came close, but something in that final moment stopped them. Maybe it was how the membership was framed. Maybe the pricing felt confusing. Maybe the checkout flow introduced just enough friction to make them hesitate. Often, the biggest blocker isn't awareness or even interest—it's the signup experience itself.

Optimizing your signup flow is one of the highest-leverage actions you can take. It improves the return on every marketing dollar and attracts higher-quality members who retain longer because they understood your core value from the start. Yet too many businesses keep pouring money into lead generation while overlooking the exact point where traffic is supposed to become revenue.

That's why your landing page and signup journey aren't just tactical tools, but strategic assets. The mechanics of conversion, including your landing page, offer framing, and purchase flow, matter just as much as the benefits you're promoting. A clunky, confusing, or unconvincing signup experience doesn't just slow growth; it actively burns your marketing budget.

In this chapter, we'll break down the anatomy of high-converting signup flows and show you how to design experiences that not only maximize conversions but also set the stage for long-term retention. Because in membership, getting someone to sign up is only the first step—but whether they complete that step depends entirely on your signup flow.

Part 1: Conversion Flow Optimization

Before diving into specific tactics, it's important to understand that conversion optimization follows a hierarchy of needs and each level must be satisfied before the next becomes effective. The foundation begins with **clarity**, ensuring visitors immediately understand what you're offering and why it matters. Without this fundamental understanding, nothing else matters. The next level is **trust**, where potential members must believe your claims and feel comfortable sharing their information. **Consistency** follows, requiring that the copy, offer, benefits, and other elements remain aligned across all touchpoints from ad to landing page to checkout flow.

Once these foundational elements are established, we move to **value**, making sure the perceived benefits clearly outweigh the cost in the visitor's mind. Only then can we focus on **ease**, creating a simple, frictionless signup process that removes barriers to completion. At the top of the hierarchy sits **urgency**, providing a compelling reason to sign up now rather than later, whether through limited-time offers, disappearing benefits, or other strategies to suggest why *now* is the best time to sign up.

Most conversion problems stem from failing at one of these levels. The most beautiful button design won't matter if visitors don't understand your offer and pricing (clarity). The most aggressive onboarding offer won't convert if prospective members don't believe your brand (trust). It's important to keep this hierarchy in mind as we explore each component of the signup experience.

Mobile-First Design: The 80/20 Reality of Conversion

Most services where I've worked acquire the majority of signups from mobile devices. Yet I still see companies reviewing only desktop landing pages, ignoring the fact that most prospective members will never see them. This doesn't mean desktop doesn't matter, especially since desktop conversions often have higher initial value and retention, but it does mean your design and optimization process should prioritize mobile experiences.

Mobile-first design requires focusing on several key elements. First, create thumb-friendly layouts with easily tappable buttons positioned in the lower two-thirds of the screen where prospective members can comfortably reach them without awkward hand stretching. Second, prioritize what appears "above the fold", the content shown before a prospective member needs to scroll. Research consistently shows that engagement drops significantly once scrolling is required, so your core value proposition and primary call-to-action must be immediately visible. Finally, ensure all form fields are autofill-enabled. Apple and Google have sophisticated systems that make entering personal and payment information nearly effortless, but they only work if your development team has properly tagged form fields to accept this auto-populated data.

The Complete Conversion Journey: From First Click to Confirmed Member

The conversion process for a membership service typically follows a structured flow designed to guide potential members from initial interest to commitment. While the specific journey may vary by company, the key steps remain consistent:

- **Homepage:** The starting point for visitors entering directly from a website URL. For services focused solely on paid memberships (e.g., MasterClass, Hulu, Blue Apron), this page often functions as the main pitch for conversion. In contrast, for services with a free engagement tier (e.g., Spotify, Target, New York Times), this page is used to highlight value while integrating conversion messaging within the experience. Because homepages vary so widely, we'll focus on the pieces you can standardize and optimize.
- **Landing Page:** This is the primary sales pitch, which serves as a dedicated space optimized to communicate the benefits and value, show the price and any potential offer, address objections, and drive signups.
- **Credential Creation:** This is where prospective members set up their login credentials, typically an email and password, to access the service. Some companies integrate this step into the landing page or plan selection to streamline the process, but most opt for a separate, dedicated screen. Isolating this step helps keep the prospective member focused on completing their account setup without distractions, reducing the risk of drop-off before payment.
- **Plan Selection:** If a service offers multiple membership options (e.g., monthly vs. annual), this step presents the choices. Whether integrated into the landing page or as a separate step, the goal here is to make the decision feel easy and guided.
- **Payment & Billing:** This is where commitment happens. Seamless payment processing is critical, and for platforms with saved payment methods (e.g., Amazon, Walmart, Google), friction can be further reduced. Any unnecessary fields or distractions at this stage can negatively affect conversion rates.
- **Confirmation Page:** The final checkpoint, where members approve payment and legal terms. Ideally, this page should have an extremely high completion rate, meaning prospective members who reach it should

finalize their membership. Some companies require additional consent via checkboxes, while others streamline approval into a single button click.

Each of these steps plays a crucial role in converting a potential customer into a paying member. In the following sections, I'll break down strategies to optimize each stage and maximize conversion efficiency.

Step 1: The Landing Page Experience

Your landing page isn't just a webpage; it's your first impression. You have roughly 10 seconds to convince someone to stay. And whether they stay or bounce is often determined before they read your second sentence. That means visual clarity and instant communication aren't just important, they're essential.

Crafting the perfect landing page starts with a clear, structured layout that immediately communicates value and drives action. This includes:

- **Benefits Imagery:** Use imagery at the top of the page to immediately convey your core value. This draws people in and helps them understand what your membership delivers.
- **Clear, Benefit-Driven Headline and Description:** Show your logo and service name, then follow with a concise, benefit-focused headline and description. It should answer the question: *"What problem does this membership solve for me?"*
- **Transparent Pricing Information:** Display pricing early, calling out both the introductory offer and

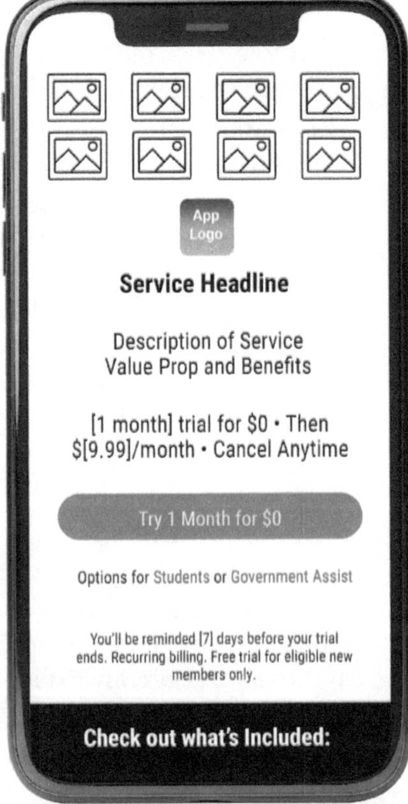

standard rate, ideally just above or below the call to action.

- **Prominent Call-to-Action (CTA):** The primary button should pop, using size, contrast, and language tied to the initial offer to drive clicks.
- **Commitment-Free Language:** Remove hesitation by calling out key reassurances like "Cancel Anytime," "30-day Money-Back Guarantee," or "You'll be reminded 7 days before your trial ends."
- **Benefits Teaser:** Signal that more value lies below. A line like "Scroll to see everything included" helps guide the prospective member journey.

All of the above should be **"Above the Fold"**. Everything below can be **"Below the Fold"**:

- **More Focus on Benefits:** Use imagery or animations to showcase the service's value and benefits.
- **Additional Plan Types:** This is a great spot to highlight variations like student discounts, family plans, or annual billing options. Some brands also link to these above the fold, near the acquisition offer.
- **Trust Signals and Social Proof:** Show testimonials, member stories, recognizable brand logos, or security badges—anything that builds trust.
- **Frequently Asked Questions:** 4–6 FAQs that reinforce value and ease concerns. These should echo key points from the page.
- **Final Signup Button:** Include a signup button at the bottom so users don't have to scroll back up when they're ready to join.

To optimize your signup flow and convert more visitors into members, address these critical elements:

- **Eliminate Friction:** Every unnecessary click or disruption increases abandonment. Remove intrusive elements like full-page cookie prompts, app redirects, or confusing promo overlays that interrupt the flow.
- **Maintain Offer Clarity:** Be consistent with promotional messaging across the entire funnel. Conflicting or overlapping offers create doubt and lead users to second-guess their decisions—or worse, abandon the process to search for a better deal.
- **Minimize Form Fields:** Every additional field adds friction. Ask only for what's absolutely necessary at signup. Non-essential details like birthdates or preferences can be captured post-conversion through onboarding or profile prompts.

- **Prioritize Speed:** Page load times should be near instant. Slow or inconsistent performance is a silent killer of conversions. Continuously test and optimize load speeds across all devices and platforms.

These fundamentals may seem simple, but they often separate high-performing signup flows from underperforming ones. Remove barriers, maintain trust, and keep the path to membership as short and intuitive as possible.

> **Resource:** Here's a template I like to use. A downloadable PSD template is available at www.membergrowth.com/screenshots

Step 2: Credential Creation

Collecting an email and password may seem straightforward, but small decisions here can have a big impact.

- Use email verification tools to filter invalid or duplicate entries without adding extra steps for legitimate users.
- Keep password requirements secure but not punishing—avoid overly complex rules that create frustration.
- Reinforce motivation: restate one core benefit and the primary reassurance (e.g., "Cancel anytime") so this step doesn't feel like a bureaucratic detour.

If you can support it, offer SSO (Apple/Google) and make it prominent on mobile. One-tap sign-in can remove an entire class of drop-off.

Step 3: Plan and Tier Selection

This is often the most pivotal point in the flow. Offering multiple plans creates choice, which can be both a benefit and a risk. Longer commitments appeal to engaged users; monthly plans reduce perceived risk for hesitant customers.

But every additional decision point introduces the chance for drop-off. Use:

- Side-by-side comparisons with one recommended option
- Clear value language like "Save 16% annually"
- Progress markers and reassurance language ("Cancel anytime," "You can switch plans later")
- Anchoring that doesn't feel manipulative (e.g., show annual savings and monthly equivalent without hiding the total)

Step 4: Payment and Billing

This is the "moment of truth." Minor improvements here can drive major lifts.

Credit cards are the baseline, but mobile-friendly options like Apple Pay, Google Pay, and PayPal can significantly reduce drop-off. If you do nothing else, prioritize Apple Pay / Google Pay on mobile. Reduce required fields, support autofill, and remove unnecessary distractions.

Remember: even an extra keystroke can cause someone to bail.

Step 5: Confirmation and Legal Acceptance

This is the last screen, where prospective members approve their payment and accept your terms. This page can either build confidence or create doubt. Here, cross-functional collaboration is essential. Your legal team needs to align on a solution that satisfies compliance while minimizing friction. The best outcome is clean, clear, minimal. Whether you surface legal terms early or at the end, make the moment feel smooth, transparent, and secure.

Organic Conversion Opportunities for Freemium Models

For services with free tiers, the challenge isn't just converting visitors on a landing page. It's moving *existing users* from free to paid—at the right moment, and for the right reason.

The key is to build **strategic hooks** directly into the experience that highlight premium value without disrupting engagement. These hooks typically fall into three categories:

- **Value-based placements:** Spotlight premium-only features, content, or experiences to remind free users what they're missing.
- **Cost-saving placements:** Frame offers around immediate financial wins, like free shipping, waived fees, or exclusive discounts.
- **Proactive messaging:** Use push notifications and in-app prompts as an internal ad system to nudge users toward upgrading at high-intent moments.

At Walmart+, we leaned heavily on these strategies—and they drove meaningful conversion volume well beyond traditional paid ads. One of the most effective tactics was integrated flow placements. For example, non-members checking out a delivery order (a \$7.95 or \$9.95 fee) or an order under \$35 (a \$6.99 fee) would see a message about starting a free trial to save instantly. Some signed up just for the one-time discount, but many entered the funnel and discovered the broader value of membership.

We paired this with strategic in-app messaging: timely reminders of Walmart+ benefits that reached users even outside the checkout flow. By embedding these prompts at high-intent points in the journey, we converted engaged free users into paying members—without relying exclusively on paid acquisition.

Part 2: Measurement, Testing, and Fraud Prevention

This section gets into the weeds, but the details matter. If we were in a workshop together, this is where I'd ask everyone to stand up, stretch, maybe take a quick walk, and then dive back in. Since we're not, I'll just suggest this: stay with me. The payoff is worth it.

When optimizing your signup flow, the real challenge isn't just driving signups—it's making sure those signups turn into valuable, long-term members. Traditional metrics like Conversion Rate only show you who signed up—not who stuck around. And that's a dangerous blind spot.

Instead, I recommend tracking a **Net Conversion Rate**, which, much like Net CAC, evaluates retained members.

Net Conversion Rate = *Paid Member Starts ÷ Total Visits*

Conversion Rate = *All Signups ÷ Total Visits*

This metric filters out the noise from free trial seekers and focuses on what really matters—true member acquisition. It gives a much clearer view of whether your growth is sustainable.

This matters because I've seen firsthand how optimizing for the wrong metric leads to costly mistakes. At multiple companies, we treated all signups equally across marketing channels, even when the retention rates varied wildly. A Net Conversion Rate approach fixes this by shifting focus from volume to quality. It ensures your funnel metrics reflect what you truly care about: acquiring members who stay.

Tailoring Landing Pages to Traffic Sources

One of the most powerful, yet often overlooked, strategies for improving conversion is customizing your landing pages based on where your traffic comes from. While many companies shy away from this due to resource constraints, how someone finds your service dramatically shapes what they need to see before they're ready to convert.

Take *organic traffic*, for example. These visitors usually arrive with intent, since they've searched for your brand or category. They've done their homework. What they want now isn't a long pitch, but a fast path to action. For them, the most effective landing pages respect that familiarity.

They emphasize efficiency: clear benefits, easy signup access, and minimal friction. The job isn't to educate, but rather to reinforce what they already believe and to help them move forward without getting in the way.

Paid advertising tells a very different story. These users may have never heard of you until they saw an ad. They clicked because of a compelling offer or a hook that piqued their interest. But they often arrive with little context or understanding of your full value. Here, education is critical. These landing pages should work harder: they need to clearly explain the value proposition, but also build trust through emotional storytelling, vivid use cases, and proof points like testimonials or brand partnerships. The goal is to move someone from curiosity to belief and to help them see how your service improves their life in real, tangible ways.

Then there's the most valuable and often the most neglected audience: *returning visitors* who previously started your signup flow but dropped off before completing it. These people were high intent as they got close, but now they're back. The key is not just reminding them of what they liked, but giving them a reason to act now. For this group, urgency converts. Whether it's a limited-time offer, a countdown timer, or an exclusive deal, adding time-sensitive incentives can nudge them to finish what they started.

Some performance marketing operators and conversion-focused teams are exceptionally good at this playbook: segment by intent, design pages accordingly, and test relentlessly. You don't need a billion-dollar infrastructure to do the same. With thoughtful segmentation and a commitment to testing, you can dramatically improve performance and meet people where they are.

Preventing Fraud Without Hurting Legitimate Signups

Fraud is a serious challenge for membership services, especially those offering valuable acquisition offers. It shows up in many forms: creating multiple accounts for resale, using fake or prepaid cards, or cycling through email addresses to exploit offers.

Left unchecked, these behaviors can put a real strain on your business, particularly when your service has hard costs during the trial period. While some fraud tactics are addressed in Ch 9: Reinforcing Value and Reducing Churn, this section focuses on those that affect the signup process.

The best programs use layered defenses that protect the business without turning away great members.

Soft gates that also improve personalization

Meal kits and curated boxes often use onboarding questionnaires not just for personalization, but as filters. Only genuinely interested users will complete them. Bonus: the answers also improve early engagement and retention.

Payment validation

One strategy every service offering free trials should consider is an authorization hold (often $0 or $1, depending on processor constraints). This verifies a card without a real charge and filters out many stolen/invalid payment methods before access is granted.

Repeat-abuse detection

By storing hashed billing signals (last four digits, expiration, card fingerprint), you can detect when the same payment method is used across multiple accounts. Combine that with checks on email, IP, device fingerprinting, and billing address for stronger protection. Some services cap trials per card or per device.

Two-factor verification

Email or SMS verification blocks recycled credentials and creates a reliable communication channel. This can reduce conversion rates, but often improves downstream retention. Walmart+ and Wonder+ verify phone numbers, while Disney+ opts for email. SMS tends to be faster and clearer—but expect some impact and use it selectively when possible.

Risk-based friction

Advanced programs use predictive models to assess fraud risk in real time (issuer patterns, prepaid card risk, channel quality, geography, velocity). Then they apply extra verification only when needed—keeping the experience smooth for the majority.

Ultimately, the goal is balance: stop abuse without punishing your best prospects. The smartest membership services make fraud prevention feel invisible—friction only appears when it's truly necessary.

A/B Testing: Finding Your Optimal Signup Flow

The specific tactics that work best for your membership business will always depend on your audience, price point, and value proposition. That's why systematic testing is crucial. As we talked about in Ch 3: Pricing for Growth and Loyalty, a thoughtful A/B testing strategy helps you move from guesswork to real insight, optimizing every step of your signup flow based on what actually works.

When optimizing signup flows, start with high-friction points early in the flow such as form fields, payment entry, or pricing presentation. These elements typically have the greatest impact on conversion, so even minor improvements can yield outsized results. While detailed tests are valuable, it's equally important to ensure your experiments run long enough to reach statistical significance.

Just as important as the tests themselves is what you do with the results. Build a centralized record of past experiments so your team can learn from what's been tried—what worked, what didn't, and what's worth testing next. This prevents you from unknowingly repeating tests and accelerates your optimization over time.

Large membership businesses run dozens of signup flow experiments every month. Netflix, for example, is known for testing every aspect of its experience, from the color of signup buttons to how pricing is displayed to the order of form fields. That relentless experimentation has helped them maintain industry-leading conversion rates, even as competition in streaming has exploded.

You may not have Netflix's resources, but you can adopt the same mindset. With focused, strategic testing, even small teams can unlock big wins and build a signup flow that truly converts.

Final Thoughts: Your Conversion Strategy as Competitive Advantage

The conversion flow of your membership business isn't merely a technical implementation, it's the critical inflection point between interest and commitment, and it can become your most powerful competitive advantage. While competitors pour resources into increasingly expensive acquisition campaigns, a meticulously crafted signup experience silently multiplies the value of every marketing dollar you spend.

The true membership innovators recognize that this moment—when a visitor transitions from curious prospect to paying member—is where fortunes are made or lost. They treat conversion not as a one-time project, but as an ongoing organizational priority that deserves constant investment, testing, and refinement. Their focus is relentless: removing friction, amplifying value perception, and tackling the psychological barriers that keep people from committing.

What separates membership businesses that scale profitably from those that plateau is their ability to transform the signup experience from a transactional checkout into a value-affirming journey. These companies map and measure every step, personalizing the experience to meet the needs and concerns of each segment. Most critically, they build institutional memory. They document what works and what doesn't, creating a flywheel of learning that compounds over time, widening the gap between themselves and competitors who start from scratch with each new product manager.

Treat your conversion flow not as a marketing tactic, but as the cornerstone of your business model. When done right, it's not just optimization. It's transformational.

Chapter 5

Marketing That Converts (and Retains)

Membership Marketing—The Art of Awareness and Conversion

Welcome to marketing: the best investment you'll ever make, or the fastest way to light your budget on fire. For a membership business, this is where you build trust, spark demand, and turn curious browsers into paying, staying members. When done right, marketing creates a growth flywheel that compounds. Done wrong, it's a money pit that spends heavily on the wrong people.

A one-time product sale can win with a single clever ad or a flash of brand fame. But memberships are commitments. They ask for an ongoing relationship. They're a promise: Pay us every month or year, and you'll keep getting value worth sticking around for. That trust isn't built in one touch; it's built in every step from first impression to first renewal.

That's why membership marketing isn't just another funnel. It's a two-step system that must work in sync:

1. **Awareness Marketing** that doesn't just make people know your name—it makes them crave the specific benefits your membership delivers.

2. **Conversion Marketing** that meets that interest with clear, low-friction ways to say yes—and turns curiosity into paying, high-LTV members who stay.

The best membership businesses master both. A big splashy awareness campaign might make people curious, but if your conversion path is broken, they bounce. The world's best checkout flow won't matter if people don't know or don't care what your membership really gives them.

In this chapter, we'll break down how to do both parts well, how to avoid the biggest traps, and how to turn every dollar you spend into not just more signups, but better signups: the kind that stick, stay engaged, and tell their friends.

Welcome to the art and science of marketing that builds a membership business with real staying power.

Part 1: Awareness Marketing: Creating Demand for Membership Benefits

Too often, companies approach awareness marketing only with a traditional branding mindset, such as big advertising buys, major sponsorships, and a focus on making the brand name as recognizable as possible. I'm not saying those actions are wrong, but if you don't also focus on the member benefits, what's the point? Every year during the Super Bowl, companies like Tubi, Paramount+, and DoorDash spend millions on high-profile brand campaigns designed to capture attention. And while these campaigns create buzz, they rarely answer the most important question: Why should I subscribe?

This is the core mistake many membership businesses make. They assume that if they get their name out there, people will naturally understand the value. But the truth is, people don't subscribe to memberships because they love a brand. They subscribe because they want a specific benefit.

I saw this play out firsthand while working with the marketing agency R/GA at SiriusXM in 2018. At the time, we were debating whether to position SiriusXM's streaming service as a standalone brand or keep it tightly integrated with SiriusXM's traditional satellite radio offering. R/GA made a point that completely reshaped how I think about membership marketing:

"People don't subscribe to Hulu because they love Hulu. They subscribe because they need to watch The Handmaid's Tale—and Hulu is the only place they can get it."

That insight was powerful because it applies far beyond streaming services. Every membership business has a set of core benefits, and those benefits are what drive signups. Most people don't join Walmart+ because they love Walmart; they join because of free grocery delivery and fuel discounts. They don't subscribe to Daily Harvest because they love the brand; they subscribe because they want healthy, ready-made smoothies delivered to their door. They don't sign up for FabFitFun because of the name; they join because they want luxury beauty and wellness products for a fraction of the price.

This is why the most effective awareness marketing campaigns don't just promote the brand; they promote the benefits that drive subscriptions.

Think of it this way: Brand marketing asks, 'Do they know who we are?' Awareness marketing for membership asks, 'Do they know what they get — and why it's worth paying for *every month*?'

Benefit-Centered Awareness and Differentiated Measurement

Traditional awareness marketing is often measured by broad metrics: search volume, social mentions, surveys asking if people recognize the brand. Those signals matter, but for membership businesses, they're not enough.

Awareness needs to be measured at the benefit level:

- Are people aware of the specific benefits this membership provides?
- Have they heard about those benefits before today?
- Which benefits feel most valuable to them?
- Which benefit would most likely trigger a subscription?

Consider Uber One. It's not enough that people recognize the name. What actually drives signups is understanding the value exchange—free delivery, lower fees, priority perks, and where those savings show up in real-life.

A helpful way to think about it: treat membership benefits like individual shows on a streaming platform. People subscribe to Netflix because of specific titles they've heard about, not because they suddenly remembered Netflix exists. Benefits work the same way—each one is a hook that creates demand.

The real goal of awareness marketing for memberships isn't simple familiarity. It's to build demand for specific benefits. Once that demand exists, conversion marketing can take over.

Case Study: The First Amazon Prime Day in 2015

A standout example of a multichannel awareness campaign done right is Amazon's first-ever Prime Day in 2015. The goal was bold: drive global awareness of Prime's full suite of benefits, such as same-day delivery, groceries via Amazon Fresh, and streaming through Prime Video and Prime Music, while also boosting membership signups. We learned quickly that demand would outpace supply and that the "deal engine" would need to mature—but the event succeeded at what mattered most: making Prime feel bigger than shipping.

This was achieved by leveraging every major marketing channel in a coordinated blitz:

- **Teaser campaigns** across social media using Amazon's owned channels, influencers, and brand ambassadors
- **Digital ads** across all major platforms
- **Short-form TV spots** (15 seconds) that leaned into the celebratory energy of Prime Day
- **Email and onsite marketing** to both existing Prime members and prospective customers

The messaging was simple but effective: exclusive deals, only for Prime members. This created FOMO and drove trial memberships at scale, many of which converted to long-term subscribers. But perhaps the most powerful outcome wasn't just the volume spike—it was how the event showcased Prime's broader value at an inflection point in the program's growth.

We ran promotions designed to deepen engagement with lesser-known benefits (Prime Music, Prime Photos, and more). Prime Day wasn't just a sales event—it was a benefit-awareness engine. It expanded perception of what Prime offered and introduced millions of people to the full value of membership.

Creating a Benefits Awareness Campaign

Brand campaigns can make a huge impact if the timing, message, and vision make an impact. There's no single "right way" to run an awareness campaign, but one of the most effective strategies is to *focus on specific benefits*, not just the membership as a whole. Partnering with a creative agency can help bring big ideas to life, but the critical differentiator is your intentionality: the goal isn't just awareness of the program, it's awareness of *why it's valuable*.

When it comes to marketing a membership, the benefits themselves must be the stars of the show. But not all benefits land the same way with every audience. A smart awareness campaign doesn't just highlight the perks. Instead, it methodically uncovers *which* benefits drive the most engagement and *why*. That requires strategy, structure, and a healthy dose of experimentation.

The first step is realizing that different benefits resonate with different audiences. A family living in the suburbs might care most about saving money on bulk purchases, while a single professional in the city may be more enticed by early access to exclusive products. Membership marketers must resist the urge to lead with every benefit at once and instead test what matters most *to whom*.

One proven tactic is benefit hierarchy testing. This involves running parallel campaigns, each spotlighting a different benefit, and then analyzing which versions spark the most engagement. For instance, a brand like WHOOP could discover that focusing on how the membership can improve sleep drives clicks with an older demo, focusing on exercise and movement wins over younger, urban shoppers. These findings then fuel larger campaigns, ensuring that creative dollars are going toward benefit themes that actually move the needle.

Bringing Benefits to Life in the Right Channels

Telling people about your benefits is one thing, but *showing* them how those benefits fit into their lives is far more powerful. This is where benefit visualization comes into play. Take HelloFresh, for example. They don't just say, "We make dinner easy." Their marketing shows a busy parent whipping up a meal in 20 minutes while helping kids with homework, emphasizing real-life examples. Similarly, fitness brands like Orangetheory Fitness might highlight a member's progress over several months, framing their journey not through intensity or exclusivity, but through relatability. These stories resonate because they feel honest and attainable.

User-generated content is another potent tool. Encouraging existing members to share their own experiences with specific benefits on social media, in video testimonials, or even through informal shoutouts, creates authenticity that polished brand messaging can't match. When prospects see real people using and loving your product, the barrier to entry feels much lower.

Don't forget to consider which marketing channels to highlight as well. Showing a beautiful graphic emphasizing quick meal prep is going to work better on platforms like Instagram, TikTok, or YouTube, whereas a cost-savings calculator will perform better directly on the website.

Framing Benefits as Solutions

The most effective membership marketing solves problems with clarity. Generic claims like "save money" don't inspire action. But "Save delivery fees on every order" does. The more you can connect benefits to specific pain points—time, stress, effort, cost—the more likely you are to create demand.

Quantification can help—but only if it's defensible. If you can credibly say, "Members typically save on delivery fees after just a few orders," people start doing the math. Comparative framing also works: "Less time meal planning," "Fewer checkout fees," "Faster access," "Better outcomes."

Clarity beats cleverness.

Bridging Internal and External Teams

While creative agencies can bring the firepower, internal alignment is what keeps the flame focused. The best benefit campaigns come from strong collaboration between outside partners and in-house teams who know the product, customer, and operational realities.

That collaboration should be ongoing, not just at the start. Regular syncs and knowledge-sharing workshops help agency teams stay grounded in what's working (and what's not). And just as important is the handoff, ensuring the messaging that works in awareness campaigns is passed to the teams responsible for conversion, so benefit framing stays consistent throughout the entire journey.

Cross-functional involvement matters too. Product, customer service, and sales teams often have insight into which benefits resonate with real members. Bring them into the development process early and often.

Measuring What Matters

To build a high-performing membership growth engine, it's essential to move beyond vanity metrics like impressions and click-through rates. These numbers may be easy to track, but they rarely reflect the real drivers of growth. What you really need to know is whether your benefit messaging is landing. Did your audience remember the specific benefit after seeing the ad? Did it boost their intent to sign up? Most importantly, did it lead to conversion or meaningful engagement?

Modern measurement solutions allow you to make brand messaging accountable—not just for awareness, but for warming up demand in a measurable, actionable way. This is where traditional brand marketing and modern performance marketing start to converge.

You also need to approach measurement differently than you would in traditional conversion marketing. While direct response channels focus on last-click attribution[5], brand-led campaigns require more sophisticated methods.

Use multi-touch attribution (MTA), which tracks a user's path across multiple touchpoints to determine what influenced the conversion, or Marketing Mix Modeling (MMM), a statistical analysis that measures the impact of different marketing activities (including non-digital ones) on sales and outcomes over time. These tools give insight into how brand and benefit messaging fuel demand, not just clicks.

And don't stop at acquisition. Channel performance must be viewed through the lens of lifetime value (LTV[6]), not just initial conversions. A flashy video ad on social might drive a lot of trials, but if those members churn quickly, it's not helping your business. Start tracking LTV by channel, and you'll uncover which touchpoints are driving long-term, valuable relationships.

The principle is simple: market the benefits, measure the benefits, and follow the benefits all the way to retention.

---

[5] **Last-click attribution** is a marketing measurement model that gives 100% of the credit for a conversion (like a subscription signup) to the final channel or touchpoint a customer interacted with before converting. For example, if someone first sees a Facebook ad, then later clicks a Google search ad and signs up, the Google ad gets all the "credit" under last-click attribution

[6] **Lifetime Value (LTV)** is the total revenue a business can expect to earn from a single member over their lifetime. If there's one metric that encapsulates the health of a membership business, it's this one. LTV = ARPU × Member Tenure OR LTV = ARPU ÷ Churn Rate

Part 2: Conversion Marketing—Turning Interest into Signups

If awareness marketing is the megaphone, conversion marketing is the net—turning attention into paying members. You can run the most brilliant awareness campaign in the world, but without a thoughtful strategy to capture and convert that demand, the investment goes to waste. Conversion marketing is about meeting prospects at the exact moment of interest and giving them every reason to act. Conversion marketing isn't about volume, but about precision. It's the art of turning curiosity into commitment, and attention into action. When done right, it doesn't just bring people into your membership, it also sets the tone for a long-term relationship.

In the next section, we'll break down the most effective tools in the conversion toolkit and how to deploy them for maximum impact.

Paid Social

Social media platforms, especially Meta (Facebook and Instagram), are powerful drivers of conversions. They offer rich targeting capabilities that let you zero in on users who look like your ideal members. Other platforms like TikTok and X (formerly Twitter) can also be effective depending on your audience. The key here is variety. Launch multiple creative campaigns and let the platforms' algorithms optimize which ads are shown to which users. You might discover that a value-focused message resonates with one segment, while lifestyle imagery drives conversions in another.

Display Ads

Display advertising, banners and sidebars you see across the internet, can be especially effective for retargeting, something we'll talk through shortly. Services like Google's Display Network let you follow up with people who've visited your site but haven't signed up yet. This is where frequency matters: by staying in front of someone who's already shown interest, you keep your membership top of mind. Smart marketers sign up with several display ad networks to test reach, cost, and conversion performance. The goal isn't just clicks; it's signups.

Search (Paid and Organic)

Search marketing is about showing up when people are actively looking for something related to your offering. Search Engine Marketing (SEO) ensures your content ranks well for relevant search terms, while paid search lets you guarantee visibility. Here's the trick: don't just rely on branded terms that call out your service name. Yes, those are cheap and you should bid on those terms to ensure competitors don't buy your brand terms but also test non-branded terms like "best fitness membership." These reach people who don't yet know your brand but are clearly in the market for a solution.

Some brands skip paid search altogether, assuming users will find them organically. That can be a missed opportunity. Paid search ensures you're in the top results and helps you control the message users see first.

Affiliate Marketing

Affiliate marketing brings third-party partners into the fold such as bloggers, publishers, influencers, and review sites, who promote your membership in exchange for a commission on signups. This performance-based model can be highly efficient, especially if you equip affiliates with the right tools: tracking links, compelling creative assets, and attractive commission terms.

The most successful affiliates aren't just the biggest websites; they're trusted voices whose recommendations carry real weight. For example, a frugal-living blog might be the perfect partner for a value-focused membership, while a parenting site could excel at promoting a kids' education subscription.

That said, not all affiliate-driven signups are equal. Some members may join only to chase cash-back or bounty rewards, which can drag down retention. This makes affiliate programs a channel that demands careful testing, segmentation, and ongoing quality monitoring.

Most companies manage affiliates through established networks. These platforms handle tracking, reporting, and payments, while giving you tools to recruit and manage partners.

Influencer Marketing

Influencers can be incredibly effective conversion partners, but only if the fit feels authentic. The best influencer campaigns don't just endorse a membership; they show the influencer using it, benefiting from it, and weaving it into their actual life. This is especially true for micro- and nano-influencers. They may have smaller audiences, but their engagement tends to be deeper, and their followers are more likely to trust and act on their recommendations.

It can be better to have 50 conversions from someone with 10,000 followers than five from a mega-influencer with a million. In this world, trust beats reach.

What Actually Matters: CAC, Not Clicks

It's tempting to focus on surface-level metrics like impressions/reach (CPM[7]) or clicks/traffic (CPC[8]), but those numbers are irrelevant if they don't convert into paying members. The most important metric at this stage is Customer Acquisition Cost (CAC[9])—how much you're spending to acquire each new member. Every campaign, creative decision, and budget allocation should ultimately ladder up to this number.

But CAC doesn't exist in a vacuum. Not all channels serve the same purpose, and measurement needs to reflect that. For example, search might yield highly qualified, ready-to-convert users with lower CAC, while influencer marketing or mid-funnel campaigns might require higher costs because you're creating demand. To account for these differences, use attribution modeling or assign channel-specific CAC targets.

Equally important is tracking Lifetime Value (LTV) by channel. A cheaper acquisition isn't valuable if those members don't stick. Understanding how each channel contributes to long-term retention and value helps you balance short-term efficiency with sustainable growth.

---

[7] **CPM (Cost Per Mille):** A common advertising metric that measures the cost of 1,000 ad impressions ("mille" is Latin for thousand). For example, if a publisher charges a $20 CPM, it means you pay $20 for every 1,000 times your ad is shown—regardless of whether anyone clicks on it.

[8] **CPC (Cost Per Click):** An advertising metric where you pay only when someone clicks your ad. For example, if your ad is shown 10,000 times, but only 200 people click, and your CPC is $1, you'll pay $200 total.

[9] **Customer Acquisition Cost (CAC):** The average cost to acquire a new member. CAC = Total Marketing and Sales Spend ÷ Number of New Members Acquired

Don't Forget Retargeting

One of the most effective forms of conversion marketing is retargeting. If someone visits your site or even lands on your checkout page, they've raised their hand. That's your moment. You can implement retargeting using tracking pixels—tiny bits of code from platforms like Meta or Google that allow you to serve targeted ads to these "warm" leads across the web. Done well, retargeting feels timely and helpful, not intrusive. It's the digital equivalent of the salesperson who remembers your name and follows up just as you're about to make a decision. Make sure to invest heavily and efficiently here to make the conversion net as strong and wide as possible.

The Power of Email Marketing

When someone shows an interest in your membership, by entering their email on a website, claiming a partner offer, or starting, but not completing a signup flow, you've opened a valuable conversion window. Email marketing, when done well, can be one of your most cost-effective tools for turning that interest into action.

The key is to build a thoughtfully structured email sequence that highlights different angles of your membership without overwhelming the reader. Each email should focus on a single, clear call to action—signing up—while addressing different motivations and potential objections.

A typical conversion sequence might look like this:

- **Initial Welcome**: Thank them for their interest and introduce the core value of your membership, while mentioning an acquisition offer to drive urgency.
- **Benefit Deep-Dive**: Focus on one or two high-impact benefits, explained in practical terms.
- **Social Proof**: Showcase testimonials, user stories, or impressive stats to build trust and credibility.

- **Special Offer**: Introduce a time-limited discount or extended trial to create urgency.
- **Final Reminder**: Reinforce the offer with a clear deadline and a nudge to act now.

The goal is to create momentum by building curiosity, reinforcing value, and ultimately lowering the friction to join. And don't forget: consistency in tone and visual branding across emails helps build familiarity and trust.

Direct Mail: The Comeback Channel

Direct mail is having a quiet renaissance. While receiving a postcard or letter through "snail mail" may seem old-school compared to digital channels, its physical nature is exactly what makes it stand out. In an age of endless screens and inboxes, a well-designed piece of mail has a presence that few digital ads can match. The key to success with direct mail lies in targeting and testing.

Focus on high-intent audiences, such as lapsed members, cart abandoners, or lookalike segments, and work with seasoned direct mail experts to fine-tune your campaigns. Design matters in this channel, so it's important to use eye-catching visuals, bold headlines, and a clear, compelling value proposition. Include a short, memorable URL and a QR code to make signup as seamless as possible. You're not just sending a flyer, you're putting your brand on someone's kitchen counter, where it might sit for days, subtly nudging them to act.

While direct mail is traditionally used for acquisition, don't overlook its potential for engagement. I've seen strong results using mailers to drive onboarding behavior and reinforce early habit formation. It's a channel worth testing beyond the initial signup phase.

Creative and Offer Strategy

No matter how smart your targeting or efficient your channels, conversion ultimately hinges on compelling execution. That means pairing strong creative with the right offer and making it as simple and attractive as possible for someone to say "yes." Creative should be consistent across all touchpoints, reinforcing your value proposition in ways that are both visually and emotionally engaging.

Test various creative angles, such as emotional storytelling, product demos, lifestyle imagery, or bold value statements. What resonates may surprise you. A critical part of this is messaging hierarchy: test whether leading with core benefits, specific offers, or tailored persona-driven messaging performs best at different stages of the funnel. Often, subtle shifts in message order can significantly influence performance, especially as users move from awareness to consideration to conversion.

Your offer strategy should be equally dynamic and precise. Whether it's a free trial, a discounted first month, or a "first month free" campaign, you should be testing permutations across different audiences and channels. As covered in Ch 3: Pricing for Growth and Loyalty, offer effectiveness is highly context specific. A 30-day trial might outperform on paid social because of low friction, while a discounted annual plan might drive better results via search or affiliates where intent is higher.

Always remember, urgency is your accelerant. Whether through expiring discounts, countdowns, or messaging like "Join by Sunday for this bonus," your campaign must make clear why someone should act now. The best-performing conversion campaigns consistently give people a compelling reason to move today—not tomorrow.

Measurement: Optimizing for Lifetime Value, Not Just Acquisition

One of the most common mistakes in membership marketing is focusing on the wrong outcome. Too often, success is judged by how many people sign up for a trial. But that metric can be dangerously misleading. A member who cancels after one month is fundamentally different from one who stays for a year, yet most acquisition models treat them the same.

Traditionally, marketers calculate Customer Acquisition Cost (CAC) using initial conversions without considering how long those members stay. This is a flawed model. Optimizing campaigns around cheap signups who churn quickly doesn't grow your business—it burns cash on the wrong leads. The solution is to adopt Net CAC, a more accurate measure that filters out early cancellations. Instead of tracking everyone who signs up, focus on those who stay beyond your promotional window or key early milestones.

Net CAC = *Marketing spend ÷ Paid Members Converting from Trial*

CAC = *Marketing spend ÷ All Trial Signups*

If your promotional period is long (e.g., six months), use early engagement signals as proxies for retention. Are new members completing onboarding? Using key features? Hitting meaningful engagement milestones in the first 30 days? These behavioral indicators can refine your CAC model long before long-term retention data arrives.

This more disciplined approach might make your CAC look worse in the short term because your denominator shrinks.

But it ensures you're optimizing for quality, not just volume. Over time, that leads to stronger retention, higher lifetime value, and sustainable, scalable growth.

Seth Harris – Vice President, DTC Strategy & Operations, CNBC.

Quality has to be paired with consistency. If you sell me a markets product, don't turn it into political news on Tuesday. People pay for a promise—scope, tone, cadence—and the fastest way to destroy trust is to wander off-brief. Our job is to meet that promise every day, and to check our own work the unglamorous way: read the analytics, talk to customers, and close the loop with product. I'll stop someone at a conference who says, "Love the content, but your DVR doesn't go back far enough," and DM the team on the spot. Why wouldn't I? That's real feedback from real people. If you're not doing that, you're decorating a storefront, not running a business.

Where is this all headed in the next three to five years? I think we're living through "peak subscription"—not in the sense that growth is over, but in the sense that the market has matured. For decades the expectation was that content on the internet should be free.

Today, across generations, the expectation is that the *good* stuff costs money. Paywalls aren't a sin; they're a statement of value. Winners will be the publishers and creators who invest in premium reporting or truly differentiated content—then deliver it with ruthless clarity about who it's for, where it lives, and why it's worth returning to. Everyone else will be commoditized.

With that maturity comes a harder retention game. We survey constantly, but we also expand coverage in ways that track how people actually make decisions now. When the zero-rate era ended and money finally had a time value again, "income investing" moved from niche to mainstream. So, we launched more income content.

When options became a big thing for retail traders, we invested in education and ideas there too. And we're steadily shifting more value behind the paywall. Right now, 70–80% of our content sits in front of it. Over the next few years that ratio will invert, because great journalism has to be paid for by the people who use it.

People often bring up Netflix—"case study of our time." What they sometimes miss is that Netflix prioritized *utility* first, content second. They beat Blockbuster by removing friction: DVDs to your door, then streaming so you never had to wait. Only after they owned the habit did they go all-in on originals. Today every streamer has a distinct positioning—Apple leans prestige, Netflix serves breadth and discovery (it knows I'm a sucker for a good Norwegian war film).

The challenge isn't just "too much TV"; it's the paradox of choice. Consumers will consolidate to the two or three services that meet their taste and time windows best—and the rest will be turned on and off as needed. Our lesson from that world is the same: utility first, then distinctive content that keeps you from churning on a Sunday night.

Generationally, attention is more fragmented, but I don't think "short attention spans" is the most useful frame. The better question is: *Where does your brand play inside those spans?* TikTok, before it was TikTok in the West, was ByteDance video. I was an early user. Brands rushed in and misread it as "just another social platform," when in practice it was an entertainment algorithm and a communication format. Snapchat was similar—people called it "social," but it was a messaging product with a camera-first UX. If your brand doesn't belong in that context, don't force it. If it does, play the native game, not the ad-reel version of it.

Demographics matter, too. Our average TV viewer may be 60–65; our subscribers skew younger but are still older than most "creator economy" audiences. These folks have investable assets and clear utility expectations.

The Robinhood cohort—fractional shares, options as sport, a habit loop that looks like live betting—requires a totally different product and tone. Pretending those two mindsets are the same is how you build for no one.

On competitive sets, I think in layers. If you ladder up to brand, Bloomberg and The Wall Street Journal are the obvious comps. But on the subscription product we've built—retail-investor focused, day-to-day market activity, picks and calls—the real comparables are the Seeking Alphas, Motley Fools, and TheStreet-type offerings.

The nuance is obvious to insiders but invisible to a guy trading from his kitchen table in Florida. That's on us to explain through experience, not slogans.›

Ask me which memberships I admire, and I'll give you two that taught the world something: Amazon and Peloton. Amazon made two-hour delivery not a perk but a norm. That bundle—logistics superpower plus a benefit stack that keeps getting better—should be studied by anyone selling memberships. Peloton—hardware plus software plus community—didn't invent the bike; they invented the *relationship* with the bike. They stumbled into apparel and over-extended on hardware, then refocused on the few products that deliver habit and identity. Read their 10-Ks and you see a company relearning its genius in public.

Uber is another useful analogy. People thought they were "fixing taxis." The real insight was that they changed *car ownership economics* for entire segments—urban dwellers who suddenly didn't need a personal vehicle. The promise wasn't glamour; it was operational: tap the button, a car shows up in a reasonable time, it's cleaner than a cab, the payment is invisible. In media, the corollary is simple: I log in, it works, the content I paid for is there, it teaches or entertains me, and I leave smarter—or at least satisfied—every single time. If you can't keep that promise at the most basic layer, the brand promise doesn't matter.

Some closing principles I keep returning to:

• **Honor the promise you sold.** Scope, cadence, and tone are as much a contract as your terms of service.
• **Utility before novelty.** Make the core task fast and reliable; earn the right to surprise me afterward.
• **Be audience specific.** Build for real behavioral clusters, not a persona Frankenstein.
• **Move value behind the paywall with purpose.** If you don't value your work enough to charge for it, don't expect your audience to.
• **Close the loop in public.** Ask, listen, and fix. Nothing builds trust faster than visible responsiveness.

The market will keep producing winners and losers. Winners will keep compounding trust—through quality, consistency, and usefulness—until the membership feels less like a fee and more like a *home base*. That's the business I want to run, and the one I'll pay for myself.

Final Thoughts: Connecting Awareness and Conversion

When executed effectively, awareness and conversion marketing form a virtuous cycle. Awareness sparks interest by showcasing specific, compelling benefits. Conversion captures that interest and transforms it into new members. And when those members are satisfied, they become advocates who fuel future awareness and push more potential members into the funnel.

The best membership businesses turn this into a marketing flywheel—one that continuously drives growth, lowers customer acquisition cost, and increases retention over time. They understand that marketing doesn't stop at signup. It continues throughout the entire member lifecycle.

Building Your Marketing Flywheel

To create a self-reinforcing marketing engine:

- **Start with benefit-driven awareness**. Identify the two or three benefits that consistently drive signups and anchor your awareness campaigns around them.
- **Design seamless conversion paths**. Every awareness touchpoint should make it effortless to join. Don't make potential members hunt for the "Join Now" button—meet them with it.
- **Optimize for long-term retention**. Build acquisition strategies that prioritize high-value members—even if it raises your initial CAC. You're playing the long game.
- **Test relentlessly**. The most successful membership marketers are constantly experimenting—across channels, creatives, offers, and messaging. They treat their funnel like a product: always in beta.

Mastering this dual approach—awareness centered on benefits, conversion optimized for longevity—won't just help you acquire more members. It will help you acquire *better* members. Members who stay. Members who engage. Members who refer others like them.

When you focus on what really matters, including communicating value, minimizing friction, and measuring success through retention, you build something far more powerful than just a marketing campaign. You build a membership business with staying power. But every channel and creative decision needs to answer: are we attracting members who will stay?

Remember: the best membership marketers don't just market for signups. They market to members who stick around, use what they pay for, and tell their friends. That's how you build a flywheel that doesn't just ›spin—it compounds.

Chapter 6

Unlocking Scale:
Distribution and Strategic Partnerships

The Hidden Growth Lever: Strategic Partnerships & Bundling

When membership businesses hit growth plateaus, the default response is to push harder on acquisition—spend more in the same channels, launch a new promo, or tune referral incentives. These tactics have their place, but they often produce diminishing returns and rising customer acquisition costs. Meanwhile, the most sophisticated membership companies unlock growth through a different lever altogether: strategic partnerships and bundling.

The right partnership transcends typical marketing initiatives and becomes a structural component of your membership's value proposition. Unlike short-term campaigns, well-crafted partnerships create durable acquisition channels, drive deeper retention, and elevate perceived value by aligning with a trusted brand or service. They allow you to tap into new customer segments that would be prohibitively expensive to reach otherwise. At the same time, they reduce churn by embedding your offer into a broader value ecosystem.

In Part 1 of this chapter, we'll explore how to identify, structure, and scale these partnerships. In Part 2, we'll shift focus to the complex but critical decision of distributing your membership through third parties. This includes not just Apple's and Google's app stores, but also platforms like Amazon Channels, YouTube TV, and Roku, which control valuable gateways to streaming and subscription audiences.

Each channel comes with trade-offs—from revenue share and data access to discoverability and customer ownership—and those choices carry long-term strategic implications.

Part 1: Membership Partnership Strategies That Drive Growth

What Makes Partnerships Work: The Four Pillars of Successful Bundling

A well-executed bundle creates disproportionate value when built on four foundational elements.

First: Complementary Value Creation.

The most effective collaborations pair services that enhance each service without competing for the same type of benefit. For example, if T-Mobile bundles with Netflix, it creates a comprehensive "entertainment + connectivity" solution. Similarly, if American Express pairs its card, which includes airport lounges and travel discounts, with airport security service CLEAR, it's addressing two aspects of the same travel journey. The key is finding offerings where 1 + 1 = 3 in terms of perceived member value. When services complement each other rather than compete, members

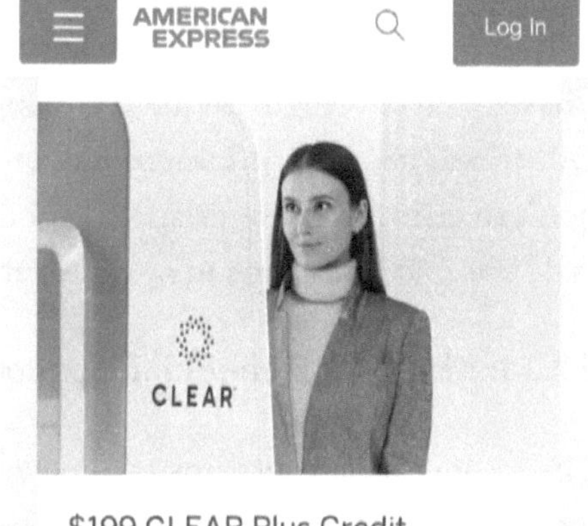

$199 CLEAR Plus Credit

Your Card benefits can help you experience ease, speed and comfort at the airport. You can receive up to $199 in statement credits per calendar year after you sign up and pay for a CLEAR Plus Membership (subject to auto-renewal) with your eligible American Express Card.*

see the bundle as solving multiple needs rather than pairing random unrelated offerings.

Second: Audience Alignment.

Ideal partnerships target audiences with meaningful overlap in demographics or psychographics, but with different acquisition channels or customer bases. This creates efficient customer sharing without cannibalizing either business. The Chase Sapphire and DoorDash partnership exemplifies this approach, as both target urban professionals with disposable income, but they reach these members through entirely different touchpoints and contexts.

Chase gains a high-frequency benefit that increases card usage, while DoorDash acquires premium customers without paid marketing. That said, don't over-index on overlap—sometimes the best partnership expands your "addressable" audience in a way your existing channels never could.

Third: Mutually Beneficial Economics.

The strongest partnerships create clear financial benefits for both parties, whether through revenue-sharing based on new subscriber growth, reduced customer acquisition costs compared to traditional channels, enhanced retention metrics that increase lifetime value, or competitive differentiation that supports premium pricing. The economics should be transparent and balanced, with both partners seeing measurable value from the relationship. One-sided deals inevitably collapse when the disadvantaged partner realizes they are subsidizing another company's business without corresponding returns.

Fourth: Brand and Mission Compatibility.

The most enduring partnerships pair brands with compatible positioning and values. This kind of alignment ensures consistent messaging and experience across both services, strengthening rather than diluting either brand. When Kaiser Permanente offered free access to Headspace, it combined healthcare with mindfulness. The partnership felt natural to members because both services supported the same underlying passion for health and wellness.

Negotiating Successful Partnerships: A Practical Guide

Great partnerships aren't built on good ideas alone. They require strategic alignment, data-backed proposals, and operational excellence. The most successful membership businesses start by identifying partners whose audiences align with their ideal members but aren't direct competitors. They prioritize existing relationships, overlapping member interests, complementary business models, and similar scale and growth trajectories. And they think beyond their category—some of the most valuable partnerships are "journey-based," spanning industries but anchored in the same customer moment.

When entering partnership discussions, lead with data, not just vision. Strong proposals include member overlap analysis, engagement projections, financial models, and case studies from similar collaborations. Larger deals often require executive or even board-level approval, so equipping champions of the partnership with compelling numbers and a clear business case helps justify approval. Membership partnerships are uniquely suited to win-win structures, but expectations must be clearly defined. Whether it's revenue share, acquisition bounties, or minimum guarantees, both sides should see tangible business benefits and a clear path to return on investment.

While some partnerships launch with a splash, most begin with small pilots. These test runs, backed by clear metrics and defined exit paths, build trust and reduce risk. They also create space for collaboration and course correction before scaling.

Finally, operational planning makes or breaks a deal. Ensure seamless data sharing, joint marketing, clean onboarding flows, and measurable success criteria. Even the best strategic ideas will fall apart without disciplined execution.

The Partnership Playbook: An Extended Trial from Amazon and Grubhub

In July 2022, Amazon Prime and Grubhub+ announced a partnership that demonstrated how smart membership bundling can unlock significant value for both companies and their customers. Prime members were offered 12 months of Grubhub+ (normally $9.99/month) for free, giving them unlimited delivery and exclusive perks at select restaurants. After the year ended, the membership would auto-renew unless canceled, creating a seamless conversion path to long-term retention. This wasn't just a promotion; it was a strategic alliance built around complementary value.

For Grubhub, this partnership addressed a critical challenge: how to accelerate growth in a market increasingly dominated by DoorDash and Uber Eats. By tapping into Amazon's massive Prime member base, Grubhub gained instant reach without incurring massive acquisition costs. By many accounts, uptake was meaningful early, growth that would have required tens or hundreds of millions in traditional marketing spend.

Amazon also benefited strategically. The partnership added a high-perceived-value benefit to Prime, one that could justify the membership cost for frequent delivery users and allowed Amazon to re-enter the restaurant space without building a delivery operation from scratch. After shutting down its restaurant business in 2019, partnering with Grubhub offered a low-risk, high-reward path to expand service utility and deepen engagement.

While the exact terms are unknown, it's likely that Grubhub offered a wholesale rate to Amazon or accepted the trial as a marketing expense, betting that a strong share would convert. The deal generated lots of press and gave both services a visibility boost with relatively low advertising costs.

Most importantly, this partnership leaned into behavioral psychology. By offering a long free trial with habit-forming potential, the deal increased the odds of post-trial retention. It also marked a shift in membership strategy, from competing for the same wallet share to teaming up to drive more perceived value and shared usage.

The question becomes less "What else can we build?" and more "Who can we partner with to strengthen the promise we already sell?"

The Partnership Playbook: An Embedded Benefit from American Express & Walmart+

A key driver of growth for Walmart+ is its partnership with American Express Platinum. On paper, these services couldn't appear to be more different. Walmart serves middle America with an average customer earning around $53,000 annually[10], while American Express Platinum cardholders have a staggering average household income of $474,000[11]. This is where the strategic focus of this partnership becomes clear.

American Express recognized that even affluent consumers appreciate everyday value and convenience of grocery delivery, and Walmart saw an opportunity to expand its membership to a new group of members.

The partnership works by offering cardholders a statement credit for their $12.95/month Walmart+ charge and American Express pays Walmart a wholesale rate for cardholders who activate this benefit. For American Express, the addition of Walmart+ to its growing suite of lifestyle benefits helps justify the Platinum card's substantial $895 annual fee. This creates another "sticky" benefit that increases the psychological cost of cancellation, even among high-income members who could easily afford the AmEx card. For Walmart+, this partnership opened access to an entirely new segment of consumers: affluent households who might ordinarily shop at higher-end retailers, but who still value the convenience of Walmart's delivery services for essentials and household staples.

---

[10] https://www.businessinsider.com/meet-the-average-wal-mart-shopper-2015-6

[11] https://monkeymiles.boardingarea.com/whats-average-household-income-net-worth-amex-platinum-cardholder/

The Partnership Playbook: Telcos & Credit Cards Provide Great Examples

Telecommunications companies and credit card issuers have emerged as the most sophisticated architects of membership partnerships, constantly expanding their value propositions through strategic partnerships. If you want examples of how these come to life, a great place to start is by evaluating how each of these services utilizes its vast network to launch partnerships. Here are some examples:

- **T-Mobile** has built its "Un-carrier" strategy around partnerships, bundling services like Netflix, Apple TV+, MLB.TV, and Paramount+ into various plans. This approach transforms a utilitarian service (wireless connectivity) into a comprehensive entertainment hub, dramatically increasing switching costs for customers who would lose multiple subscriptions by changing carriers.
- **Verizon** has countered with its own ecosystem, featuring Disney+, Hulu, ESPN+, Apple Music, and gaming perks. These partnerships aren't merely promotional, as they represent a fundamental evolution in how telcos define their value proposition, moving from connectivity providers to lifestyle enablers.
- In the financial sector, **Chase** has pioneered the "super-app" approach with partnerships spanning DoorDash, Lyft, Instacart, and Peloton, creating a comprehensive benefits ecosystem that activates across various spending categories. **Capital One** has followed suit with its own entertainment and dining-focused partnerships, including access to exclusive culinary experiences and entertainment venue perks.

These companies understand that in a world where core services such as wireless plans and credit cards are increasingly commoditized, differentiation comes from creating unique membership ecosystems that consumers can't easily replicate by switching to competitors.

Resource: Want to see more examples of partnerships? Head over to my website, www.membergrowth.com/screenshots and browse to the Partnerships section.

Partnership Offers: Driving the biggest bang for the buck.

Strategic membership partnerships typically fall into two primary offer categories, each serving distinct business objectives. The first approach is called **Extended Trials,** which offers a long free trial (typically 12 months, but it can be shorter or longer) as a complementary benefit to members of another service. These extended periods provide sufficient time for new members to integrate your service into their routines, forming habits that increase conversion likelihood when the trial concludes. The extended trial model works particularly well when 1) your service requires time to demonstrate full value, 2) members benefit from repeated engagement to experience core benefits, and 3) when your onboarding can be optimized for habit formation within the trial period.

The second approach is called **Embedded Benefits,** which permanently embeds your service as a benefit within another. This approach creates enduring distribution channels, stable revenue streams, and significantly enhances retention for both partners. The bundled membership model excels when the services create complementary daily or weekly usage patterns. Together, the bundles solve multiple related customer needs. The combined offering creates a stronger value proposition than either service alone, and both partners benefit from each other's retention strength.

Framework: Be the Aggregator or Be Aggregated

Bundling is turning into the default shape of distribution. As ecosystems expand, every membership business faces the same fork in the road: *be the place where other services get discovered, or be one of the services discovered inside someone else's bundle.*

This isn't a superficial packaging decision. It determines who owns the customer relationship, who controls the data, who sets the rules—and ultimately, who holds the leverage.

Path 1: Be the Aggregator

Aggregators win by becoming the default starting point. They simplify choice, centralize access, and make convenience feel like value. Amazon is the obvious example. But you see the same playbook across industries: Chase and AmEx bundling benefits, Verizon packaging services, YouTube and Netflix shaping how content is surfaced and consumed. The common thread isn't "exclusive content." It's reduced friction—one place, one login, one bill, and a growing set of reasons to stay.

The upside is power. Aggregators own the relationship and the data. They can monetize through multiple streams—subscriptions, upsells, ads, and partner economics. And because discovery starts with them, value compounds: each new partner makes the bundle stickier, which attracts more customers, which attracts better partners.

The downside is complexity. Aggregation demands real investment: technology, partner management, and experience orchestration. And partners will negotiate hard—on economics, on visibility, and on whether they're truly being featured or simply "included."

The best aggregator strategy is simple: build a marketplace where convenience is the value proposition. Curate aggressively. Make discovery effortless. Layer in partnerships that broaden the offering without diluting your core identity. You're not just bundling—you're becoming the interface customers rely on.

Path 2: Be Aggregated

For many companies, aggregation is the smarter move—at least at first. If you're a niche player, a premium service, or an emerging brand with strong product-market fit but limited scale, bundling into a bigger ecosystem can unlock distribution you could never buy efficiently.

Think of services like BritBox or Crunchyroll inside larger content bundles, or niche wellness and commerce brands that grow faster once they're placed in the path of an existing audience.

The upside is reach. You piggyback on trust and distribution. Customer acquisition costs drop. Discovery accelerates. And you get trial at scale among people who might never have found you organically.

The trade-off is margin and access. Aggregators take a meaningful cut—often 30–50%—and you typically lose direct ownership of the customer relationship and behavioral data. That weakens your ability to personalize, cross-sell, and build loyalty outside the aggregator's walls.

The best approach is to treat aggregation as a channel, not your entire business. Choose partners that complement your brand, not dilute it. Use the bundle to drive awareness and early adoption, while continuing to build direct relationships where you can own the data, the pricing, and the long-term lifecycle.

Quick recap

- **Be the aggregator** if you have scale + infrastructure and want to own the relationship, data, and monetization.
- **Be aggregated** if you have strong product-market fit but need reach—just don't let it become your only growth engine.

Building Partnerships that Last: The Path Forward

The distribution decisions you make today will shape your membership business for years to come. What separates enduring membership partnerships from short-lived promotions is their foundation in mutual value creation. The most successful collaborations generate ongoing benefits for both parties, creating self-reinforcing systems rather than zero-sum competitions. When American Express bundles Walmart+ or when T-Mobile includes Netflix, both partners gain advantages they couldn't achieve independently, whether through access to new audiences, enhanced value propositions, or improved retention metrics.

To build partnerships that drive sustainable growth for your membership business, focus on three essential elements. First, identify truly complementary services that align naturally with your members' existing behaviors and needs. Second, structure arrangements where both parties receive quantifiable benefits, creating new value rather than merely redistributing existing revenue. Third, design your partnership to foster habit formation, giving members enough time to incorporate both services into their routines through thoughtful onboarding and engagement strategies.

Beyond the initial implementation, measure impact beyond surface-level acquisition metrics. The true value of strategic partnerships often materializes over time through improved retention, increased engagement, and enhanced lifetime value. These metrics take months to fully reveal themselves. Finally, consider limited trials before full-scale commitment. This allows you to refine the offering based on actual member feedback while limiting downside risk for both parties.

Perhaps the most powerful aspect of partnership-driven growth is its controllability. Unlike many acquisition channels where you're perpetually feeding the growth engine, partnerships can be structured with defined timelines and renewal points. When a partnership delivers a wave of new members who form habits, you can renew, renegotiate, or end the relationship—with many members staying because the behavior stayed.

In today's increasingly crowded subscription landscape, standalone membership services face unprecedented challenges in breaking through the noise. Strategic distribution partnerships offer a path forward, not just as marketing tactics, but as fundamental business model innovations that create more compelling, integrated member experiences. The future of membership isn't just about what your service offers in isolation; rather, it's about how your service fits into an ecosystem of value that makes members' lives better in multiple ways that reinforce each other.

Part 2: The App Store Dilemma: Strategic Choices for Distribution

For any membership business, distribution is everything. You can have the best product in the world, but if prospective members do not have a convenient way to sign up and pay, your growth will stall before it even begins. One of the most consequential distribution decisions membership businesses face today is whether to sell subscriptions through Apple's App Store, Google Play, or streaming video platforms from Amazon, YouTube, Roku, and more. On the surface, it seems like an easy choice, since billions of users already use these platforms. However, there is a hidden cost that has a massive impact on profitability.

The 30% Commission Reality

Apple and Google take a 30% cut of all in-app purchases for the first 12 months. After that, the fee drops to 15% for recurring subscriptions[12]. However, for high-volume membership businesses, this first-year impact can be staggering. For a $10/month service with 1 million members, the first-year commissions alone total $36 million. That kind of toll changes pricing strategy, marketing math, and ultimately product investment capacity.

The Case For: Why Membership Businesses Accept App Store Subscriptions

Despite the high fees, many brands embrace in-app purchases because the benefits can outweigh the costs, especially for companies focused on rapid user growth.

Reason 1: Frictionless Conversion

One of the biggest obstacles in converting a potential member is payment friction. With in-app purchases, prospective members can subscribe instantly with a single tap or Face ID verification as the entire signup flow happens within a familiar environment with stored payment information. This seamless experience dramatically reduces drop-off rates at the critical moment of conversion.

---

[12] Note: Percentages and rules vary by platform, region, and developer program; confirm current terms before modeling.

Reason 2: Built-in Discovery and a New Marketing Channel

The App Store and Google Play serve as powerful discovery platforms, which can also serve as efficient paid marketing channels. On the editorial side, apps can appear in category-specific searches and browsing or on editorial features. Also, "App of the Day" placements drive massive visibility.

In addition, companies can purchase certain App Store placements, which give more flexibility to maximize marketing spend. Apple and Google tend to favor apps with conversion in editorial placements. Paid placements are much more efficient when they can tie directly to a trial offer.

Reason 3: Member Trust and Credibility

Many prospective members feel more comfortable subscribing through Apple or Google since payment information is secured by these companies and subscription management is centralized in a familiar place, and cancellations can be made easily. This built-in credibility and familiarity can improve not just conversion rates but also willingness to pay premium prices.

Reason 4: Simplified Subscription Management

App stores handle the technical complexities of subscription billing, such as automatic retry logic for failed payments, streamlined renewal processes, standardized receipts and tax handling, and grace periods for subscription recovery.

For early-stage companies without robust billing infrastructure, these features can save significant engineering resources and reduce subscriber churn because of payment failures.

The Case Against: Why Some Membership Businesses Bypass App Stores

For many companies, retaining control over pricing, member data, and revenue models is more important than convenience. These businesses bypass in-app subscriptions entirely and instead push users to sign up on the web.

Reason 1: Preserving Margin Integrity

Keeping 100% of revenue allows businesses to reinvest more into product development, marketing, and onboarding offers without sacrificing profitability. For a mature membership business with millions of members, the difference between paying 15-30% commissions and keeping that revenue can represent tens or even hundreds of millions of dollars annually.

Reason 2: Owning the Member Relationship

When a member subscribes through the App Store, Apple and Google own the transaction, not the business. This creates significant limitations, as the membership service has some barriers to directly communicating about billing issues, has limited personalized retention offers based on usage patterns, and may make it difficult to implement sophisticated winback campaigns. These restrictions make it harder to personalize retention efforts, run direct marketing campaigns, and manage cancellations effectively. For businesses where lifetime value is driven by relationship management, these limitations can be deal breakers.

Reason 3: Strategic Pricing Flexibility

App store policies restrict many common membership pricing strategies, such as targeted discounts or promotions, additional tiers and bundling, and constraints on price changes, especially by restricting grandfathering existing subscribers during price changes. This is also impactful during retention as personalized save offers, pause options, and downgrades are more difficult, if not impossible, using App Store billing.

Hybrid Approaches: Getting the Best of Both Worlds

Many companies struggle with the trade-off between app store distribution and direct web acquisition. However, some innovative businesses have developed hybrid strategies that maximize both reach and revenue while working within platform constraints. Examples include:

- **Token & Credit Systems:** Rather than processing full subscriptions through apps, some companies use token-based approaches. For example, Audible does not allow subscriptions through the App Stores, but members can use their credits to download audiobooks directly in-app. This preserves convenience while protecting margins on their core revenue stream.
- **Freemium & Limited Access:** These models offer basic functionality in-app while directing premium conversions to the web. For example, YouTube provides standard video viewing in-app but requires prospective members to visit the web for YouTube Premium subscriptions. This strategy maintains broad mobile reach while channeling high-value conversions to commission-free channels.
- **Platform-Specific Pricing:** Some companies openly differentiate pricing between channels, passing through some or all of the margin loss to new members. For example, Amazon Music Unlimited charges $12.99/month for in-app purchases but offers lower rates on their website: $10.99/month for Prime members and $11.99/month for non-Prime members. This approach passes some of the platform fee to consumers who prefer the convenience of in-app purchases while preserving margins and offering incentives for direct purchasing.

Navigating App Store Policies

Large companies have historically found ways to route users to web purchase flows despite platform restrictions—sometimes through careful language, sometimes through policy changes over time. Smaller developers typically have less leverage and may face stricter enforcement.

Regulatory scrutiny of app store rules is intensifying worldwide, and distribution strategies that include both an app presence and strong direct channels offer the best adaptability.

Recent U.S. court rulings and regulatory pressure have begun to weaken platform control over external payment links. The practical implication for membership businesses is meaningful: maintaining a strong direct channel alongside your app presence can improve flexibility, reduce commission exposure over time, and future-proof your distribution strategy.

Wrapping It Up: Which Strategy Should You Prioritize?

The App Store dilemma represents one of the most consequential strategic decisions for membership businesses today. Rather than viewing this simply as a technical choice about payment processing, successful companies recognize it as a fundamental business strategy that shapes everything from unit economics to member relationships. The right approach depends on your specific context.

The decision hinges on five key factors: your margin structure, growth stage, target audience, offering complexity, and lifetime value drivers. High-margin businesses in early growth stages with simple offerings often benefit from the frictionless conversion of app stores despite the fees. Meanwhile, companies with thin margins, complex offerings, or those heavily dependent on relationship management for retention may find direct signups essential for sustainable growth. Your specific audience matters too, as consumer-focused services targeting younger demographics typically see stronger results from in-app purchases, while B2B offerings and higher-priced subscriptions often convert effectively through web channels.

Your distribution strategy should evolve alongside your business maturity. New membership businesses might start with in-app purchases to maximize early distribution and conversion, then gradually introduce web signup options as their brand strengthens. Established businesses already using app stores should segment members by channel to understand lifetime value differences and experiment with hybrid models. Those considering removing in-app purchasing must implement phased transitions with clear value propositions for web signup, robust mobile-optimized experiences, and preparation for potential short-term conversion impacts.

Final Thoughts: Unlocking Distribution

The best membership businesses do more than chase short-term conversions—they engineer distribution strategies that create long-term, defensible advantages and maximize lifetime value. True distribution isn't just about where transactions happen; it's about building durable, profitable relationships with members over time. And remember: great companies evolve. Your distribution strategy today should serve the current moment, but it must also stay flexible enough to adapt as your business, customers, and market shift. The key is to be deliberate now, and fearless about adjusting later.

Part 2:

Building the Growth Foundation

Chapter 7

First Impressions:
Onboarding and Early Wins

Onboarding and the First 30 Days—Securing Long-Term Retention

A couple of years ago, I made a splurge purchase: a seriously high-end meditation chair marketed to athletes and celebrities. I'd first tried it at a marketing event and instantly loved it.

The experience was unlike anything I'd used before—part physical recovery, part guided meditation, synced in a way that made mindfulness feel immersive and deeply effective.

Still, it wasn't cheap—this was a big purchase, and I braced for a frustrating setup when the massive box finally arrived. What I got instead surprised me.

The unboxing experience was seamless. Every part was clearly labeled, the instructions were intuitive, and setup took less than ten minutes. But what really set it apart?

A few hours later, I got a call from the company inviting me to schedule a 1:1 onboarding session. That session made all the difference. The trainer walked me through how the machine worked, recommended programs based on my goals, and gave me simple strategies to build it into my daily routine.

It wasn't just technical support—it was confidence-building. And it created momentum. I didn't just understand the product; I was excited to use it. I saw how it could fit into my life. I felt as though the company genuinely wanted me to succeed.

That kind of white-glove onboarding works when you're selling a premium, low-volume product to an early adopter. But most businesses don't have that luxury. So, the real challenge becomes this:

How do you recreate that same sense of clarity, confidence, and personal connection—at scale?

Nailing the onboarding moment may be the most critical step in turning fleeting curiosity into long-term engagement. The best membership businesses understand this, treating onboarding not just with the same care as acquisition, but with even greater strategic focus.

Think of onboarding as the foundation of a house. No matter how beautiful the architectural plans or how premium the materials, a weak foundation compromises everything built on top. Similarly, even the most compelling membership offer will collapse without a thoughtful onboarding experience to support it.

In this chapter, we'll explore the psychology behind successful onboarding, walk through a proven four-part framework, share a practical set of onboarding metrics for measuring success, and identify the critical pitfalls that undermine even well-intentioned efforts. Whether you're launching a new membership or optimizing an existing one, you'll learn to craft an onboarding experience that doesn't just welcome members—it converts them into long-term advocates who stay, pay, and spread the word.

Part 1: Why First Impressions Set the Course

Too many companies make the same critical mistake: After signup, they simply display a "Thank you for subscribing" message or send a generic confirmation email. That does nothing to reinforce the value of the membership or encourage engagement.

This approach creates a dangerous gap between acquisition and activation. The member has committed to trying your service, but they haven't yet experienced what makes it valuable. In this limbo state, doubt and second thoughts flourish. The longer a new member goes without experiencing value, the more likely they are to forget, disengage, or cancel.

That's why it's essential to obsess over what happens immediately after signup. Ask yourself:

- Does the member immediately understand the key benefits of the service?
- Do they know how to engage with those benefits right away?
- Is the onboarding flow personalized to their needs?
- Have you removed all friction between signup and first-time usage?

The goal is simple: Guide new members toward meaningful engagement as quickly as possible. Not just any engagement, but interactions that deliver on your core value proposition and create the foundation for ongoing usage.

The Psychological Journey of New Members

The first 30 days aren't just about retention—they're about transformation. What begins as curiosity must become connection.

Most companies treat onboarding like a checklist. But for the member, onboarding is a guided tour through a series of psychological states—each one shaping whether they become loyal, lapse, or leave.

New members also experience a cognitive bias known as the honeymoon effect—a brief window of elevated optimism where hopes are high and possibilities feel endless. That makes the first 24–48 hours the most leveraged moment in the entire lifecycle. Get this wrong, and everything after becomes an uphill battle.

Here's what that first month typically feels like—from the member's point of view.

The 30-Day Emotional Arc

Day 0–2: The High (Post-Purchase Excitement)

They've said yes. Now they're looking for confirmation they made the right choice. Momentum is high, and they want a quick "win."

Risk: Silence feels like regret. Confusion kills excitement.

What to do: Welcome fast. Deliver value immediately. Make the next step obvious.

Day 3–7: The Reality Check

They start exploring, and expectations meet execution. If anything feels hard, unclear, or underwhelming, doubt creeps in.

Risk: "This isn't what I thought it was."

What to do: Reduce friction. Provide proactive guidance. Give fast paths to early wins.

Day 7–14: Competence Building

They either start feeling empowered—or overwhelmed. This is the fork in the road where confidence forms.

Risk: "I don't get it," turns into disengagement.

What to do: Teach progressively. Make mastery feel achievable. Help them build comfort step by step.

Day 14–21: The Value Question (Value Assessment)

This is when the mental math starts: *Is this worth it?* Sometimes it's explicit (they check cancellation). Sometimes it's subconscious (they compare cost to value).

Risk: Value feels invisible—even if it exists.

What to do: Make value unmistakable. Show usage, savings, progress, and the benefits they haven't tried yet.

Day 21–30: Habit or Drift (Habit Formation)

If the member has momentum, the membership shifts from something they try to something they rely on. It becomes routine. Identity begins to attach.

Risk: If no rhythm forms, usage fades—and churn becomes likely.

What to do: Create cadence. Establish rituals. Reinforce repeatable actions that become automatic.

Design for the Journey, Not Just the Signup

Onboarding isn't a one-time tutorial—it's a system designed to move members through these phases. When done right, it doesn't just reduce churn. It creates connection, competence, and long-term loyalty.

Part 2: From Insight to Action: A Four-Step Onboarding Framework

The section above is the member's internal timeline—the psychology. This next section is your build sheet—the operating system.

In other words, the emotional journey tells you what members feel. The onboarding system tells you what you do about it.

Below is a practical system that aligns to the 30-day arc. It's designed to increase early engagement, reduce churn, and turn curiosity into connection. Each component reinforces the next—so the member's experience feels guided, not random.

1) Show Immediate Value (Don't Just Say "Thank You")

The moment a member joins, optimism is high, but they're also looking for reassurance. Your job is to deliver a fast "moment of value" that confirms: *This was worth it.* The worst thing you can do is to make new members figure out the experience on their own.

What immediate value looks like:

- **Streaming services:** Immediately suggesting personalized content they can watch now
- **Fitness apps:** Presenting a beginner workout they can complete in 10 minutes
- **Meal kit services:** Showcasing their first delivery and the meals they'll soon enjoy
- **Retail memberships:** Highlighting an exclusive discount they can use immediately

2) Build Competence with an Interactive Walkthrough (Not an Information Dump)

A guided experience beats an information dump every time.

Instead of throwing every feature at new members at once, break the experience down into simple, digestible steps, so members build confidence fast. The goal is not just understanding. It's competence.

For some services, this looks like a tutorial. But most people don't have the patience for a long walkthrough. A better approach is to guide members contextually, in the moments that matter.

Tools that work:

- **Tooltips:** Highlight key features with short, actionable explanations at the right moment
- **Progress bars and checklists:** Give members clear steps and show progress toward activation
- **Personalized recommendations:** Use onboarding questions to tailor the experience
- **Incentivization:** Some services offer a credit or bonus for completing key onboarding actions

At Walmart+, for example, we tested giving a $10 credit to members who took three key actions in their first week. This approach can be risky—there's always the chance you're simply paying for activity that doesn't translate into long-term retention—but

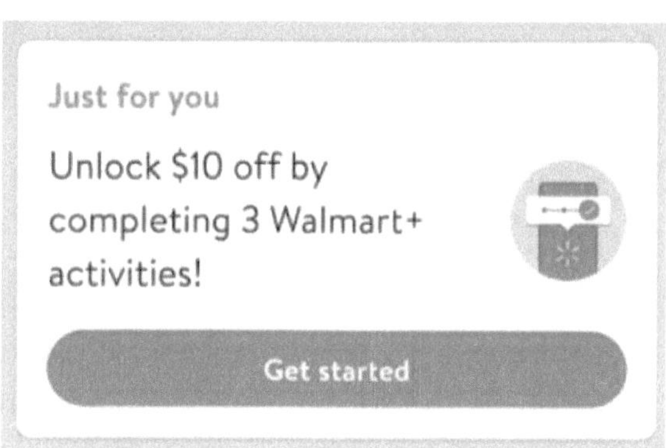

it can work when the actions align tightly with behaviors that drive lasting engagement.

3) Orchestrate the Experience Across Channels (Don't Rely on One Touchpoint)

To truly guide new members toward activation, you need multiple touchpoints across multiple channels—working in concert, not in silos.

Each channel plays a distinct role in this journey. **Email** excels at delivering deeper explanations and serves as a reference point members can return to later. **Push** notifications provide timely nudges that spark immediate action and keep momentum high. **In-app messages** appear contextually while members are actively using your service, prompting engagement at just the right moment. **Onsite placements** act as persistent visual cues, subtly reminding members of available benefits and guiding attention toward high-value actions.

When these channels are orchestrated thoughtfully, onboarding feels personalized, consistent, and intuitive—not disjointed or overwhelming.

This comes to life through a cohesive 30-day communication plan that's mapped out, tested, and continuously optimized. Ideally, each day aligns around specific member actions you want to drive, with consistency across email, push, in-app messaging, and onsite placements.

Every message should include one clear call to action and a defined success metric. For example:

- "Explore benefits" is vague and hard to measure
- "Claim your first free personal training session" is specific, testable, and value-focused

Your sequencing should reflect the actual member journey: addressing common questions, removing friction, and reinforcing key benefits at exactly the right time. Use your existing data to identify where members typically stall or succeed—and design messaging to guide them forward, one step at a time.

Personalization Is the Multiplier Layer (Not a Single Step)

One-size-fits-all onboarding doesn't work. Personalization isn't just a step—it's a multiplier that strengthens every part of the system.

Effective personalization starts with what you already know:

- If a member joined through an ad for fitness supplements, spotlight related discounts or content
- If they joined through a student offer, highlight savings and flexibility that fit student life

This is a "warm start": using early signals to make the first experience feel designed for them.

Stated preferences captured during signup add another layer. If members identify goals or interests, onboarding should prioritize content and features that speak directly to those goals. This builds immediate relevance and trust.

Behavioral data deepens personalization further:

- If a member is consistently engaging with one feature, highlight more advanced tools or content in that area
- If they haven't logged in since signing up, shift outreach toward reactivation and reminding them of what they're missing

Membership type matters too:

- **Trial members** require urgency—drive engagement before the window closes
- **Annual members** may benefit from a broader, more gradual onboarding journey

Ultimately, personalization proves you understand your members—and demonstrates it through thoughtful, responsive guidance. When done well, it transforms onboarding from a generic sequence into a member-specific journey that increases activation, deepens value, and drives long-term retention.

Case Study: Netflix's Evolution

Netflix has refined its "time-to-play" experience over years of testing. New members are typically asked for a few quick preference signals—genres, titles they like, or profile choices—and then are routed straight into personalized recommendations so they can press play fast. Netflix doesn't waste the first session on lengthy tutorials. Instead, it prioritizes the fastest path to the core value: something great to watch right now. Contrast that with traditional cable subscriptions, which often overwhelm new customers with hundreds of channels and no guidance. More choices don't create a better experience; curation and momentum do.

Part 3: Measure What Matters in the First 30 Days

If you can't measure onboarding, you can't improve it. The goal isn't more emails, more tooltips, or more steps. The goal is getting members to use their benefits as quickly as possible and then creating a habit of continued usage. Because in the first month, members aren't just evaluating your product. They're deciding whether your membership deserves a place in their life. Onboarding is a race against doubt.

That's why the first 30 days need a scoreboard. Not vanity metrics. Not "activity for activity's sake."

You need signals that tell you, early, whether members are finding value, building confidence, and forming momentum.

Here are the practical onboarding metrics I recommend:

1) Time-to-First-Value (TTFV): How long does it take a new member to experience the core benefit?
This is the heartbeat of onboarding. The shorter the TTFV, the lower the buyer's remorse—and the faster trust forms. For example, first stream watched, first workout completed, first delivery placed, first savings redeemed.

2) Activation Milestone Rate ("Aha" Rate): What percentage of new members reach the minimum set of actions that proves value within the first 7 days?
This is your "they got it" metric. It's not about using everything—it's about crossing the threshold where the membership feels real.

3) Day 1 / Day 7 Key Benefit Adoption: What percentage complete the single action that best predicts retention—within 1 day and within 7 days?
Some behaviors are destiny. For Spotify, it might be creating a playlist. For Walmart+, it might be placing the first delivery. Find the one action that separates "tourists" from "future loyalists," and measure it relentlessly.

4) First-Week Depth: How many high-signal actions does a new member complete in the first 7 days?
Depth matters. One action can be curiosity. Multiple actions signal momentum. The question isn't "did they show up?" It's "did they start building a pattern?"

5) Trial-to-Paid Conversion (If Applicable): Track overall conversion— and conversion among members who hit your activation milestones.
This tells you whether your onboarding is doing its job. If people who hit milestones still don't convert, the issue isn't onboarding—it's your offer, pricing, or perceived value.

6) Early Churn / Refund Rate: How many cancel before day 7 or day 30? If you offer refunds, track refunds as a pain signal—not just a financial metric. Early churn is rarely random. It's almost always friction, confusion, unmet expectations, or delayed value.

7) Onboarding Completion Rate: If you use checklists or setup steps, what percentage finish—and where do they drop off?
This is one of the most actionable diagnostic metrics you can have. Every drop-off point is a story: "this was too hard," "this didn't feel worth it," or "I got lost."

8) Net Promoter Signal (Early NPS / CSAT): A short pulse at day 7 or day 14 can reveal confusion early enough to fix it.

This isn't about chasing a perfect score. It's about catching issues while the relationship is still forming—before silence turns into churn.

Pro Tip: Pick One Onboarding North Star

The biggest mistake teams make is tracking too much—and owning nothing. To avoid that, choose a single onboarding North Star metric and make it the shared scoreboard across all teams. For example: *"% of new members who complete 2+ core actions in week one."*

When onboarding is measured clearly, it becomes manageable. And when it's managed well, something powerful happens: members stop feeling like they're trying a service—and start feeling like they've joined something that fits.

Part 4: Empathy at Scale—Automating the 1:1 Feel

Let's bring this back to the real goal of onboarding: building connection, not just completion.

Like the meditation chair I mentioned at the start of this chapter, a fitness company I consulted with nailed onboarding early on because they could do it manually. The team personally contacted every new member, asked about goals, scheduled a quick onboarding session, and helped them build a simple plan. It worked—members who went through that experience were far more likely to stay active months later.

Then the company grew. The high-touch approach became too expensive and too slow.

The move wasn't to abandon the experience—it was to translate it.

We broke down what the "human" onboarding delivered and rebuilt those moments with systems:

- **A warm start:** tailor the first experience based on what brought them in (ad source, signup path, stated goals).
- **Guided steps:** a short checklist that leads to early wins (not an overwhelming tour).
- **Timed nudges:** email + push + in-app prompts that hit the right moment, not just "day 3 because day 3."
- **Confidence loops:** progress signals, reminders of benefits used, and simple next actions that make the member feel capable.

Quick exercise: Onboard Your Best Friend

If your best friend joined today:

- What would you show first?
- Where would they get confused?
- What's the smallest "win" you'd want them to get in the first 10 minutes?
- What would you tell them to do in week one to build a habit?

That's your onboarding blueprint. Build the journey so it feels like that level of care—delivered consistently to everyone.

Automation done right doesn't feel robotic. It feels like empathy at scale.

Final Thoughts: The 30-Day Rule

If you get the first 30 days right, everything that follows becomes easier. You'll have members who understand your value, build usage habits, and feel confident navigating your service. But if you miss this window, no amount of discounting, retargeting, or winback campaigns will bring back what was lost.

Retention isn't an afterthought. It's a strategy that starts the moment a member joins. Onboarding is where your brand promise meets lived experience. When you get it right, you don't just acquire members; you create advocates who stay, engage, and spread the word.

Above all, remember:

Onboarding isn't a technical step. It's the start of a relationship.

The clarity, care, and confidence you provide in those early moments set the tone for everything that follows.

Make those first 30 days count. Because onboarding isn't just a phase—*it's the foundation.*

Chapter 8

Engaging Members Through Support and Listening

Keeping Members Engaged—The Art of Long-Term Retention

You've guided someone through the funnel and delivered a strong onboarding experience. They've tasted the value and started forming a routine. But this is where membership businesses get humbled: value doesn't retain people automatically. If your service isn't habit-forming, consistently improving, and visibly worth the price, members drift. And when something breaks—delivery misses, content disappoints, a billing issue hits—members don't just churn because of the problem. They churn because of how you handle it.

This chapter is about the middle game: keeping members engaged after onboarding, pulling them back when usage fades, and using service moments, even the messy ones, to turn frustration into loyalty.

Part 1: The Engagement Spectrum—and What to Do About It

After onboarding, members usually fall into one of three states:

1) Engaged members
They're using the core benefit and getting recurring value. Your job is to *deepen the habit*: expand feature adoption, increase frequency, and keep the experience fresh so "using" becomes "belonging."

2) At-risk members

They've used you a little, but the pattern is fading. Your job is to *rebuild momentum*: remove friction, surface the next best action, and make returning feel effortless.

3) Dormant members

They've effectively disappeared. Your job is to *re-engage them quickly*—or gracefully let them go without training them to expect discounts.

The strategy only works if you can reliably identify who is where—and move people up the curve over time.

Tracking Engagement & Creating Member Cohorts

You can't improve what you don't measure. Your first job is to track engagement patterns and categorize members into clear cohorts. Rather than treating all members the same, break them into meaningful engagement segments.

Here's an example of how you could evaluate usage patterns, but it's important to realize that the usage amounts will vary drastically between services. For example, a high-frequency service like grocery delivery or fitness will naturally see more frequent engagement than a lower-frequency service, such as a consumer software subscription. The important thing is to bucket your usage based on what the data shows as the engagement levels.

Here's an example of how a service could be bucketed:

Cohort	Benefit Usage Pattern	Retention Risk?
Highly Engaged	Uses 5+ times per month, multiple features	Low risk ✅
Medium Engagement	Uses 2-4 times per month, limited features	Medium risk ⚠️
Low Engagement	Used once in the last month	High risk 🗑️
Dormant	No usage in 30+ days	Critical risk ❌

The exact thresholds will vary by category. What matters is consistency: define "healthy," "slipping," and "gone," then track how many members move between states each week. Creating a dashboard around these categories is a powerful way to better understand your member base and track how your tactics influence outcomes. It turns your strategy into something visible and measurable.

For example, you might create something like this:

Cohort	Count	% of Total	% vs. Last 4 weeks
Highly Engaged	125,000	25%	+3%
Medium Engagement	200,000	40%	-1%
Low Engagement	100,000	20%	-4%
Dormant	75,000	15%	+2%

Pro Tip: Add additional filters like marketing source, plan type, onboarding offer, or payment type to get deeper insights into why members behave the way they do.

Re-Engaging Inactive Members Before It's Too Late: What to say

Most members don't cancel overnight. Churn is usually the final step in a longer process of disengagement—and that process follows predictable patterns.

The earlier you spot those patterns, the better your chances of re-engaging members before they're gone for good. Based on the analysis above, your highest-risk members sit in the Low and Dormant Engagement cohorts, with some additional churn risk present in the Medium Engagement group.

Beyond engagement tiers, you can also monitor early warning signals like:

- Shortened session duration
- Declining feature usage
- Support ticket spikes
- Payment failures or plan downgrades

The key is to identify these signals early—ideally at the first signs of friction or fading activity, not weeks after a member has already checked out.

Once you've identified at-risk members, don't default to "we miss you." Use one of five reactivation plays—each tied to a specific psychological trigger:

Play 1: What's New (curiosity + momentum)
A launch is the cleanest reason to come back: it signals the service is alive and improving.

- "New this week: [benefit]. Built for [their use case]."
- "We added something you'll love based on what you used last."

Play 2: Unlock Value (reward the behavior you want)
Incentives work best when they're conditional on a high-signal action. Reward usage, not attention.

- "Try [feature] today—get [$X credit / perk] after your first use."
- "Complete [two actions] this week and unlock [member perk]."

Play 3: Limited-Time Moments (urgency + FOMO)
Events create a deadline without feeling desperate—especially when they're seasonal or community-based.

- "Member Week starts today—exclusive [perk] ends Sunday."
- "This month only: [bundle/perk] for members."

Play 4: Save the Relationship (earned offers, not blanket discounting)
Use modest offers for members showing cancellation intent or consistent decline—paired with a reason to re-engage.

- "Before you go: here's a month to explore [new benefit]—on us."
- "Renew your annual today and we'll add [bonus] to your account."

Play 5: Show Progress (endowment effect + identity)
Members hesitate to cancel when they see what they've already accumulated.

- "You've saved $___ / completed ___ / unlocked ___ so far."
- "Pick up where you left off: your next step is ready."

Re-Engagement: Where to Say It

Start with channels that reach members *when they're not using you*: **push + email**. In-app prompts are powerful, but only if someone opens the app.

A simple rule:

- **Email = explanation and narrative** (why this matters)
- **Push = timing and action** (do this now)
- **In-app = context** (do this here)

Make every message earn its place: one clear call to action, one success metric. Don't optimize for opens and clicks—optimize for behavior lift:

- Did they return?
- Did they use the core benefit?
- Did they complete the next best action?

A note on images/creative: In multiple tests I've run, plain-text, direct emails often outperformed heavily designed templates for high-intent lifecycle messages. You'll notice many of the most important emails from Amazon are very text-forward. Clarity often beats polish when the goal is action.

Offer discipline matters: don't give your best deal to every dormant member. Reserve high-value offers for segments with the highest probability of returning—and measure incrementality, not redemptions.

When used well, Email and Push don't just nudge members back—they remind them why they joined in the first place. And they do it in a way that feels helpful, not desperate.

Next, let's explore how to reinforce value once you've re-engaged them.

Part 2: Build the Engagement Engine: Cadence, Triggers, Rewards

The best retention is a product that gives members a reason to return before they drift.

Most strong memberships run on a simple loop:

Trigger → Action → Reward → Next best action

- **Triggers:** content drops, replenishment cycles, weekly recommendations, expiring credits, seasonal moments
- **Actions:** one or two core behaviors that predict retention
- **Rewards:** visible progress, savings, status, personalization, community signal
- **Next best action:** always make the next step obvious

If onboarding is how members learn the value, this engagement engine is how they *live it*.

Making Value Come Alive

One of the most powerful retention levers is making membership value visible. When members can clearly see what they've saved, earned, learned, or completed, the membership stops feeling like a recurring expense and starts feeling like a compounding asset. Progress becomes motivating, and the service becomes harder to give up.

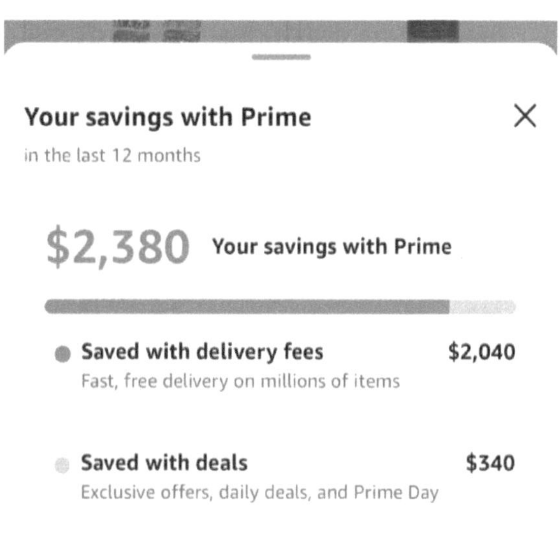

This matters across the lifecycle, but it becomes especially powerful after onboarding, when members are subconsciously asking: *Is this worth it?* Your job is to make the answer obvious.

Great membership businesses do this in different ways: **Peloton** highlights workout streaks and achievements. **Calm** sends weekly recaps that show meditation minutes and consistency. **Walmart+** and **Amazon Prime** surface savings calculators. **Duolingo** uses streaks, levels, and badges to turn practice into a game. And **Spotify Wrapped** has become a cultural moment by visualizing listening habits in a way that feels personal, shareable, and identity-building.

To create effective value tracking for your members:

1. **Identify your tangible benefits:** What concrete value do members receive? (Money saved, time saved, goals achieved, etc.)

2. **Create visual representations:** Design simple, clear visualizations that highlight this value (progress bars, savings counters, achievement badges)

3. **Place these indicators prominently:** Ensure members see this value representation during normal service usage

4. **Send periodic summaries:** Email weekly or monthly recaps that reinforce the total value received

5. **Celebrate milestones:** When members reach significant value thresholds, acknowledge and reward their loyalty

6. **Branded Currency:** Consider offering discounts or member bonuses through branded currency instead of straight price reductions. For example, Uber One delivers its 6% member discount on rides by issuing rewards in Uber Cash. While this approach requires additional development, it unlocks a powerful retention lever: members can be reminded that they'll lose their earned credits if they cancel, creating a stronger incentive to stay.

Remember: Delivering value isn't enough; members need to notice it.

Max Nimaroff – SVP, Retention, Oats Overnight

Membership Is Where Creativity Meets Discipline

I've spent the better part of the last decade building, scaling, and evolving membership and retention programs and the truth is, I didn't set out to become a "membership guy." I fell into it because it sat at the intersection of two things I care deeply about: creativity and long-term value creation.

As of this week, I joined Oats Overnight as Senior Vice President of Retention. It's a few-hundred-million-dollar business that started in the most unlikely way…by a professional poker player making oatmeal in his kitchen. He was successful at poker but burned out on the lifestyle. He wanted to build something more sustainable, something people genuinely enjoyed, and it turned out he was onto something.

What drew me to the company wasn't just the product; it was the mindset. Oats Overnight is run by people who think differently. Many of them come from poker backgrounds, which means they're comfortable with probability, long-term thinking, and calculated risk. That's exactly the kind of environment where retention work thrives. If your job is to create ongoing value, you need space to experiment.

This isn't my first time doing this kind of work. I've built membership programs at DoorDash, AG1, and now Oats Overnight. At this point, I've done it enough times that I can say with confidence: retention is not a function—it's a philosophy.

How DashPass Taught Me What Membership Really Means

At DoorDash, I joined early in the life of DashPass. Today, it's one of the largest subscription programs in the world; easily a top-five consumer subscription in the U.S. But when I arrived, it was much smaller and far more limited.

Originally, DashPass offered reduced service fees and free delivery at a subset of restaurants. That was fine…but it wasn't enough. My first major move was expanding eligibility to nearly every restaurant on the platform. That single change dramatically increased the perceived value of the membership.

From there, we layered in benefits deliberately and creatively:

- Credits for pickup orders, not just delivery
- One membership across both DoorDash and Caviar
- A reimagined Summer of DashPass campaign with thousands of participating restaurants
- Annual subscription commitments
- Loyalty challenges and streak-based incentives
- Exclusive menu items and limited-time offers

Each addition wasn't about novelty; it was about deepening the relationship. Membership only works when customers feel like the product is getting better *because* they're members.

Over time, my role evolved. Earlier in my career, I had to fight harder for unconventional ideas. As I gained seniority and trust, resistance dropped, and my ability to place bigger bets increased. That freedom matters. The best retention ideas often sound strange before they work.

Why Retention Became My Lane

My background isn't traditional marketing. In college, I studied public health at Johns Hopkins, mostly because it was the easiest major that still let me minor in business. But after graduating, I took three foundational jobs back-to-back that shaped how I think.

First, I worked in market research, learning how to ask good questions and interpret customer insights. Then I moved into product marketing, helping sales teams understand how to position value. Finally, I joined a strategy group where I learned analytics, data fluency, and structured problem-solving.

Those three skill sets…customer insight, product thinking, and strategic analytics…became the foundation of my career. What started as corporate strategy evolved into product strategy, and eventually into retention as a specialization.

Retention became my edge because most people in the space come from lifecycle marketing backgrounds. I don't. I approach it as a generalist with a creative bias. And that difference matters.

Retention Is a Creative Discipline

What I love most about this work is that it gives me permission to create.

Not everyone who is creative ends up being an artist, filmmaker, or musician. For a long time, I didn't even realize how creative I was, because I didn't fit the traditional mold. But retention work is one of the few corporate roles where creativity isn't optional—it's essential.

You're constantly asking:

How do we surprise customers?

How do we make this feel fresh?

How do we turn utility into delight?

I write on Substack now, and that's helped me reconnect with creativity in a more traditional way. But I've been exercising my creative muscle for a decade inside businesses…designing experiences, incentives, narratives, and moments that make people feel something.

That's the secret most companies miss: retention is emotional.

Membership Isn't a Generational Trend—It's a Survival Advantage

People often ask whether membership models are more popular with Gen Z. I don't think that's quite right. Membership businesses have always existed. What's changed is that they survive better.

If you look at large, enduring companies over time, many of them are membership-based. That's not an accident. Membership forces you to orient around the customer, not the transaction. When your business is built on ongoing relationships, you're naturally more adaptable.

That said, younger generations do change the execution. Social media has made emotional connection mandatory. Brands now have to communicate through content, culture, and values…not just features. Membership businesses tend to be better at this because they're already invested in long-term engagement.

At the same time, we're seeing a renewed hunger for real-world connection. Paradoxically, the more digital everything becomes, the more people crave belonging. Successful membership programs understand this. They're not just selling access—they're cultivating fandom.

The Brands That Do It Best

As a consumer, there are three membership brands I admire most.

Netflix sets the standard for cultural relevance. They don't just release content—they create moments. Costco is the gold standard for trust and value discipline. And Spotify may be the best example of personalization at scale…sending fans personalized experiences that make them feel seen.

What all three have in common is depth. They go incredibly deep in the areas that matter most to their customers. That level of sophistication is only possible when you have a recurring relationship.

Reinventing Oatmeal (Yes, Really)

At Oats Overnight, the magic lies in turning a boring category into something fun. Flavor variety is central; we launch new flavors constantly, listen obsessively to customer feedback, and iterate fast. The product is also designed for modern life: drinkable oatmeal for people on the go.

This is a classic example of taking a tired category and reimagining it through convenience, creativity, and customer obsession. The membership layer simply amplifies what's already working.

Where This Is All Going

If I had to summarize where membership models are headed, I'd say this: fandom is becoming non-negotiable. The future belongs to businesses that turn products into platforms for identity and belonging. I often think about how a simple product could evolve the way the NBA has. At its core, it's just basketball…but around it exists culture, community, merch, content, betting, and storytelling.

Any product with a passionate audience has that potential. The job of membership leaders going forward is to unlock it: to turn customers into advocates, advocates into fans, and fans into the front line of growth.That's the work I love. And I think we're just getting started.

Part 3: Customer Service as a Strategic Advantage

Too many companies view customer service as a cost center and something to minimize rather than optimize. For membership businesses, this is a costly mistake. Customer service isn't just about fixing problems; it's a powerful retention tool that can transform frustrated members into loyal advocates.

When members encounter issues, they're at a critical decision point. Great customer service doesn't just solve problems; it reinforces the value of membership at moments when that value is being questioned. In membership, a resolved issue isn't neutral—it's a chance to increase trust and raise the psychological cost of leaving.

Here are five areas to focus on for driving the best customer service possible:

Focus 1 - Solve Problems Fast: Speed matters more than most companies realize. For membership businesses, this means offering multiple support channels (chat, email, phone), empowering frontline agents to solve problems without escalation, creating self-service options for common issues, and setting and measuring response time targets.

Focus 2 - Reinforce Membership Value in Every Interaction: Train support teams to go beyond problem resolution and actively remind members of the benefits they receive. This can be as simple as: "Thanks for being a Prime member since 2019! I see you've saved $327 in shipping this year. Let me help resolve this delivery issue right away." This approach subtly thanks the member and reminds them of accumulated benefits, putting the current problem in perspective.

Focus 3 - Follow Through After Resolution: The support experience doesn't end when the immediate issue is fixed. Implement a follow-up system to ensure the solution worked as intended, gather feedback on the support experience, offer a small gesture of appreciation such as a small promo code for a bigger issue, and provide relevant benefit information based on their issue. Surveys are a key way to meet these goals, so always ask for feedback on the communication.

Focus 4 - Focus on Root Cause Analysis: While you should always focus on solving member problems as quickly as possible, you also need to identify what caused the problem in the first place and how it can be prevented in the future. Amazon's Correction of Errors process, described below, provides an excellent framework for this approach.

Focus 5 - Documentation is an Imperative: Creating both member-facing and agent-facing documentation is key to ensuring all solutions are approached in the same way. Let's chat about that in more detail.

Documentation: The Self-Service Engagement Strategy

While personal support remains essential, great documentation can significantly enhance the member experience while reducing support costs. This refers to articles, frequently asked questions, and AI chatbots that help answer simple questions from your members. Self-service resources empower members to solve problems independently and discover new value in your service. Here's how I like that documentation to be structured:

- **Structure as Questions and Answers:** Format your documentation around the questions members actually ask, not how your company thinks about features. This makes information more discoverable and useful. Use actual support queries to identify common questions.
- **Study Best Practices:** Examine how leading companies in your space structure their help content. Apple's support site, Spotify's help center, and Amazon's help pages are excellent examples of clear, navigable documentation. Use these examples to help guide what you build.

- **Create Comprehensive Resources:** Develop your documentation with clear, jargon-free language, step-by-step instructions, and visual aids. Always cross-link between related topics and provide regular updates as features change.
- **Implement a Feedback Loop:** After each help article, ask: "Did this answer your question?" When someone says "no," capture what information was missing and improve the article accordingly.

Case Study: Amazon's Correction of Error (COE) Process

When a significant customer-impacting issue occurs, Amazon initiates a Correction of Errors (COE) process using a structured problem-solving framework to analyze failures, identify root causes, and implement long-term fixes. It's a core part of Amazon's operational excellence, ensuring that mistakes aren't just corrected but systematically prevented from happening again.

I helped write one of these during my time at Amazon, and I remember it vividly. The process was both brutal and brilliant. It demanded complete transparency, forced us to walk through every misstep in painful detail, and took an enormous amount of time. But the result was worth it: a clear roadmap to prevent future failures—and a team that was better because of it.

Here's how the process works:

The COE is Triggered: A COE is initiated when an issue causes customer impact, financial loss, or operational inefficiency. The team responsible for the area is tasked with writing the COE.

The COE Document: This detailed postmortem follows a structured format:

- **What Happened:** A clear, factual timeline of events leading up to the incident.
- **Customer & Business Impact:** Who was affected and to what extent.

- **Root Cause Analysis:** Using the 5 Whys methodology to uncover the true underlying cause. This takes time and focus to uncover.
- **Immediate Fixes:** Actions taken right away to fix the issue.
- **Preventative Measures:** Long-term changes to ensure the problem never recurs.

Leadership Review: Senior leaders review COEs to ensure real corrective action is being taken, with the expectation that similar issues should not be repeated.

Documentation & Learning: Completed COEs are stored in a knowledge base, allowing other teams to learn from past mistakes and prevent similar issues.

Why It Works: The COE process is brutally honest, but never about blame. It's designed to fix systems, not people—and to fix root causes, not just symptoms. For membership businesses, adapting this kind of process can transform customer service from reactive troubleshooting into a proactive engine for continuous improvement.

Imagine if every time a member churned, or a benefit failed to deliver value, your team performed a mini-COE—not to punish, but to learn. That kind of discipline doesn't just reduce mistakes. It builds trust, inside and out.

Final Thoughts: Engagement as the Engine of Growth

In the increasingly crowded membership economy, engagement is no longer just a metric. It's your moat. Companies that master the art of keeping members active, satisfied, and emotionally invested build deeper relationships, stronger brand affinity, and ultimately, more resilient businesses.

As I continue to mention in this book, the key isn't to drive signups, but to engage and retain the members you do acquire. You do this by creating so much consistent value that members feel like they'd be giving something up by leaving.

As strategies evolve, one thing remains constant: engagement is earned in every interaction. It's built through seamless experiences, habit-forming value, and a relentless focus on solving member problems before they become reasons to leave.

And when problems *do* arise—as they always will—don't waste them.

Bill Gates once said, *"Your most unhappy customers are your greatest source of learning."*
Listen to them. Learn from them. And use that feedback to turn a frustrated member into a loyal advocate.

The membership businesses that thrive will be the ones that treat engagement as their growth engine, not just a retention tactic. When you do that, you don't just keep members. You create advocates. And that's when your membership truly starts to scale.

Chapter 9

Reinforcing Value and Reducing Churn

The Moment of Truth: Keeping Members and Preventing Churn

No matter how strong your value proposition is, every member will eventually consider canceling. Some will feel financial pressure. Some will outgrow the need. And some will drift simply because nothing has reminded them why they joined in the first place.

Retention matters throughout the journey, but renewal is when the decision becomes real. It's the moment members look at what they're paying, weigh what they're getting, and choose whether the membership still belongs in their life. That makes renewal your best opportunity to reinforce value, remove friction, and make staying feel obvious.

Renewal is where loyalty is tested—and where retention finally pays off. Because one truth doesn't change in membership: keeping a good member costs less than replacing one. Yet too many companies still spend most of their energy on acquisition and treat retention as cleanup. It's time to flip that.

Churn Prevention Framework

Before diving into specific strategies, let's establish a framework for thinking about retention:

1. **Prevention** - Proactive measures taken before members consider leaving

2. **Intervention** - Actions taken when members signal intent to cancel

3. **Recovery** - Strategies to bring back those who have already left

This chapter focuses primarily on the first two components, with the third, "winback," covered in the next chapter.

Part 1: Leading Up to the Time of Renewal

The period before a member's renewal is a crucial time to reinforce the value of your service. If they haven't been actively engaged, their decision to renew is up in the air. Here's how to approach this window effectively.

Engaging Dormant Members: Wake Them or Let Them Be?

In the previous chapter, we discussed the importance of re-engaging dormant members—specifically those who haven't used their benefits in 30, 60, or 90 days. The standard best practice is to nudge them back into usage with personalized messages, special offers, or curated content.

However, as renewal time approaches, some membership businesses adopt a "let sleeping dogs lie" approach, intentionally avoiding reminders that aren't legally required for dormant members who may have forgotten about their subscription altogether. The reasoning: if they're not using the service but also not canceling, why risk drawing attention to their inactivity?

In practice, many memberships carry a "quiet" segment—members who pay but use very little for stretches of time. Maybe they intend to return, maybe they forgot to cancel, or maybe they're simply not price-sensitive. Regardless of the reason, there are times when not reminding them (beyond what's legally required) may be the smarter move.

That may sound unfriendly to members, but I'm not advocating hiding anything. Transparency should always be a baseline. Rather, it's about choosing whether to actively prompt a decision or allow inertia to play out. The right approach depends on your business model, your audience, and how long someone has been a member.

My recommendation: for first-time renewals, double down on engagement. These members need to experience the value you provide to renew. But for long-term dormant yet retained members, consider placing them in a "low-touch" category, where they receive minimal communication. Many will stay simply because they still see future potential, or because canceling just isn't a priority. If you do low-touch, make sure you're still meeting clear billing descriptor + accessible self-serve cancellation + required notices.

Optimizing Renewal Emails: Turning Compliance into Opportunity

In many jurisdictions—and on some platforms—businesses are now required to send renewal reminder emails that clearly state when a membership will renew and at what rate. Unsurprisingly, these emails often prompt the highest share of cancellations. I'll be honest: at previous companies, we pushed back hard against these requirements, worried they'd drive mass churn.

Eventually, we had no choice but to comply, but it wasn't the disaster we expected. Yes, some members did cancel, but many appreciated the transparency. We saw a drop in customer service complaints about unexpected charges. More importantly, we realized we could embed value-reinforcing messaging alongside the legally mandated notice. Rather than resisting these requirements, I've learned to embrace them, and even go beyond the requirements by sending proactive renewal reminders in non-mandated states as that can turn a legal burden into a strategic advantage.

Here's what advantages that can provide:

- **Marketing edge**: You can highlight your transparent renewal policy in acquisition campaigns ("No surprise charges—we'll always remind you before billing").
- **Testing ground**: You can refine your messaging before laws expand to more regions.
- **Trust builder**: Proactively communicating reinforces your brand as member-first and transparent.

- **Messaging control**: By sequencing your communications, you shape the narrative *before* the renewal email lands.
- **Technical simplicity**: One consistent approach avoids state-by-state segmentation and operational complexity.

The timing of these emails is just as important as the content. A well-timed sequence can turn a moment of potential churn into a moment of reaffirmation. Here's how:

1. **Value recap (3–10 days before renewal)**: Send an email highlighting recent usage, savings earned, content consumed, and benefits discovered. Make the members feel that their subscription has been working hard for them.

2. **Renewal reminder**: Open with a quick summary of the value received, then clearly state the upcoming renewal terms.

3. **What's next (1–3 days after renewal)**: Reinforce upcoming features, content drops, or improvements to keep anticipation high.

Think of it like a "value sandwich." You're surrounding a compliance-driven message with two pieces of compelling engagement. That way, the question shifts from *"Do I still want to pay for this?"* to *"Why would I stop now?"* Done right, renewal reminders don't just check a legal box. They deepen trust, reinforce value, and reduce avoidable surprise-driven churn.

Part 2: How to Improve Renewals at the Critical Moment of Choice

It's easy to assume that when a member clicks "Cancel," they've made up their mind. But many aren't looking to leave—they're looking for options.

They may be confused about their benefits, need a short-term pause, or want reassurance that they're getting value. That's why the cancellation flow shouldn't be treated as an exit door—think of it as a checkpoint, a moment to re-engage, clarify, and potentially course-correct.

In the next section, we'll explore smart, member-first ways to improve the cancellation experience—turning a potential loss into a chance to retain trust, value, and even loyalty.

The High-Level Path for Handling Cancellation Requests

Regulators have made it clear that "dark patterns" and overly difficult cancellations can backfire—legally, financially, and reputationally. Don't make the same mistake.

You shouldn't hide the "Cancel" button—but you don't need to promote it front and center either. The key is transparency and respect.

Place the cancellation option in a logical, intuitive spot within account settings, clearly labeled with language like: "Cancel or Change My Membership."

Members shouldn't have to dig through five screens or contact customer support just to leave. If someone has truly decided to cancel, they'll find a way. Your goal isn't to block the exit—it's to give them a reason to pause and reconsider.

Because if they leave feeling tricked or frustrated, your chances of winning them back are close to zero.

What to Do When a Member Clicks "Cancel"

When a member initiates cancellation, that click is more than an endpoint—it's a critical moment of influence. Your job is to make them think twice, not by begging them to stay, but by reminding them what they're about to lose—both emotionally and factually.

Show them the value they've already received:

- What they've saved
- What they've used

- How often they've engaged

People are far more likely to stay to avoid losing something valuable than to gain something new. This is your chance to frame that loss with clarity and confidence.

Don't Force a Binary Choice

Sometimes the reason for cancellation isn't dissatisfaction—it's timing, price, or even temporary fatigue. That's why flexibility is more powerful than finality.

Instead of presenting a "stay or go" decision, offer smart alternatives:

- Downgrade from annual to monthly
- Switch to a lighter or lower-cost plan
- Pause the membership (a powerful option for services with seasonal drop-off)

Save offers can also work well here—we'll explore those in more detail shortly. The key is to meet the member where they are and offer a path forward that fits their needs.

Always Capture the Why

Whatever the outcome, don't waste the moment. A well-crafted exit survey can deliver insights you won't get anywhere else. Keep it simple, focused, and actionable:

- Use pre-selected options like "Too expensive," "Didn't use it enough," "Didn't see the value," or "Life change"
- Avoid vague options like "Other" unless you allow for context
- If one reason dominates (e.g., "Too expensive" accounts for the majority of responses), that's a red flag—either your pricing/packaging is off, your value isn't landing, or your cancellation reasons are too coarse.

You can even go a step further: reach out to a few churned members for a quick, open-ended conversation. Ten minutes of candid feedback from someone who has left is often more valuable than ten hours of internal speculation.

Post-Cancel ≠ End of the Relationship

Even after someone cancels, your opportunity to re-engage isn't over.

A well-timed post-cancellation message—something like "You're about to lose access to X. Want to come back?"—can reignite interest, especially for those who canceled impulsively or without realizing the impact.

These messages shouldn't feel desperate. They should feel clear, empathetic, and rooted in clarity + loss aversion, not guilt.

This is your first winback moment—the start of a longer strategy that we'll unpack in the next chapter.

Churn Prevention Strategies That Work

The best membership businesses don't rely on a single tactic. Instead, they layer multiple strategies to address different cancellation mindsets. Below are four of the most effective.

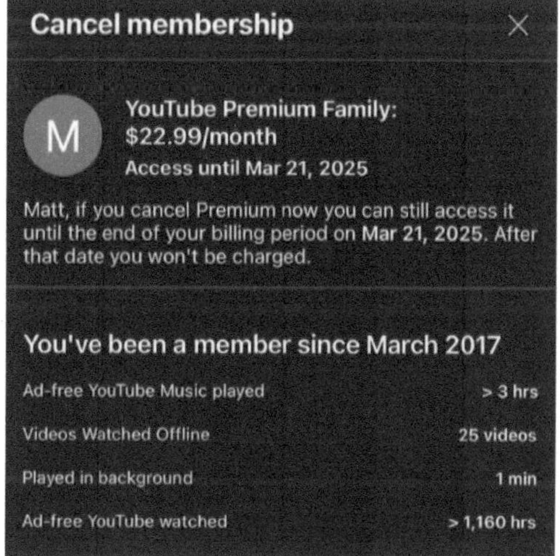

Strategy 1: Remind Members What They're Getting

One of the most powerful ways to reduce churn is to surface the value the member has already received. This might include savings, content consumed, credits used, or milestones achieved. Even simple reminders can trigger second thoughts about canceling. Examples:

- **Amazon:** highlights major benefits and includes a savings calculator that shows how much you've saved with your membership.
- **Disney+:** provides personalized content recommendations to remind users what they'll miss if they leave.
- **Uber One:** show savings and remind members what benefits they'll lose.

Whether personalized or general, this approach taps into a member's emotional and financial investment to make them second-guess their decision to cancel.

Strategy 2: Use Loss Aversion to Reframe the Decision

Loss aversion is the idea that people feel the pain of losing something more acutely than the joy of gaining something. Use this by emphasizing what they'll lose if they cancel, especially if the membership includes expiring perks or earned credits. Examples:

- **Audible:** Any unused audiobook credits are forfeited immediately when a member cancels.
- **ClassPass:** Remaining credits expire on the final day of membership and cannot be rolled over.
- **American Express:** If you cancel your Rewards account and don't hold another eligible Amex product, all unredeemed points are lost.
- **Adobe Stock:** Unused image licenses are forfeited upon cancellation of your subscription.

These aren't just policy details. Instead, they're powerful psychological nudges. By framing what's being given up, not just what's being saved, you encourage the member to reassess the decision to leave.

Strategy 3: Offer a Pause Option

Sometimes churn is circumstantial, not emotional. A "Pause Your Membership" feature gives members a way to opt out temporarily without severing the relationship. Even if few use it, just offering it reduces total churn by giving hesitant members a middle ground.

Examples:

- **Spotify** and **Hulu** allow users to pause subscriptions
- **Equinox** and **ClassPass** offer seasonal holds
- The **New York Times** provides break periods for subscribers

This is especially useful for seasonal services or content-heavy platforms where interest may wax and wane.

Strategy 4: Use Save Offers—Strategically

Save offers can be one of your highest-performing tools. A well-placed discount or bonus can lift "save rate" (percentage of members who initiate a cancellation but end up staying) by a meaningful amount right away. But there's a catch: used incorrectly, they can backfire by training members to expect a deal and game the system.

Here's how to do it right:

- **Start small**: Test low-risk options like trial extensions instead of immediate discounts.
- **Segment smartly**: Use behavioral data to target the most likely savers, not everyone who cancels.

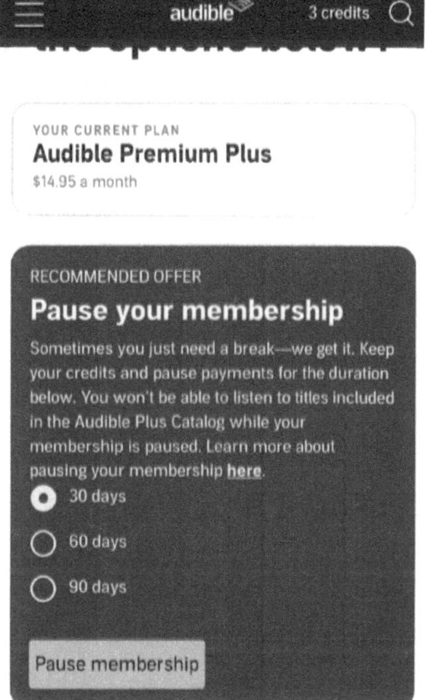

- **Escalate cautiously**: When testing discounted membership save offers, start with a smaller amount, say 20% off an annual plan, before going to a large discount such as 50% off an annual plan. That way you can alleviate risks of devaluing the brand and creating a demand for continuous large discounts.

Also, watch the legal landscape. Some regions prohibit save offers within the cancellation flow. In that case, surface them in the confirmation message or follow-up email. And finally, don't let save offers stand alone. Pair them with messages about future value, upcoming launches, or long-term benefits. For example, "We'd like to extend a special offer so you can experience

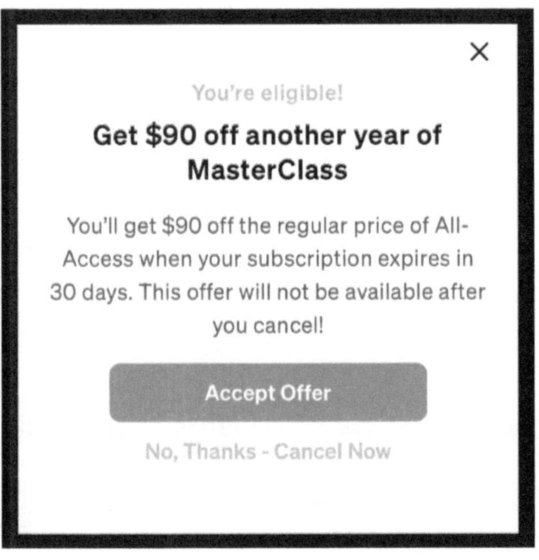

the new benefit launching next month." Remember, discounts buy time, but it's what you do with that time that earns trust.

When done right, these strategies shift the cancellation conversation from, *"Should I leave?"* to, *"Why would I?"* They turn a moment of doubt into a second chance. And they remind every member that your service is worth staying for.

Part 3: Churn - What It Is, How to Measure It, and What to Do About It

Churn is the silent killer of membership businesses. While growth metrics like new signups tend to grab the headlines, high churn means you're running hard just to stay in place. If too many members leave, growth stalls, no matter how good your acquisition looks.

As a reminder, churn is the percentage of members who cancel or fail to renew within a given time period.

Churn Rate = (Lost Members ÷ Total Members at Start of Period) x 100

- Example: If you start the month with 10,000 members and lose 500 members, your churn rate for that month is 5%.

The lower your churn rate, the more predictable, scalable, and profitable your business becomes. Yet many services wait too long to address churn, lulled by strong retention from early adopters. But as you expand into broader audiences, you tend to have fewer sticky members, and churn inevitably rises. That's why churn prevention shouldn't be an afterthought. It should be a core part of your strategy from the start.

Remember, your overall churn rate is a blended number. The real insights show up when you track churn by cohort tenure—how many members cancel in month 1 vs. month 6 vs. month 18. That's because early-tenure churn and long-tenure churn usually have different causes.

Industry Benchmarks and Expectations

I often get asked for a "typical" churn rate for a membership service. Generally, monthly churn often lands in the low single digits to mid-single digits, which implies that less than half of your members will still be around after one year. That's after converting from a free trial to paid membership. However, standout businesses perform far better. For example, Peloton historically has 1.4% monthly churn, SiriusXM is 1.6%, and Netflix is ~2%.

It's also important to consider how a business's life stage impacts churn. Churn is typically highest early in a member's tenure[13], often spiking to 20–30% in the first paid month, especially when members see their first charge hit their credit card. Over time, churn decreases significantly as members become more engaged and invested. This means services in growth mode, with a large share of newer members, will naturally show higher overall churn than mature businesses with a more tenured, loyal base.

The Two Types of Churn—Why Members Leave and How to Prevent It

Not all churn is the same. Some members cancel by choice, while others leave because of backend issues like failed payments. The biggest mistake businesses make is treating both types of churn the same way. Instead, you need a two-pronged strategy—one for voluntary churn and one for involuntary churn.

Type 1: Voluntary Churn—When a Member Actively Cancels

Voluntary churn happens when a member makes the conscious decision to leave by canceling their membership. Common Reasons for Voluntary Churn:

- **Lack of Perceived Value:** The member doesn't believe they're getting enough for what they pay
- **Price Sensitivity:** They like the service but can't justify the cost
- **Bad Onboarding Experience:** They never built a habit around using the service
- **Life Circumstances:** Job loss, moving, seasonal shifts (e.g., fitness memberships in summer)
- **Better Alternatives:** A competitor offers a more attractive deal

---

[13] **Member Tenure** – The average length of time a member stays subscribed.

If voluntary churn is high, you're losing the battle of perception. Members don't see enough ongoing value to keep paying for your service.

How to Reduce Voluntary Churn

You might feel like this is a recap of everything we've covered so far—and that's exactly the point. Because nearly every element of a successful membership business converges here. Voluntary churn isn't solved with a quick fix. It's the byproduct of an experience that fails to deliver ongoing value. Retention isn't a phase in the funnel—it's the outcome of getting everything else right. And it starts with one mindset shift: obsess over the value your members receive, not just what you offer on paper.

Your membership needs to feel indispensable. Benefits shouldn't just sound impressive on a landing page—they need to deliver in the real world. If members aren't regularly using and appreciating what they're paying for, doubt creeps in. And once someone starts questioning the value, you're already on the defensive.

Pricing plays a bigger role than most realize. Members are constantly weighing what they're getting against what they're paying. Ask yourself: Does the price feel fair? Does a deep onboarding discount create sticker shock at renewal? Or does the monthly or annual fee feel like a no-brainer for the value delivered? Missteps here—even subtle ones—can drive churn among satisfied but cost-conscious users.

But here's the thing: retention doesn't start at renewal—it starts the moment someone joins. The first 30 days are pivotal. If new members don't quickly feel the value, they're far more likely to leave.

Onboarding isn't just about explaining the service—it's about immersing members in it. Their first purchase, first stream, or first benefit usage should happen fast. The goal is simple: by the time they stop to evaluate, they've already built a habit.

That said, even the best onboarding can't compensate for a clunky experience. If members are confused by a feature, frequently contacting support, or ignoring parts of your service altogether, don't settle for surface fixes. Go upstream. Find the root cause. Then empower your team to fix it—really fix it—with meaningful product and experience improvements, not temporary workarounds.

One often overlooked strategy is reminding members of the value they've already received. Personalized usage summaries—"You've saved $142 this year," "You've listened to 63 hours of exclusive content," "You've unlocked 22 member perks"—trigger the sunk cost effect. When people see how much they've used, saved, or gained, they're less likely to walk away. Canceling starts to feel like leaving value on the table.

And remember, not every cancellation is permanent. Some members are just overwhelmed, in transition, or tightening their budgets. Flexible options like pause, downgrade, or limited-tier access can salvage relationships with people who aren't ready to fully leave—but also aren't fully lost.

Most importantly, treat churn like a data problem, not just a behavioral one. Run regular cohort analyses. Segment by join date, acquisition channel, plan type, and engagement behavior. Look for inflection points: When do members start to drop off? What features correlate with retention? Where do habits break? These signals aren't just insights—they're roadmaps.

When you stop treating churn as a lagging metric and start seeing it as a mirror of product-market fit, the game changes. You stop reacting—and start designing. That's when retention becomes not just an outcome, but a competitive advantage.

Type 2: Involuntary Churn—When a Payment Fails

Not every member who churns intended to leave. Sometimes, their departure isn't a choice, but a technicality. This is what we call involuntary churn, and it happens when a member's payment method fails, resulting in a lost member even though they may still value the service.

There are several common reasons this happens. The first reason is that credit cards expire. At any given time, several percent of stored cards are out of date.

Members may have insufficient funds, especially if they're using debit or prepaid cards, which are often chosen specifically to avoid ongoing charges.

Sometimes, legitimate transactions are flagged as fraud by a bank's automated systems. Other times, members call their credit card companies and complain, resulting in the dreaded "chargeback." And occasionally, the issue is on your side, where technical hiccups in the billing flow can quietly fail transactions that would otherwise succeed.

The good news is that involuntary churn is one of the easiest types of revenue loss to fix. A few well-placed systems can save a meaningful percentage of at-risk members.

Fraud and Churn: The Silent Killer

But not all involuntary churn is due to technical failure—sometimes, it's intentional abuse hiding in plain sight through fraud, which refers to activations from bad actors who exploit the system. These are members who game promotions, use stolen credit cards, abuse trial loopholes, or take advantage of bonuses, incentives, and referral programs. They create a double hit: inflating acquisition and engagement numbers in the short term, then driving up churn and costs when they inevitably disappear.

The challenge is that these accounts look like engaged members at first glance. They redeem offers, trigger bonuses, and in many cases use high-cost benefits like free delivery, streaming, or credits. But they were never real members. If you don't isolate them, they'll distort your retention data, inflate your forecasts, and mask the performance of legitimate members.

Here's a real example of how this played out at Walmart+. We launched a referral program where a new member would receive $20 off their next Walmart purchase after paying for their first month. The referred also received a $20 bonus. Initially, it looked like a huge success. Signups spiked, and we leaned into the program as a powerful acquisition engine by tapping into our most engaged members to spread the word.

But once we dug into the data, the cracks started to show. A significant percentage of these new signups were fraudulent. Scammers created fake accounts to game the referral system, funneling bonuses back to themselves while racking up free benefits. These accounts churned quickly, but not before distorting our engagement metrics and driving up costs.

Because they appeared "engaged," we baked their behavior into our retention models and forecasts. That turned out to be a costly mistake. Once we analyzed the deeper retention and cost data, it became clear: we were off-plan, spending heavily on members who had no intention of staying.

To fix the problem, we tightened the referral program controls to reduce abuse. We developed models to detect and segment fraudulent accounts from our core member base, excluding them from retention reporting while continuing to track their presence. Ultimately, we determined it was too difficult to effectively gate the referral program and made the decision to shut it down.

The lesson was clear: not all growth is good growth. If you don't filter for quality, top-line metrics can lie. What looks like traction might be a red flag. Growth, engagement, even retention only matter if they're coming from real, high-intent members. Otherwise, you're building your forecasts, and your future, on a shaky foundation.

Chargebacks: What They Are and What to Do About Them

A chargeback occurs when a customer disputes a charge on their credit or debit card with their issuing bank, and the bank forcibly reverses the transaction. In essence, it's a forced refund, usually because the customer:

- Doesn't recognize the charge
- Believes the charge is fraudulent
- Claims they never received the service/product
- Forgot they signed up or didn't realize it was a recurring membership
- Attempted to cancel but was charged anyway

In membership, this is especially common with subscription renewals.

Why Chargebacks Matter, especially in Membership

In a membership model, chargebacks aren't just a financial loss. They're a signal. And too many can cause real damage, including:

1. **Lost Revenue**: Not only do you lose the transaction amount, but you may also pay a chargeback fee (typically $15–$50 per incident, depending on your payment processor).

2. **Increased Operational Risk**: Card networks and processors monitor dispute/chargeback rates, and high levels can trigger monitoring programs, rolling reserves/withholds, higher processing costs, or even termination of your ability to process payments.

3. **Damaged Brand Trust**: A chargeback often means the member felt their only recourse was to call their bank—not you. That's a failure in communication or user experience.

4. **Skewed Metrics**: Chargebacks can quietly inflate your gross revenue numbers and artificially lower churn, making your LTV and CAC calculations misleading if not tracked properly.

Common Chargeback Triggers in Membership

- **Involuntary churn**: A member's card is declined, but you keep trying to charge them—and they eventually dispute the transaction.
- **Surprise renewals**: Auto-renewing without clear reminders (especially after long trials or discount periods).
- **Ambiguous billing descriptors**: The customer doesn't recognize the merchant's name on their statement (e.g., "WMTPLUSWB22").
- **Poor cancellation UX**: If canceling is difficult, customers may feel scammed and go straight to the bank.

In a well-run membership business, chargebacks should be rare—and when they do happen, they should be treated as product signals, not just financial annoyances. High chargeback rates often mean one thing: you're not meeting the member's expectations—or worse, they don't even realize they *are* a member. Fix that, and you fix churn, trust, and profitability all at once.

Building a Fraud Detection Model

The key to minimizing fraudulent churn isn't just catching bad actors after the fact. It's spotting them before they drive up your costs or distort your data. That's where a risk-based fraud detection model comes in.

At its core, this model works by identifying behavioral and technical patterns that are statistically linked to abuse. For example, you might see clusters of signups coming from the same IP address or geographic region, especially when paired with disposable email domains or nearly identical usernames. Prepaid and debit cards from certain issuing banks often show higher fraud rates, particularly when tied to promotional abuse. A well-built model can evaluate these characteristics, but also understand who signs up, uses a costly benefit, and then cancels right away. These patterns on their own may not prove anything, but together they form a reliable signal.

Once you centralize this data, ideally in a single member-level table, you can begin to score members on their likelihood of fraud. This can be done through a simple rule-based system or a machine learning model trained on past fraudulent behavior. Many companies complete this work internally, while others partner with their billing platform or an external agency to help push this important work forward.

From there, you're no longer stuck reacting. You can take proactive action, such as:

- At acquisition, introducing light friction for high-risk signups, such as two-factor authentication or lengthy quizzes
- Limiting access to high-cost benefits until certain engagement or identity thresholds are met
- Segmenting out likely fraud accounts from reporting, so your retention metrics reflect real customers
- And most importantly, sweeping your base to remove accounts flagged with high fraud scores before they trigger expensive incentives or distort cohort data

This model doesn't just protect your budget. It gives you cleaner, more accurate insights. You avoid offering bonuses or save offers to members who were never going to retain. You build forecasts that reflect genuine member behavior. And you focus your growth efforts on people who are actually likely to stay.

Fraud will always exist on the edges of any scaled program. But by applying a data-driven model, you can keep it as an edge case and ensure your business is built on real, high-quality membership.

Actions to Reduce Involuntary Churn

What follows are the most important actions you can take to reduce involuntary churn—the kind caused by failed payments, outdated cards, or overlooked billing issues. These aren't just operational fixes; they're strategic levers to protect the integrity of your revenue stream, strengthen member trust, and ensure your growth is built on a stable, high-quality foundation.

Action 1: Proactively Update Expiring Cards

To reduce chargebacks and involuntary churn, the first step is ensuring payment credentials stay current. Tools like Visa Account Updater and Mastercard Automatic Billing Updater automatically refresh expired or replaced cards, preventing failed transactions before they ever reach the member. Payment methods like Apple Pay, Google Pay, and PayPal also handle updates on the member's behalf, which makes them valuable acquisition channels as well as retention tools. Be sure your platform is integrated with these services and that your processor has card updater functionality turned on. A simple backend adjustment here can quietly protect significant revenue.

Action 2: Build a Smart Dunning and Retry System

Dunning—the process of following up on failed payments—is often mishandled. A single email and a billing retry isn't enough. Treat failed payments as urgent retention moments. Offer a 14- to 30-day grace period during which you retry payments at strategic intervals. Use in-app messages, push notifications, SMS, and even phone calls for high-value customers. Don't just wait for members to update their cards—make it easy for them and ensure you're automatically retrying cards in the background in case issues resolve without their input. A well-designed dunning flow can recover more revenue than most marketing campaigns.

Action 3: Offer Flexible Payment Methods at Signup

Involuntary churn often starts at acquisition. If a member's preferred payment method isn't supported, you're setting up a problem later. Enabling digital wallets like Apple Pay and Google Pay can reduce friction at checkout and handle card maintenance invisibly. Monitor how many new members are signing up with prepaid or virtual cards (e.g., from services like Privacy.com). These often block recurring payments and inflate churn. If necessary, prompt for a backup payment method when members use debit or prepaid cards. The goal is to reduce the risk of billing failure before it starts.

Action 4: Communicate Clearly and Transparently

Many chargebacks happen not because the value wasn't delivered—but because the member didn't recognize the charge. That's a communication failure. Use a clear billing descriptor (e.g., "Walmart+ Membership" instead of "WMT-WB-2023"). Send pre-renewal reminders, especially for annual plans. And ensure that pricing and renewal terms are shown clearly during signup—not buried in fine print. If a member is surprised by a charge, they're more likely to call their bank than your support team. Don't give them that reason.

Action 5: Make Cancellation Simple and Honest

If canceling takes more than a few clicks, members will either become frustrated—or skip you and go to their bank. Either outcome is a loss. Let people cancel easily. But more importantly, offer options to pause, downgrade, or delay cancellation if appropriate. These off-ramps often recover members who would have churned, while avoiding the negative sentiment that drives chargebacks. Making exits easier is not a threat to growth—it's part of building long-term trust.

Action 6: Monitor and Dispute Chargebacks Effectively

Chargebacks should be tracked with the same urgency as churn or acquisition. Assign ownership. Use your payment processor's reporting to identify trends and catch issues early. When a chargeback does occur, respond quickly and with clear evidence—like signup IPs, usage logs, and cancellation timestamps. Winning a dispute protects revenue but also keeps your chargeback rate in check. Too many disputes will land you on processor watchlists or lead to withheld funds. Prevention is ideal, but active defense matters too.

Action 7: Build Feedback Loops to Learn and Improve

Treat every cancellation and every chargeback as a signal, not just a transaction. Ask members why they're leaving. Analyze dispute reasons and group them by theme. Use this insight to surface broken experiences or mismatched expectations. In cases where a bad experience is clear, proactively issue a refund before the member feels compelled to initiate a dispute. It may cost you in the short term, but it protects your chargeback rate and preserves brand trust.

Michael Ribero – SVP, Global Consumer Revenue, Condé Nast

The Long Game of Membership: Value, Retention, and the Power of Belonging

I've been working in and around subscription and membership models for more than two decades, long before the word "subscription" became fashionable. My entry point was not consumer media or lifestyle brands, but finance. As an investment banker in the early 2000s, I watched software companies shift from on-premise licensing models to cloud-based SaaS platforms. That transition fundamentally changed how businesses thought about revenue, relationships, and long-term value.

What struck me even then was that while the technology was new, the underlying principles were not. Whether you're selling enterprise software or a consumer subscription, success depends on one thing: sustained value delivered over time. The mechanics may differ, but the contract with the customer is the same. You're asking them to commit not for a moment, but for a relationship.

That belief has guided my work ever since—from B2B platforms to consumer subscriptions, and now through my role in media at Condé Nast. The channels, formats, and expectations have evolved dramatically, but the membership thesis remains remarkably consistent. A membership only works when the value compounds.

From Ownership to Access

The rise of subscriptions coincided with a broader cultural shift—from ownership to access. Consumers no longer want to buy once and be done; they want relevance, personalization, and continuity. But too many companies misunderstood that shift. They believed that slapping a subscription price on a product was enough. It isn't.

A successful membership model isn't about charging people repeatedly—it's about earning the right to stay in their lives. That requires delivering value not at a single moment, but repeatedly, predictably, and meaningfully. When a product or service can improve someone's life over time—and when that improvement is visible and felt—the membership model becomes not only viable, but powerful.

Media's Great Unbundling—and Rebundling

Media offers one of the clearest case studies in how membership models evolve. Newspapers were subscription businesses long before digital transformation entered the conversation. But the internet triggered a massive unbundling of value. Classifieds moved to Craigslist. Reviews went to Yelp. Recipes found new homes elsewhere. What had once been a single, comprehensive product fractured into dozens of specialized experiences.

Today, we're seeing the opposite trend: rebundling. Platforms like Netflix didn't just create content; they rebuilt the experience around discovery, convenience, and frictionless access.

Their success wasn't solely driven by great programming—though that matters—but by the holistic user experience. Ad-free viewing. Intuitive interfaces. Personalized recommendations. Seamless discovery.

For younger generations raised on streaming platforms, the old model of linear television feels almost unwatchable. Excessive commercials and rigid schedules simply don't align with modern expectations. Netflix, Disney+, and others didn't just change content delivery—they rewired consumer expectations.

Distribution Is the Differentiator

One of the most overlooked aspects of Netflix's success is its role as a distribution engine. The most valuable advertising real estate in the world today may well be the Netflix homepage—not because it creates content, but because it can introduce content to massive, engaged audiences at scale.

Netflix also understands something subtle but important: not every piece of content needs to be exceptional. Some content exists to anchor attention. Background viewing, comfort viewing, familiar formats—these play a crucial role in retention. In traditional television, networks like HGTV mastered this years ago with low-cost, high-engagement programming that people left on all day. The goal wasn't obsession; it was presence.

Membership is often about becoming the default.

The Loss—and Reinvention—of Shared Experience

One unintended consequence of infinite choice is the erosion of shared cultural moments. When everyone watched the same show at the same time, conversations flowed naturally. Today, content consumption is fragmented. People binge different shows on different schedules, making communal discussion harder.

Interestingly, online communities are stepping in to fill that gap. Forums, fandoms, and social platforms now serve as the connective tissue that linear media once provided. In many ways, membership today is as much about belonging as it is about access.

Brands That Get It Right

Outside of media, several brands exemplify strong membership thinking. T-Mobile stands out for its challenger positioning—casting itself as the outsider taking on entrenched incumbents. American Express continues to balance premium status with broadening accessibility, using a closed-loop system that benefits both consumers and the company.

In healthcare and wellness, platforms like Calm, Headspace, and One Medical demonstrate how ongoing value is essential. Mental health, preventative care, and convenience are not one-time needs—they're continuous. These brands succeed because they understand that membership must evolve alongside the customer's life.

Building for Audiences, Not Just Products

At Condé Nast, much of our work today revolves around understanding audiences deeply and building offerings that serve them at different levels of commitment. Some brands that appear niche on the surface—like Architectural Digest—unlock significant opportunity when you look beyond traditional consumer models. By creating products for professional designers, we expanded from inspiration to education and business enablement.

Segmentation is another critical lever. Not all members want the same thing. Some seek casual engagement; others want premium, insider access. By analyzing data, behavior, and fandom, we can create tiered experiences that align with varying degrees of passion and willingness to pay.

We're also exploring bundling across brands—recognizing that while each title has a distinct identity, many readers have overlapping interests. When done thoughtfully, bundling increases value while reducing friction, allowing members to explore a broader ecosystem without feeling nickel-and-dimed.

Starting from Scratch: Advice for New Membership Businesses

For companies just beginning their membership journey, my advice is simple but often ignored: start with retention. Before scaling, before marketing aggressively, before chasing growth, ensure that your existing members are staying.

Retention is the clearest signal of product-market fit in a membership business. Benchmark against comparable services. Understand where you stand. If members aren't sticking around, growth will only amplify the problem.

I'm also a strong believer in member-driven growth. People buy from people. Especially in niche or B2B communities, existing members are often your most effective—and least expensive—acquisition channel. When members advocate on your behalf, acquisition costs drop and trust rises.

At the premium end of the spectrum, referrals often drive nearly all growth. That's not accidental—it's a byproduct of delivering undeniable value.

Awareness Still Matters

Even the best membership offering fails if people don't understand it. One of the great challenges today is reach. Traditional mass media once made awareness easy. Now, attention is fragmented across platforms, feeds, and formats.

The goal is simple but demanding: ensure that when a potential customer is ready to consider a solution, your brand is already on their mental shortlist. Membership isn't just about what happens after the sale—it's about being visible, credible, and relevant long before it.

The Enduring Truth of Membership

At its core, the membership business model isn't about transactions—it's about trust. It's about showing up consistently, delivering value repeatedly, and evolving alongside your audience. The technology will continue to change. Platforms will rise and fall. But the fundamental promise remains the same.

Earn the relationship, and the revenue will follow.

Final Thoughts: Retention Is the Real Growth Engine

If there's one idea I hope stays with you, it's this: membership doesn't scale by chasing more people. It scales by earning the right to keep the people you already have.

Retention isn't defense. It's the engine. It turns trials into subscribers, subscribers into advocates, and advocates into your most efficient acquisition channel. The best membership businesses don't accept churn as the price of growth. They treat it as a problem worth solving—because every point of churn you prevent becomes momentum you can build on.

So how do you tackle this challenge at the critical moments in a member's journey?

- **Understand why members leave.** Use surveys, exit interviews, and usage data to diagnose patterns in churn and identify root causes—then fix them systematically. Make churn reporting a consistent, visible part of your operating rhythm, with the same prominence as acquisition metrics.
- **Show members their value.** Consistently remind them of the benefits they've used, the money they've saved, and the meaningful experiences they've gained. If you don't actively tell that story, don't assume members will connect these dots themselves.
- **Give them choices beyond cancellation.** Don't force a binary stay-or-go decision. Offer ways to pause, downgrade, or switch plans based on changing needs. Often, members don't want to leave entirely—they just need a different relationship with your service.
- **Prevent involuntary churn.** Use account updater tools, smart payment retries, and flexible billing methods to keep loyal members from slipping away because of something as trivial as a failed payment.

When you shift your mindset from "how do we get more members" to "how do we create more value for the members we have," you unlock the true potential of the membership model. That's because acquisition fills your bucket, but retention plugs the holes of a leaky bucket. Both matter, but only one compounds over time.

Chapter 10

The Levers Behind Continuous Growth

Winback, Referrals, Gifting, and Monetization: The Continuous Growth Levers

Think back to the labyrinth analogy from earlier in the book: the member journey twists, evolves, and loops back on itself. Some members return after a pause. Some change plans. Some bring others with them. And some—through the right nudge at the right time—reignite their engagement after falling away. What looks like an exit is often just a fork in the path.

This is the magic of a well-designed membership ecosystem: it becomes self-sustaining. Former members come back. Existing ones bring in fresh faces. And the business continues to grow—not through aggressive discounting or constant paid acquisition, but through deliberate, member-first strategy.

At the center are three often underutilized levers: winback (bringing members back after they cancel), referrals and gifting (turning advocates into growth), and monetization (expanding revenue per member through pricing, tiers, partner offers, and, when appropriate, ads). Together, they create a flywheel where churned members return, active members recruit others, and new plans and packages increase revenue—all without compromising the experience that brought people in the first place.

But while these levers hold tremendous potential, they're easy to misuse. If executed poorly, they can erode trust, inflate vanity metrics, and weigh down the long-term health of your business. In this chapter, we'll explore how to deploy these growth strategies effectively, responsibly, and with an eye toward building something that lasts.

Part 1: Winning Back Churned Members - They're Not Gone, Just Taking a Break

Most companies treat churn like a funeral. A member leaves, and that's the end of the story. But the truth is, many cancellations are circumstantial, not emotional. People cancel when they move, when their financial situation changes, when life slows down or speeds up. Often, they don't want to leave forever. They're just taking a break.

That's why a great winback strategy is one of the most powerful and underappreciated tools in your growth arsenal. Former members already understand your value proposition. If they return, they tend to re-engage more quickly and often stick around longer because the learning curve is gone.

Understanding Why Members Leave

The foundation of an effective winback strategy is understanding why members leave. Churn is not a one-size-fits-all problem, as members cancel for different reasons, and each requires a tailored approach. A member who leaves because of price sensitivity will respond very differently than someone who churned because they didn't engage or found a better alternative.

As discussed in the previous chapter, one of the most powerful tools for diagnosing churn is the exit survey, along with any feedback collected during or after the cancellation process.

The more clearly you understand the *why*, the better positioned you are to win members back, and even more importantly, to reduce future churn. At a high level, most churn falls into four main categories:

1. **Price**: The initial promotional offer ended, or the ongoing price became too expensive

2. **Benefits**: The member no longer sees enough value, either because of life changes or because they've consumed what they needed

3. **Experience**: Poor experiences, such as delivery issues, technical problems, or bad customer service

4. **Other**: Unexpected or unique reasons that require deeper investigation

The best winback strategies start with these insights. Companies that consolidate this data, spot patterns, and align on short-term and long-term fixes are the ones best positioned for sustainable growth.

Winning the Member Back: The Four Pillars of Effective Winback Campaigns

To bring lapsed members back into your ecosystem, you need more than a one-off email or a blanket discount. Effective winback campaigns rely on four foundational components: **Channel, Messaging, Timing, and Offer.**

Pillar 1: Channel

The most effective and cost-efficient channels for re-engaging churned members are email and push notifications, but email should lead. After cancellation, many members disable or ignore push, and in some cases platform policies limit what you can promote via push. Retargeting via digital ads can be a strong complement: it costs money, but it extends reach and adds visibility. You don't need to spend aggressively—just enough to stay present, especially when paired with email.

One important guardrail: respect channel permissions. If a member unsubscribes from email or opts out of marketing, honor it. Winback should feel like an invitation, not a chase.

Pillar 2: Messaging

The goal of winback messaging isn't just to remind people your service exists, it's to show them that it's improved, evolved, or become more relevant since they left. Tailor the message to their likely reason for churning:

- Left due to value? Highlight a new benefit.
- Left due to content fatigue? Spotlight recent releases.
- Left due to a technical issue? Show what's been fixed.
- Left due to price? Announce a new plan or feature mix.

If personalization isn't possible at scale, lead with one strong, broadly appealing "what's new" moment, and pair it with the single action that gets them back to value fastest. The message should feel like an invitation, not a pitch.

Pillar 3: Timing

While it may seem logical to reach out immediately after cancellation, it's often better to wait. Giving members a brief pause creates the feeling of a "clean break" and reduces the risk of early email unsubscribes. More importantly, it gives your service time to evolve, so you can genuinely say, "Here's what's new."

The sweet spot for many brands is 30-90 days post-cancellation. When you do re-engage, avoid over-messaging. One email isn't enough, but 10 is too many. A series of 2–3 emails around a unified theme, spaced a few days apart is usually most effective.

Pillar 4: Offer

Just as in acquisition, the right offer creates urgency. But what kind of offer works best for winback? It depends on your audience and timing:

- **No offer (direct to membership):** This works when you've launched a meaningful new benefit, feature, or seasonal push that creates urgency on its own. These returned members tend to be more committed and have higher lifetime value.
- **Free trial:** A trial re-engages members without asking for immediate payment. It's ideal when showcasing new features or benefits and works well for those on the fence.
- **Discounted membership:** This option provides immediate revenue and a longer runway to re-establish habit but can complicate future renewals if members balk at returning to full price.

A simple ladder helps avoid "discount addiction": start with value-first (no offer), then a low-cost offer (trial or credit), and reserve deep discounts for the small slice that needs it.

Measuring Winback Success

When evaluating winback campaigns, look beyond simple conversion rates. The key metrics to track include:

- **Winback rate**: The percentage of churned members who return
- **Retention after winback**: How long returning members stay before churning again
- **Cost per winback**: How much are you spending to bring each member back?
- **Lifetime Value of returned members:** and how it compares to both new members and continuously retained members
- **Incrementality:** lift vs. a holdout group (where possible)

A successful winback program brings back members who stay and continue to find value. That requires ongoing analysis and refinement based on the data you collect.

Part 2: Referrals and Gifting - The Promising but Tricky Acquisition Levers

Referrals and Gifting promise low-cost, high-quality growth. But only if you can design them with the right incentives, timing, and structure.

Referrals: Turning Members into Advocates

One of the most appealing growth strategies for a membership business is referrals. Giving engaged members an incentive to talk about your service and bring in new members seems like an obvious win. In theory, it's perfect: members are rewarded for spreading the word, and the company gains high-intent signups without relying on paid advertising.

Unfortunately, referrals are notoriously hard to implement effectively. In fact, at every company where I've worked, referral programs have consistently underperformed against pre-launch forecasts. One core issue is that most members aren't thinking about who else to invite. They're focused on using the service themselves. And when people *do* refer others, it's often for the wrong reasons. Fraud is rampant: bad actors create fake accounts or abuse promo structures to game the system.

That's why when launching a referral program, you need to build in controls from day one. Think carefully about how to "gate" participation to ensure that the people being referred, and the ones doing the referring, are likely to become legitimate, long-term members. Many of the lessons from Ch 9: Reinforcing Value and Reducing Churn apply here too: a program that looks good on paper but fails to deliver real value can backfire.

Despite these challenges, referrals *can* work when designed with both incentive alignment and fraud prevention in mind. Here are a few proven strategies:

- **Double-sided incentives:** Reward both the referrer and the referred member. This creates mutual motivation and feels more like a shared benefit than a transaction.
- **Tiered rewards:** Offer increasing rewards based on multiple successful referrals. This encourages your most enthusiastic members to become true advocates.
- **Quality controls:** Require a credit card to start the trial, delay rewards until after the first successful paid renewal or an activation milestone, or only pay out once the new member has been active for a set period.

- **Personalized sharing options:** Make it easy to refer via email, social media, or messaging apps, whatever feels most natural to the member. Less friction equals more follow-through.
- **Target your best members:** Promote referral programs to your most engaged and satisfied members. They're far more likely to refer others who will stick.
- **Use fraud detection tools:** Monitor suspicious behavior (shared IP/device, repeated payment methods, repeated addresses), cap rewards, and remove bad actors quickly.

One more unlock: trigger referrals at moments of delight. Ask right after a member hits an "aha" moment or a milestone—not in a generic newsletter.

The key to a successful referral program is striking the right balance: make it easy for real members to refer others, while creating just enough friction to keep fraud out. Do that well, and referrals can become a reliable, high-quality growth channel over time.

Gifting: Turning Members into Marketers

Gifting is another common membership growth strategy that often generates excitement. The premise is simple: let current members buy a membership for someone else. On paper, it feels like a win-win. Members get to share something they love, and companies acquire new members without paid marketing. However, like referrals, gifting often underperforms against expectations.

The biggest challenge is that most memberships rely on ongoing engagement, and gifted memberships frequently go unused. The recipient didn't actively choose the service, so while they may feel obligated to give it a try, they often lack the intrinsic motivation that drives long-term retention. That said, some companies have found smart ways to improve gifting performance by reframing the offer or focusing on timing. A few proven approaches:

- **Limited-time experiences:** Rather than gifting a full membership, let members share premium access for a short period. For example, Calm's 30-day trial for referrals goes well beyond the typical 7-day trial and offers bonus incentives if members hit certain referral thresholds.

- **Strategic timing:** Align gifting campaigns with natural gift-giving seasons like the holidays. Disney+ sees meaningful spikes in gift subscriptions during December, positioning itself as an affordable yet thoughtful present.

- **Two-for-one promotions:** MasterClass's "Buy One, Give One" campaign turns gifting into a secondary benefit of a standard purchase. It not only encourages gift-giving but also prompts action from those who might have hesitated to buy for themselves.

- **Business-to-business gifting:** Corporate gifting often drives better results than individual campaigns. LinkedIn Premium, for example, has had success partnering with employers to offer gift memberships as part of professional development perks.

Most importantly: gifted members need a different onboarding path. Treat them like a new segment with dedicated messaging ("here's how to get value fast"), a clear start date, and a clear "what happens next" moment when the gift period ends.

Part 3: Monetization - Maximizing Revenue Without Destroying Trust

So far, this book has focused on growing your membership base and increasing retention. But there's another essential lever in the growth equation: Average Revenue Per User (ARPU[14]).

The challenge is that you want to grow revenue per member without compromising trust and without damaging the quality-price perception that attracted members in the first place.

Let's explore the three most effective strategies to do this right: raising prices, expanding your plan offerings, and incorporating advertising and partner offers.

Option 1: Raising Prices Without Losing Members

Few topics create more anxiety for membership leaders than raising prices. The fear of backlash, cancellations, or bad press often leads companies to delay adjustments long past when they're financially justified. But the reality is simple: price changes are inevitable. Costs rise, benefits expand, and long-term sustainability requires periodic adjustments.

---

[14] **Average Revenue Per User (ARPU)** – The average revenue generated per member over a given period, typically per month. ARPU = Total Revenue from Members ÷ Number of Active Members

The key isn't *whether* you raise prices, but *how* you do it. Done poorly, a price increase feels like a betrayal. Done well, it becomes an opportunity to strengthen your relationship with members.

Look at Amazon Prime. Since its launch, Amazon has raised Prime's annual fee four different times, raising it from $79 in 2005 to $139 in 2025. Yet instead of revolt, Prime has continued to grow. Why? Because each increase was tied directly to added value: grocery delivery, new streaming content, Prime Day events, faster delivery options, and more. Members weren't just paying more—they were *getting more.*

That's the playbook. Lead with value, not price. Frame the increase as progress, not profit-taking. Show members how the product they're using today is worth far more than when they joined.

Principles of Successful Price Increases

1. **Communicate Transparently:** Announce early (60–90 days before the increase). Surprises breed resentment, while transparency builds trust. Always explain the "why," tying the change to new benefits or improved service.

2. **Reward Loyalty:** Grandfather long-term members for a set period, let them lock in the old rate for one more year, or offer a goodwill gesture (e.g., two free months of premium service). Recognition reduces churn risk.

3. **Time It Strategically:** Align increases with positive momentum—a new feature launch, a content expansion, or a milestone moment. Never roll out an increase when members are already frustrated.

4. **Provide Options:** Offer flexible payment plans (monthly or quarterly), add tiers so members can choose their level of investment, or bundle in new perks to soften the impact.

5. **Test Before Rolling Out:** A/B test communication framing and sequencing, not just the number. Even subtle changes ("$2 more per month" vs. "less than a coffee per week") can dramatically shift perception.

Handling Pushback with Empathy

Even with the best strategy, some members will object. The difference between losing them and saving them often comes down to *how you respond.*

Use an Empathy-First Response Framework:

- **Acknowledge:** "I understand this increase impacts your budget, and I appreciate you sharing your concern."
- **Validate Value:** "Here's what's been added to your membership and how it supports your goals."
- **Explore Options:** "Let's review payment plans or other tiers that might be a better fit."
- **Future Focus:** "What would need to happen for you to feel great about this investment going forward?"

Common objections and responses:

- *"I can't afford the increase."* → Highlight new benefits, offer flexible plans.
- *"You haven't delivered enough value."* → Probe specifics, show how benefits align with their needs.
- *"Others charge less."* → Differentiate—highlight outcomes only your membership delivers.
- *"This feels like a cash grab."* → Be transparent—show where the dollars are going and how they directly improve the member experience.

The Takeaway

Raising prices doesn't have to trigger panic. In fact, when approached as an ongoing discipline—tested, measured, and communicated with empathy—it can be one of your strongest levers for long-term growth.

The goal isn't to keep prices static. It's to ensure members always feel that the value they receive exceeds the price they pay. When you get that balance right, a price increase isn't a risk—it's a reinvestment in the relationship.

Option 2: Expanding Plan Types—Meeting Members Where They Are

Another powerful way to grow ARPU is by expanding your plan offerings. Not every member has the same needs or the same willingness to pay. By introducing multiple tiers, you can unlock value from both ends of the market.

Premium plans can serve your power users with high-end features such as faster delivery windows, exclusive content, better audio/video quality. Meanwhile, stripped-down versions can attract price-sensitive members who might otherwise churn or never join at all.

But the key is clarity. Each plan should have a clearly defined purpose, distinct benefits, and a logical path for upgrades. Think of how streaming services offer ad-supported, standard, and premium tiers, or how meal kits add premium recipes or faster shipping as upsells. Remember, even your entry-level plan must deliver your core value proposition, and premium tiers should enhance, not unlock, that experience.

A Deeper Look: The Power (and Risk) of Household Plans

Among plan expansions, household plans deserve special attention. They're popular for good reason—members love them. They reduce account sharing, and they boost retention by getting multiple people invested in your service. But they're also tricky.

Take Spotify: its individual plan is priced at €11.99/month, but its real ARPU is closer to €4.39 because of widespread use of Family and Duo accounts. When multiple users share one plan, it's great for retention, but not always great for revenue per user.

And there's cannibalization risk. If multiple family members already pay separately, rolling out a household plan could cut your revenue, even as it improves experience.

For that reason, household plans often make the most sense once growth starts to plateau. At that stage, the goal shifts from explosive acquisition to deepening loyalty.

Once launched, monitor usage and abuse patterns to evaluate if restrictions are needed. For example, Netflix has added measures to reduce password sharing and introduced paid add-ons in many markets, which changed the economics of household access.

Used well, household plans are a retention machine. But they require discipline, controls, and a clear understanding of the tradeoffs.

Option 3: Advertising - A Monetization Lever Best Used at Scale

Eventually, some membership businesses introduce advertising or partner offers as secondary revenue streams. Done poorly, ads feel intrusive and out of place—especially for paying members.

Done well, advertising can be additive. The key is relevance, restraint, and respect. Think about how Costco promotes partner services or how platforms offer sponsored placements that align with user intent. These aren't random banner ads—they're curated extensions of the experience.

Two guardrails:

- **Give members choice** (e.g., ad-supported tier vs. ad-free).
- **Protect the core experience** (no "tax" on the primary value proposition).

Advertising tends to work best when you have real scale—enough members to attract strong partners and still keep the experience feeling premium. If your base isn't large enough, the upside can be modest while the downside is real: distracting placements, eroded trust, and annoyed members. Treat ads as a late-stage lever, roll them out carefully, and reinvest a meaningful share of the revenue into better benefits so members can clearly feel the trade.

Denise Karkos – GM, Champs Sports (part of Dick's Sporting Goods)

I first worked with Matt at SiriusXM, where I led marketing for both SiriusXM and Pandora. The subscriptions team didn't report to me, but our work was intertwined every day. Matt sat on the subscriptions side, and I ran growth, brand, and e-commerce. To make any pricing strategy real, we had to meet in the middle—value proposition, offer design, channels, creative, and customer experience all moving in the same direction. What struck me early on was Matt's energy and discipline: customer-obsessed, systems-minded, and relentlessly empirical about what truly changes behavior.

Those years were a study in duality. During COVID, we needed to act with empathy first. People couldn't get through to call centers. The idea that a subscriber might sit on hold for hours to cancel wasn't acceptable, so we stood up customer-centric capabilities fast—like enabling online cancellation. That was the right thing to do in the moment. Then, as the world reopened, we had to re-accelerate growth and restore profitability— rebuild the demand engine, fortify retention, and prove why the product was worth paying a premium for. That arc—for the customer and for the business—shaped my philosophy on membership: it's not a marketing trick; it's an operating model. If your promise in the app isn't dependable at 5:30 p.m. on a Tuesday, no amount of promotion will save you from churn.

Today I'm the GM of Champs, one of Foot Locker's banners. It's fun—like running a focused company inside a larger one. We're a classic retail model with a loyalty program, and I think there's real upside in evolving toward membership where it makes sense. But I'm careful. I've seen too many teams slap the word "membership" on a points program. That's not it. True membership reduces friction, increases frequency, and feels like a relationship that gets better the more you use it. If a program doesn't do those three things, it's not a membership; it's packaging.

If you ask me how companies compete, I'll always come back to three levers: price, product, and customer experience. Anyone can copy price. Product advantages are precious but often perishable. Customer experience— consistently, distinctively delivered—is the hardest to replicate and the most enduring. That's where membership lives. You earn the right to charge a premium when the experience is so tuned to the customer that alternatives feel clunky by comparison. At SiriusXM, a big part of my job was clarifying that value proposition by tier, so people understood what they were paying for and felt good about it.

My roots are both analog and digital. I started in 1993 as a media buyer— radio, print, out-of-home—literally riding boards in the Midwest to make sure a billboard wasn't covered by a tree. By 1995, at Hill Holliday in Boston, clients were asking about "the internet," so I dove into digital and later moved to Digitas. That blend—brand craft and growth accountability—still defines how I lead. Yes, algorithms can do a lot of "marketing" now, but they don't absolve you from old-school fundamentals: talk to customers, watch them use the product, sit in service queues, visit stores. You can't outsource your curiosity.

Generationally, I'm Gen X. My team skews younger. I value what they bring: pace, fluency, and an instinct to use technology as a force multiplier. They're resourceful and fast. They find legitimate shortcuts—especially now with AI—to speed insight and delivery. Do they always prize the same human interactions I grew up valuing? Not necessarily. Ordering on an app and skipping the conversation with the barista isn't a deficit; it's a choice about where to spend limited energy. They're conserving for the connections that matter more to them. As leaders, our job isn't to judge that; it's to design experiences that map to it.

Ask me for my own "can't live without it" membership and I'll point to the Starbucks app. It nails the basics: order clarity, pickup predictability, points that accrue quickly enough to feel rewarding, and consistency in airports— where time is the scarcest resource. That's membership done well: save me minutes and mental load, predictably.

Costco is another great case study in model and discipline. And for brands with long-tenured advocates, I'm a huge believer in a "top 1%" strategy: study the outliers in depth—whether defined by revenue, profitability, tenure, or advocacy—and build deliberate programs around them. Outliers aren't just bigger versions of the top 10%; they're often different in kind. Understand those differences and you uncover playbooks that don't show up in the averages.

Culturally, this is both the best and the hardest time to build membership. Best, because the mechanisms for extreme loyalty are there—software, data, logistics, ubiquitous mobile, and the social graph. Hardest, because consumers are exquisitely discerning about values, transparency, and congruence. If you don't know your brand's non-negotiables—what you will and won't do—and you can't hold that line when news cycles get choppy, you will get found out. The consumer you met twenty years ago is not the consumer of today; today's customer reads the fine print. They expect you to mean what you say.

When it comes to "what would you change?" my answers sound simple, but they're not easy:

- **Engineer frequency, don't announce features.** Shiny new perks are tempting, but compounding value comes from making the core actions easier and more rewarding every time.
- **Default to annual when it's genuinely better for the member.** Annualization stabilizes retention and lets you invest in long-horizon experience improvements—if you've earned the trust first.
- **Design from the moments of truth backward.** If rush pickup windows slip or fees creep into "free" benefits, the relationship erodes. Operational integrity is brand integrity.
- **Wrap your outliers.** Know your top 1% deeply and build a deliberate, human program around them. Advocates are priceless, and they don't happen by accident.

This is also where Matt shines. He resists the "museum of perks" tendency and pushes teams toward a short list of high-frequency wins that matter most to the core customer. He designs for fit. He insists that the promise be something the operation can keep on its worst day, not just its best.

If I zoom out on my own journey—from billboards to digital, from finance to music to retail—the throughline is the same: passion for the customer and accountability for growth. You can port that across categories because it doesn't depend on a channel or a fad. It depends on a posture—curious, candid, and willing to adjust when the customer teaches you something. That's also why membership is so powerful when it's done right: it converts your posture into a product. The more I use it, the more it feels built for me. The more it feels built for me, the more I use it.

Would I launch a membership in this climate? Yes—if I knew exactly whom it was for, what problems it solved weekly, and which operational muscles I'd need to build so the promise is kept every time. I'd publish our values and stick to them. I'd start with usage, not advertising. I'd measure friction relentlessly and remove it. And I'd reserve a special place for the customers who carry the brand on their backs—reward them, learn from them, and make them feel seen.

That's the work. Not a bag of parts, but a promise and a practice—kept in thousands of small ways, day after day. That's where loyalty lives. And that's why Matt's book matters. It doesn't just argue for membership; it teaches teams how to build one that deserves to exist.

Final Thoughts: The Membership Growth Flywheel

Every tactic in this chapter is powered by one truth: if your product isn't worth paying for, no growth strategy will save it. But if you're solving a real problem, delivering consistent value, and putting members first, growth doesn't just happen. It compounds.

Winback becomes meaningful reintroductions. Referrals and gifting become trust transfers. Monetization becomes a value exchange.

When orchestrated thoughtfully, these levers reinforce one another, creating a flywheel that strengthens with every spin. The best membership businesses don't rely on a single growth lever—they build a system, integrating winback, referrals, and monetization into one cohesive strategy:

- Thoughtful re-engagement brings lapsed members back
- Returning members refer new ones who are more likely to stay
- Referrals reduce acquisition costs and increase trust
- Monetization grows revenue per member without eroding loyalty
- That revenue funds better onboarding, new features, and deeper value
- Which improves retention—and the flywheel turns again

This is durable, scalable growth: not brute-force acquisition or endless discounting, but maximizing the value of every moment in the member journey—whether someone is new, returning, or on the edge of churn.

Do this with intention, rigor, and empathy, and growth stops being something you chase. It becomes something you sustain.

Part 3:

Structure, Accountability and Action

Chapter 11

Designing the Team
Behind the Membership Engine

Solving for the How

Up to this point, we've talked about what to build and why it works. We've mapped the levers, named the moments that matter, and traced the arc from curiosity to commitment. But membership isn't won in theory. It's won in the daily work—the invisible choices and repeatable habits that turn a promise into an experience.

Because the truth is simple: membership is not a product. It's a relationship. And relationships don't scale on ideas alone. They scale on people, systems, and discipline—on clean data, clear ownership, steady reporting, aligned goals, and a culture that treats the member experience as sacred.

This part of the book is about that operating system. The "how" behind the growth. The structure that keeps teams moving in the same direction as complexity rises. The accountability that makes progress measurable. The rituals that turn good intentions into durable outcomes.

Building the Right Team Structure

One of the most critical decisions you'll make as you scale your membership business is how to structure your team. Get it right, and alignment compounds: decisions get faster, experimentation gets sharper, and the experience feels seamless to members. Get it wrong, and even the most talented people create friction—duplicated work, slow handoffs, unclear ownership, and momentum that leaks out in a hundred small ways.

The hardest part is that teams aren't machines. People are variable. Everyone brings different strengths, blind spots, instincts, and rhythms. Structure isn't just boxes on an org chart; it's the choreography of how those differences turn into progress instead of noise.

I'm usually listening to music when I'm thinking through ideas, which might be why this metaphor sticks. A great band solves the exact same problem: getting distinct individuals to create something consistent and effortless for the audience.

In most bands, there's a clear creative leader—usually the lead singer or primary songwriter—who sets direction and holds the sound together. Think Bruce Springsteen and the E Street Band. Thom Yorke and Radiohead. Jerry Garcia and the Grateful Dead. They don't play every instrument, but they carry the vision and shape the output. Around them, the drummer, bassist, guitarist, and others bring their craft and judgment, all aligned around one shared goal: the song the audience experiences.

The leader brings the skeleton of a track, and the band brings it to life. The result is greater than the sum of its parts, not because of hierarchy, but because everyone shares accountability for what comes out the speakers.

Now imagine a different setup. Instead of rallying around a leader, every musician reports into their instrument silo. Drummers to the Head of Drums. Bassists to the Head of Bass. A "CEO of Music" oversees the whole thing. Musicians are assigned to different bands as needed.

There are benefits to this structure: drummers learn from drummers, bassists share techniques. But there's a cost. When allegiance shifts to the silo instead of the band, the magic fades. Chemistry weakens. Feel flattens. And the music loses its groove.

In business terms, the first model is journey-aligned ownership: a vertical team structure built around a customer outcome. You see it most often in startups and product-led organizations, where a single team owns the work end-to-end. It shines when speed matters, accountability is non-negotiable, and the experience needs one clear direction.

The second model is the classic matrix: functional teams that roll up to the CEO. It dominates in large organizations, where people report into functions like marketing, product, or engineering while working cross-functionally on initiatives. The matrix is built for specialization and scale—but it often introduces complexity, slows decisions, and blurs accountability. Worst of all, it can push the member out of the center. Teams optimize their own function, and the experience across the member lifecycle becomes nobody's job in particular.

Both models have their place. But growing a membership business isn't like launching a one-time product. It's not transactional. It's relational—a living, breathing, ever-evolving experience. It's more like keeping an album fresh night after night, city after city, for years.

To do that, you need more than functional excellence. You need harmony. You need clear structure, aligned ownership, and someone who sees the full picture—someone who can orchestrate the sound. Because in the end, you don't just need soloists. You need a band leader and a setlist.

In this chapter, I'll break down why most traditional structures fail—and how to fix them. You'll see why organizing teams around the member journey leads to faster execution, stronger results, and more scalable growth. Instead of isolating people by function, I'll show you how to assign clear ownership of specific stages of the member lifecycle, creating sharper accountability and performance. And in the next chapter, you'll learn how to reinforce that accountability with the right metrics, reporting, and measurement systems.

Because at the end of the day, you can hire the best people in the world—but if your structure fragments accountability, you'll spend more time debating who owns what than fixing what's broken.

Part 1: Why Most Membership Companies Get Their Structure Wrong

When I moved from Amazon to SiriusXM, I felt the pain of shifting from journey ownership to a matrix structure. But it wasn't until I joined Walmart that I saw the full impact of what happens when no one truly owns the member journey. Huge meetings filled with stakeholders, no clear owners, endless debates over "who owns what." A simple question like, "Who owns the marketing budget for Walmart+?" could trigger hours of discussion, only to end with a punt.

Walmart's larger org structure wasn't going to change overnight, if at all. But here's what I realized: you don't need a full-scale reorg to see the benefits of vertical alignment. What you need is explicit ownership. When accountability is mapped across the member journey, most of the value shows up—without ever redrawing the org chart.

Why Traditional Org Structures Sabotage Membership Success

In traditional organizations, responsibilities for the membership journey are fragmented across departments with competing priorities:

- **Marketing**: Celebrates acquisition milestones while often being blind to retention outcomes. Success is measured by new signups, regardless of whether those members stay or go.
- **Business/Growth/Commercial**: Experiments endlessly with pricing and offers without authority to align messaging across touchpoints. They change pricing structures but can't ensure consistent communication to members.
- **Product**: Optimizes the signup flow in isolation, without insight into which acquisition channels are driving traffic or what expectations were set pre-conversion.
- **Finance**: Focuses on short-term profitability metrics while lacking influence over the customer experiences that drive lifetime value.

The critical problem is that no single team owns the complete member journey. From the member's perspective, this creates a disjointed experience with different messaging styles across emails and the app interface, confusing transitions between free and paid status, and support agents who don't have visibility into the offers or promotions that brought the member in initially. And when metrics decline, the blame game begins:

- *Marketing points to Product for low conversion*
- *Product blames Marketing for low-quality traffic*
- *Business/Growth criticizes Finance for limited test budgets*
- *Finance questions everyone's efficiency as churn rises*

Meanwhile, retention—the single most important driver of membership economics—is owned by no one. It's everyone's job in theory, but no one's in practice. What follows is the classic dysfunction: 20+ people in a room debating issues, no one empowered to make a decision, and action items that dissolve into the space between org charts, while speed and innovation suffer as consensus-building replaces decisive action. I've seen this happen far too often in my career.

Contrast this with organizations that treat membership like an operating system: clear owners, aligned goals, and clear decision rights at each stage of the journey.

For most companies, though, the membership experience plays out like a badly run relay race where batons get dropped at every handoff, and the runners spend more time yelling at each other than moving forward.

In the next section, I'll show you how to fix this and how to structure your teams around the member journey in a way that creates clarity, speed, and true accountability. Because if you want to build a world-class membership business, you need more than good ideas. You need someone in charge of making them happen.

Part 2: Reimagining Your Organization Around the Member Journey

So the fix isn't another standing meeting or a new "cross-functional pod." It's simpler—and harder: name an owner for every critical stage of the member journey, and give them the authority to move it.

When you shift your structure to align with each critical phase of the member journey, you unlock a new kind of accountability. Every stage, from awareness to winback, has clear leadership, focused resources, and direct ownership of outcomes. This directly addresses the problems we identified earlier: eliminating finger-pointing, removing decision paralysis, and creating clear ownership of the entire member experience.

Below is a journey-aligned blueprint mapped to the **Membership Flywheel™**. Treat these as "functions" you must own—not mandatory job titles. In smaller orgs, one leader may own multiple functions.

1. **Value Proposition & Benefits**: Own the "why"—why members join, why they stay, and how benefits evolve.
   - Ownership: Core value prop, benefits roadmap, competitive differentiation, member insights

2. **Pricing & Offer Strategy**: Own price architecture and promotions without training members to wait for discounts.
   - Ownership: Pricing, discount strategy, tiering, elasticity testing, LTV optimization

3. **Awareness & Conversion Marketing**: Own acquisition quality measured by downstream retention, not just CAC.
   - Ownership: Messaging, channel mix, net CAC by channel, promise integrity

4. **Distribution & Partnerships**: Own bundles, affiliates, and strategic channels beyond paid media.
   - Ownership: Partnerships, bundle economics, co-marketing, corporate programs

5. **Signup & Conversion Flow**: Own the "last mile" from intent to paid.
   - Ownership: Checkout conversion, drop-off points, payment options, identity/account setup

6. **Onboarding & Early Engagement**: Own day 0–30 activation and time-to-first-value.
   - Ownership: 7/14/30 engagement, TTFV, onboarding completion, early habit formation

7. **Ongoing Engagement & Customer Service**: Own habit reinforcement and experience quality over time.
    - Ownership: Benefit depth/breadth, CSAT, NPS, proactive retention plays

8. **Churn & Renewals**: Own save flows, renewal experience, cancellation learnings, and churn forecasting.
    - Ownership: Renewal rate, save rate, churn reason analysis, churn forecasting

9. **Member Growth Loops**: Own winback, referrals, gifting, upsells, and tier expansion.
    - Ownership: Winback rate, referral activation, upsell conversion, ARPU growth

What makes this structure powerful is that every stage of the journey has an owner. There's no more "it's everyone's job." Each function has a measurable scoreboard and a clear decision-maker.

Here's a visual of what this looks like:

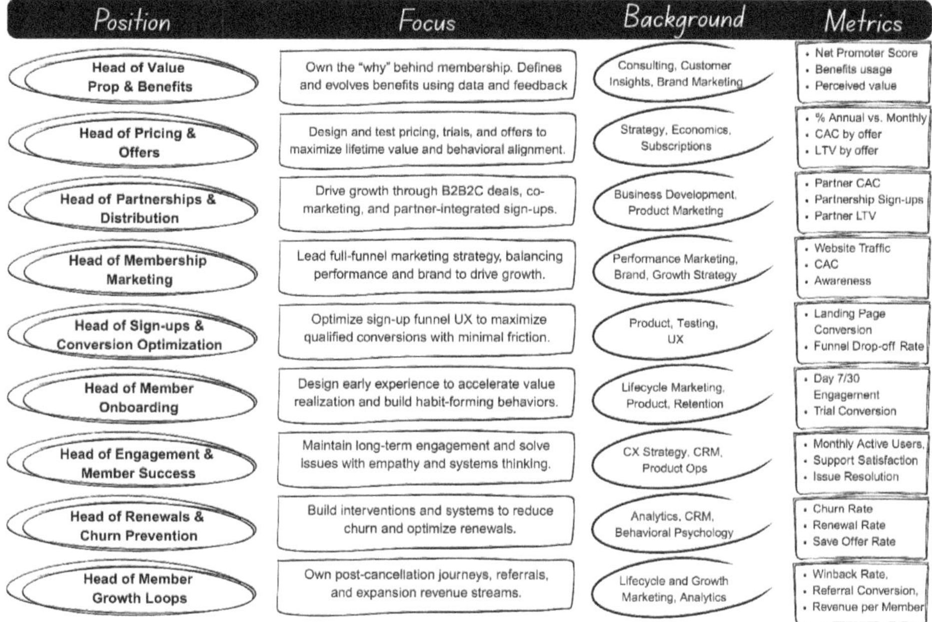

Managing Handoffs and Collaboration

A journey-aligned model doesn't eliminate collaboration—it makes it intentional. The handoffs are where member experiences break, so treat them like contracts: shared definitions, shared metrics, and clear escalation paths.

- **Signup ↔ Onboarding:** Align on the promise and the first win (Time-to-First-Value, activation milestone).
- **Onboarding ↔ Engagement:** Align on the habit metric (week-one depth, week-two return).
- **Engagement ↔ Churn:** Align on risk signals and response speed (save rate, time-to-intervention).

Each handoff becomes a collaboration point—not a blame opportunity.

The Chief Membership Officer: Orchestrating the System

In a band, the leader isn't the best at every instrument. Their job is bigger than that. They hold the song together. They set direction, call the tempo, and make the tradeoffs that keep the experience coherent—so the audience hears one thing, not a collection of parts.

A membership business needs that same kind of leader.

At the top sits a Head of Membership—whether you call it Chief Membership Officer, VP Membership, Membership GM, or Head of Subscriptions—someone accountable for the membership P&L and the end-to-end outcomes of the member journey. For the sake of the rest of the book, I'm calling this person Membership GM.

If recurring revenue is your core economic engine, this role has to be senior enough to resolve tradeoffs across all teams. Because membership isn't a feature you bolt on. It's the business model. And without a band leader—someone responsible for the full sound—you end up with talented teams playing well in isolation while the member experience falls out of tune.

The best membership leaders focus on three things:

1. **Strategic direction:** setting the vision and Flywheel priorities

2. **Decision frameworks:** defining how tradeoffs get made and resources get allocated

3. **Data synthesis:** connecting signals across the journey to spot systemic issues early

In practice, the Membership GM functions as the single point of accountability for the membership operating system. Teams execute day to day, but this role sets the direction, aligns priorities, and holds the organization to a shared scoreboard.

The Membership Chief of Staff: Execution Excellence

To make this model operational, the Membership GM needs a strong right hand, a VP or Director-level Chief of Staff who brings discipline, clarity, and execution muscle across all nine teams. This isn't an executive assistant role or a project manager. It's a force multiplier.

The Membership Chief of Staff ensures that planning, reporting, and decision-making operate at scale. They resolve bottlenecks before they become blockers. They run the business reviews, manage cross-functional initiatives, and keep the entire membership operation focused on what matters most.

Their key responsibilities include:

- Driving initiatives that span multiple stages of the member journey
- Standardizing processes for goal setting, resource planning, and performance tracking
- Identifying misalignments early and surfacing decisions for executive attention
- Leading operating rhythms like quarterly business reviews, all-hands, and leadership syncs

I base this role on the effectiveness of what I saw firsthand with Amazon's Technical Advisor (TA) structure: a trusted thought partner who drives strategic alignment while enabling day-to-day execution to senior executives.

At Amazon, these roles often rotate high-potential leaders through an executive's business for a fixed period, giving them deep exposure to decision-making and operating mechanisms.

In the membership context, this same dynamic unlocks tremendous value. The Chief of Staff to the Membership GM helps connect dots across the member journey that might otherwise remain disconnected. They see patterns in data, inconsistencies in execution, and opportunities for improvement that specialized teams might miss. They become the institutional memory of decisions, the keepers of standards, and often the voice of the member in rooms where functional priorities might otherwise take precedence.

Just like at Amazon, this role can also serve as a launchpad for future executives. The Chief of Staff gains deep visibility into every function and works side-by-side with the Membership GM on the company's most important membership priorities. It's a role that builds strategic range, operational depth, and executive presence.

Part 3: Scaling the Framework for Different Company Sizes

That was a lot—and you might be thinking, "There's no way we can build all of this right now." Fair. The point isn't to stand up nine teams overnight. The point is to ensure every critical function has a clear owner—and a clear scoreboard—so the journey doesn't fall into the cracks.

What This Looks Like at Different Stages

Startups (under 50 employees)

One person may own multiple functions. That's normal. The key is to keep the functions distinct—even if ownership is combined—by maintaining separate scoreboards and clear priorities for each part of the journey.

Mid-size companies (50–200 employees)

Start by splitting the highest-impact functions first, based on where your metrics show the biggest bottleneck. Let the numbers dictate the org build. If activation is the problem, strengthen onboarding ownership before you hire for referral loops. If churn is spiking, invest in renewals before you add new acquisition headcount.

Enterprise (200+ employees)

You can implement the full model, but coordination becomes the enemy. At this scale, structure alone won't save you—you need governance: shared dashboards, weekly reviews, and explicit decision rights so work doesn't stall in endless alignment.

What If You Can't Restructure Right Now?

You might be thinking, "There's no way I'm telling my boss to restructure the company based on this book." Fair enough. Big org changes follow results, not the other way around.

But you can apply the principles immediately. Start by assigning explicit owners to each stage of the member journey so accountability is clear, even if the org chart doesn't change. Where you have flexibility, shift reporting lines incrementally to reduce handoff friction and speed up decisions. Then update how success is measured: prioritize downstream outcomes like activation, retention, and lifetime value—not just functional KPIs like CAC, open rates, or sprint velocity. Finally, create small cross-functional pods aligned to key journey stages, with clear goals and decision rights, so teams can execute end-to-end without waiting on endless alignment.

Handling Common Objections

When I first suggested this structure at Walmart, the immediate response was: *"We're a true matrix organization—that's not going to change."* Not because the framework lacked merit, but because large organizations are naturally resistant to change.

Over time, though, my team began to embrace the mindset behind it— clarifying ownership, aligning around member outcomes, and prioritizing the full journey. That's when real progress began. You may hear similar objections.

"This will create more silos, not fewer."

Actually, it breaks down the most harmful silos, specifically the ones that separate teams from the member experience. This structure realigns accountability around the journey, with shared metrics and natural collaboration points.

"We don't have enough people to split teams this way."

That's fine. The framework scales. One person can own multiple areas, if each function has clear goals and someone responsible for delivering results. Build into the model gradually as you grow.

"Our industry is different."

Maybe in execution, but not in structure. The member journey is universal. Whether you sell streaming content, wellness services, or financial products, the stages are the same. You can adapt the tactics, but the framework still applies.

"Restructuring is too disruptive right now."

 You don't need to restructure to get started. Assign ownership, align metrics, and build momentum. As the benefits become clear, org changes will follow naturally.

Part 4: Design as a Business Growth Driver

After looking through the roles above, you may wonder how Design fits into a journey-aligned membership organization. The reality is that design is too important to be treated as an afterthought or a separate "polish layer."

Design isn't just aesthetics—it's a growth engine. It shapes friction, comprehension, habit formation, and trust. That's why design must be embedded in the membership strategy and operating rhythm.

One way to ensure this is by making the Head of Design a first-class partner to membership leadership—whether they report into Product, Engineering, or a combined Product/Tech org—with explicit shared goals tied to the member journey.

The goal is a cohesive experience across acquisition, onboarding, engagement, and retention, with consistent patterns, consistent tone, and fewer "handoff scars" between teams.

The Brand Marketing Question: Strategic Integration vs. Dedicated Function

Brand marketing often oversees creative consistency, research, and advertising development. In a journey-aligned model, those responsibilities are distributed—but brand still needs a clear owner of "the story."

My recommendation for most membership businesses:

- Keep brand strategy tightly aligned with membership strategy
- Use agencies for major campaigns unless you operate at a scale that justifies a dedicated in-house brand org
- Ensure one internal leader owns the narrative and the standards

The goal isn't to shrink brand marketing—it's to prevent brand and membership from telling different stories.

Final Thoughts: The Journey to Organizational Excellence

A great membership business isn't defined by talent alone. It's defined by alignment—clear ownership, shared scoreboards, and a system that turns effort into outcomes across the full member journey.

You don't need perfection tomorrow. You need clarity today. Assign real owners. Measure what matters. Make tradeoffs quickly. Keep the member at the center of every decision.

Because companies that get this right become more resilient, more consistent, and harder to replicate. Their advantage lies in how the organization runs, not just what it offers.

In the next chapter, we'll make that operational: how to measure alignment, diagnose breakdowns, and build a reporting cadence that keeps the membership engine getting stronger over time.

Chapter 12

Building Accountability
Systems that Drive Results

Holding the Team Accountable

In the last chapter, we tackled how to structure a membership organization, including the roles and responsibilities that bring a growth strategy to life. But even the best structure won't succeed without a second critical ingredient: accountability.

When I say "accountability," I'm not just talking about performance reviews. I'm talking about the full system of metrics, reporting, and goals that keeps teams and employees aligned, focused, and moving in the right direction.

Too often, membership businesses fall into a familiar trap: they set bold targets for growth, revenue, or retention and then watch those numbers come up short, despite their best efforts. When results lag, teams scramble to react and assign blame. Then, they roll out quick fixes that rarely solve the underlying issue.

So, what's the real problem?

Most teams are tracking outcomes, but not the inputs that drive them. They're measuring what happened, but not what made it happen.

In this chapter, we'll break that cycle. You'll learn how to shift from output-focused thinking to input-focused accountability, by building systems that track the behaviors that lead to results. We'll walk through how to identify the right input metrics, validate them, and embed them into your team's operating rhythm. Because the real power of data isn't in reporting what happened, it's in shaping what happens next.

Part 1: The Input Metric Revolution - Measuring Causes, Not Effects

Most membership businesses track output metrics like total revenue, member count, and churn rate. These are essential, but on their own, they don't offer much guidance when things go wrong.

Imagine this: your monthly report shows that first-year retention just dropped by 3%. It's a red flag—but now what?

Is onboarding too confusing?
Are members disengaging with key features?
Are competitors offering more compelling pricing?
Did your acquisition channel shift?
Or is it something else entirely?

Without leading indicators, you're left guessing. Worse, retention is a lagging indicator. By the time you see a drop, the causes may be weeks or months old.

Input metrics fix that. They're controllable behaviors that predict outcomes. They turn "improve retention" into something operational: "move this behavior that we know drives retention."

One caution up front: input metrics can become vanity metrics if teams optimize them without validating that they truly improve the outcome. That's why correlation is only a starting point, not the finish line.

Input vs. Output Metrics: The Wellness Analogy

To make this even clearer, let's step outside business and talk about something familiar: trying to get healthier. Let's say your goal is to lose 10 pounds. That target is your output metric. You might weigh yourself daily, hoping for progress. Some days you're down a pound. Others, you're up two. It's frustrating. Was it last night's meal? A missed workout? Just a natural fluctuation?

That's why most health experts recommend focusing less on weight, and more on the inputs you can control, such as steps walked, hours slept, servings of vegetables eaten, minutes exercised. These are the behaviors that, when repeated consistently, lead to long-term progress. You focus on the process, and the results will follow

The same mindset applies to membership. You may want to increase your annual retention rate, but staring at that number won't move it. What will move it are the inputs such as: Onboarding email open rates, time to first benefit used, number of benefits used in the first 30 days, and more. These metrics are actionable. You can measure them, test improvements, and optimize them. And when you do, retention likely improves, just like weight comes down when your health habits align.

Case Study: Amazon and the Power of Input Metrics

At Amazon, input metrics weren't just part of the strategy, they were the strategy. On the Prime team, one of our key output metrics was Average Revenue Per Prime Member. But instead of setting a top-down goal and hoping for the best, leadership asked a smarter question: *What behaviors cause Prime members to spend more?*

So, we dug in. We analyzed billions of lines of behavioral data, searching for patterns and asking ourselves, what actions did high-spending members take more often? And specifically, which of these actions drove a step-change increase in spend? From there, we created a list identifying the most impactful actions. One of these actions was the adoption of Subscribe & Save. The logic was intuitive: by subscribing to recurring shipments of items like paper towels or toothpaste, members eliminated the need for an in-store trip. That behavior shifted spend from other retailers to Amazon, increasing Share of Wallet.

Once we knew this was a high-impact input, we could act. We partnered across Personalization, Prime Benefits, the Homepage team, and more to ask one focused question: *What are you doing to increase Subscribe & Save adoption?*

By aligning efforts around this behavior, and embedding it into weekly reporting, we created scalable, predictable growth. Not by chasing revenue directly, but by improving the behaviors that caused it.

Case Study: Netflix and the Rise of Proxy Metrics

Amazon isn't alone in this approach. At Netflix, they use a different term—proxy metrics—but the mindset is the same. Former VP of Product Gibson Biddle explains[15]:

"Lower-level metrics—proxy metrics—are easier and faster to move than high-level metrics. Ideally, moving a proxy will improve the high-level metric (e.g., retention), and later you can prove causation via A/B testing."

In practice, Netflix looked for early behaviors that signaled intent. Did a new member take a few actions that suggested they were likely to stick—like adding titles to **My List** and starting a show quickly?

---

[15] https://gibsonbiddle.medium.com/4-proxy-metrics-a82dd30ca810

When they measured those early "intent signals," they found a useful pattern: improving them tended to improve early retention. The exact thresholds and results shift over time, but the operating principle holds: identify a proxy that predicts retention, move it, then validate causality through experimentation.

That's the power of input metrics. They turn fuzzy goals like "grow revenue" or "reduce churn" into clear, controllable levers. And once you have those levers, you stop reacting to what has already happened—and start shaping what happens next.

Part 2: Creating Input Metrics

Understanding the value of input metrics is one thing, but identifying the right ones is where the real work begins. This process isn't about guesswork; it's a mix of smart data analysis, rigorous testing, and strategic prioritization.

Start with the Outcomes That Matter Most

First, clarify the handful of big outcomes that define success for your membership business. These are the results you ultimately want to influence, such as:

- Member growth
- Number of trial starts
- Annual retention rate
- Average revenue per member
- Benefit utilization

Build an Input-to-Output Metric Cascade

Now, begin structuring your findings into a hierarchy of influence. This framework links your most controllable behaviors to your most important business outcomes. For example:

OUTPUT METRIC: 12-Month Retention Rate

↑

INPUT METRIC: 30-Day Trial-to-Paid Conversion Rate

↑

INPUT METRIC: % of Members Who Use 3+ Benefits in Week 1

↑

INPUT METRIC: % of Members Who Use a Benefit in Their First Session

This kind of mapping clarifies where each team can focus today, and how those efforts roll up to long-term success

Find the Behaviors That Predict Success

Dive into your data. Look for behavioral patterns among your most successful members by asking: What did they do early on that others didn't? You might discover that:

- Members who reordered a grocery item twice in their first week are more likely to stick
- New users who watch 3+ shows within 14 days retain better
- Members who use three or more benefits in Week 1 are more likely to convert
- Same-day app download correlates with higher long-term engagement

The best input metrics are:

- **Measurable**: You can track it cleanly and consistently.
- **Actionable**: You can influence it through design, messaging, and nudges.
- **Predictive**: It's strongly tied to increased retention and member value.

One important note: these input metrics are designed to be binary, either the behavior happened or it didn't. This makes it easier to track the percentage of members who take that action, giving teams a clean, measurable target to aim for.

Here are a few examples:

- For a **streaming service**: watching 3+ pieces of content in the first 7 days.
- For a **meal kit**: placing a second order within two weeks.
- For a **fitness app**: syncing a wearable and completing one tracked workout.

There's no universal answer—and that's the point. Your job is to identify the *specific behavior that matters most* in *your* member journey. When you find it, that metric becomes the heartbeat of your early experience. It should shape your welcome emails, your onboarding flow, your success benchmarks—everything.

Validate With Real-World Testing

Don't assume your input metrics are impactful just because they correlate with success, make sure to test them.

Does increasing the percentage of members who engage three times in their first week lift retention? By how much? Which specific interventions moved that input metric?

Controlled experiments help you separate signal from noise and ensure your teams are focusing on inputs that truly drive outcomes. The key is validating causality, not just correlation[16]. Ask yourself: Is this action driving retention, or just a sign of an already-engaged user?

Create "North Star Input Metrics"

As your membership grows, each phase of the member journey will accumulate its own set of input metrics. That's great for operational depth, but across the company, it can quickly become overwhelming.

That's why you need to define 3–5 "North Star Input Metrics:" the handful of behaviors that most reliably move your core outcomes. These are the metrics that should be:

- Reviewed weekly
- Anchor team and org-level goal setting
- Inform product and marketing roadmaps
- Receive the highest visibility from senior leadership

Once you've found your North Star Metrics, you've unlocked a critical truth: *The purpose of evaluating the member journey isn't to show everything. It's to guide every member toward that one powerful action.*

Your messaging, your user experience, your nudges, your incentives—all of it should be designed to move members toward this moment of momentum. Nail this, and you'll not only improve retention—you'll transform onboarding from a checklist into a strategic growth lever.

---

[16] **Correlation vs. Causation:** Correlation indicates a relationship or pattern between two variables—when one changes, the other tends to change too. However, correlation does not imply causation. Causation means that one variable directly causes the other to change. In business and data analysis, mistaking correlation for causation can lead to false assumptions and flawed strategies.

In the next section, we'll dive into how to embed these metrics into your operating rhythm through dashboards, reporting cadences, and role-level accountability. But for now, the goal is clear: find the behaviors that move the needle and organize your teams around driving them intentionally and consistently.

Part 3: Turning Metrics into Momentum—Building Reporting That Drives Action

You can't track what you don't consistently measure, and in membership businesses, that means building reporting systems that track not just what happened, but why it happened.

Great dashboards aren't just collections of numbers; they're storytelling tools. They connect daily behaviors to long-term outcomes, and they make performance visible and actionable at every level, from the C-suite to individual contributors.

Building a Membership Dashboard That Drives Action

The most effective dashboards combine output metrics with input metrics. When done well, they paint a complete picture of your performance and give teams a clear sense of where to focus. A well-structured membership dashboard typically includes five core categories:

- **Acquisition Metrics:** Trial signups (by offer type and plan), landing page conversion rates, signup source mix, and both Gross and Net CAC across paid and organic channels.
- **Conversion Metrics:** Trial-to-paid conversion rates by plan type, funnel completion rates, and abandoned signup recovery performance.
- **Engagement Metrics:** First-day, first-week, and first-month engagement rates, benefit utilization, and feature adoption timelines.
- **Retention Metrics:** 30-day, 90-day, and 12-month retention rates, renewal rates by tenure, and cancellation reason code breakdowns.

- **Satisfaction Metrics:** NPS, CSAT (Customer Satisfaction Score), and qualitative member feedback.

If you're just getting started, don't wait for a polished analytics tool. A simple spreadsheet updated weekly is better than nothing. What matters most is making the data visible, consistent, and actionable.

Personally, I prefer dashboards in table format as they're clear, consolidated, and easy to scan. Others lean toward charts and graphs. The format doesn't matter nearly as much as the clarity, relevance, and operational usefulness of the data.

Designing Dashboards That Actually Get Used

To make your dashboard a true decision-making tool (not just a vanity report), apply these best practices:

- **Connect Inputs to Outputs:** Don't just list metrics, show how input metrics ladder up to the outcomes they influence. This gives context and reinforces ownership.
- **Use Visual Cues for Fast Insight:** Color coding (green, yellow, red), trend arrows, and progress bars help teams see where things are off-track at a glance.
- **Include Targets and Gaps:** Every metric should show current performance, the target, and % to goal, so everyone knows if they're winning or falling short.
- **Update Frequently:** Weekly updates are ideal for most membership businesses. Some metrics, such as trial starts or daily engagement may warrant daily refreshes.
- **Customize by Audience:** Executives need high-level snapshots. Functional teams need focused views of the metrics they own. ICs may need more granular breakdowns.
- **Document Everything:** Include metric definitions, calculation logic, data sources, and update frequency, directly in the dashboard. This keeps everyone aligned and prevents misinterpretation.
- **Ensure Organization-Wide Access:** Avoid information silos. Anyone who impacts a metric should have access to that data.

Choosing the Right Tools for Your Stage

You don't need a massive BI team to get started. Pick tools that match your current complexity. For smaller teams (under 50 employees), start simple with Looker Studio (formerly Google Data Studio): it's free, flexible, and plays nicely with spreadsheets and basic databases. As you scale into the 50–200 range, tools like Tableau or Power BI become worth it for more robust dashboards and governance. At enterprise scale (200+), the priority shifts to a dedicated data team and a warehouse-backed reporting layer—using platforms like Looker, Adobe Analytics, or custom dashboards built on top of your data infrastructure.

No matter the tool, remember this: dashboards don't create accountability; people do. The real power of reporting comes not from what's on the screen, but from the decisions, conversations, and habits that data enables.

Part 4: Turning Metrics into Action: Building an Accountability and Action System

Dashboards don't drive growth. Decisions do.

You can build the right structure, define the right metrics, and ship a beautiful reporting suite—then still stall if nobody owns the numbers and nothing changes week to week. The final step is turning insight into action through an accountability system that's simple enough to run even when things get busy.

Single-Threaded Ownership: One Metric, One Owner

One of the most effective practices I learned at Amazon was single-threaded ownership. The idea is simple: when something matters, it needs a single accountable owner—not a committee.

At Amazon, major programs like Prime Day or Subscribe & Save didn't sit in a recurring meeting with vague accountability. They had a dedicated leader with end-to-end responsibility.

I've adapted that same principle to input metrics. For every North Star input metric, assign one person whose primary responsibility is to move it. In practice, that owner:

- Monitors the metric weekly and calls out variances
- Analyzes patterns, runs experiments, and maintains a backlog of next tests
- Coordinates cross-functionally to remove friction and drive measurable change

One caution: don't assign these metrics to overloaded managers. The best owners are often experienced individual contributors—senior analysts, product managers, or marketers—who are close to the work and empowered to act. Functional leaders provide oversight and remove roadblocks. The Membership GM sets direction and resolves tradeoffs. The metric owner moves the numbers.

Prioritizing Work Without Drowning in Ideas

Once ownership is clear, the next problem is focus. Most teams don't suffer from a lack of ideas. They suffer from too many.

That's where a simple Action Priority Matrix earns its keep. Rank initiatives by **impact** and **effort**, then be ruthless about where you spend time:

- prioritize **high-impact, low-effort** work first
- plan **high-impact, high-effort** work deliberately
- deprioritize low-impact work, especially when it's high-effort

This is how you avoid busywork disguised as progress. You create a roadmap that aligns effort with real outcomes, not internal activity.

Bringing It All Together: Accountability Across the Org

When done right, this creates the connective tissue between strategy and execution.

- The **Membership GM** sets the vision and Flywheel priorities
- **Functional leaders** align resources and remove roadblocks
- **Metric owners** lead the weekly rhythm of learning and improvement

That structure creates a closed-loop system: strategy flows down into measurable execution, data flows back up to inform better strategy, and every team knows exactly how their work connects to membership growth. Accountability stops being an abstract idea and becomes a habit—one that compounds.

Part 5: Overcoming Implementation Challenges

While the benefits of input metrics are clear, implementing them across a membership organization isn't always easy. Below are the most common challenges, and how to overcome them.

Challenge 1: Identifying the Right Input Metrics

Many teams either choose too many metrics (diluting focus) or the wrong ones (wasting effort).

Solution: Start with a hypothesis. Select 3–5 likely input metrics using data analysis and industry benchmarks. Then run small experiments to validate impact before scaling. It's better to go deep on a few proven drivers than to spread your attention too thin.

Challenge 2: Data Accessibility and Quality

Organizations often lack the tools or systems to track key member behaviors.

Solution: Start with what you can measure now. Build a roadmap to improve over time and consider tools like a Customer Data Platform (CDP) to centralize and connect data across touchpoints. Even a spreadsheet is better than flying blind.

Challenge 3: Organizational Resistance

Teams used to chasing output metrics may view input metrics as micromanagement or question their validity.

Solution: Begin with education. Share case studies (like Amazon or Netflix) and run pilot programs to demonstrate impact. Show the flow from input to outcome, and highlight early wins to build trust and buy-in.

Challenge 4: Maintaining Focus Over Time

Even with initial success, teams may revert to output-only thinking, especially during crises or leadership changes.

Solution: Institutionalize input metrics through weekly reviews, dashboard rituals, and even performance incentives. Consider appointing the Chief of Staff to keep input metrics top of mind across functions.

Challenge 5: Matrixed Teams and Accountability

In large orgs, shared reporting lines can blur ownership and slow decision-making.

Solution: Use a RACI matrix (Responsible, Accountable, Consulted, Informed) for each key input metric. Make sure each one has a single, clearly defined "Accountable" owner, even if multiple teams contribute.

Challenge 6: Disconnected Acquisition and Retention Teams

When acquisition and retention run separately, quality suffers. Growth becomes a volume game.

Solution: Create shared metrics. For example, tie two teams to "90-day retention of new members." This ensures marketing attracts people likely to stay and incentivizes better long-term member fit. Shared metrics are better than no accountability at all.

Challenge 7: Evolving Technology and Member Behavior

As technology and effective marketing channels shift, some input metrics may lose relevance.

Solution: Hold quarterly "metric validation" sessions to reassess what's working. Be willing to adapt while keeping core behavioral drivers consistent.

Challenge 8: Input Metrics Don't Become Part of Culture

Without cultural buy-in, even the best systems fizzle out.

Solution: Leaders must walk the walk. Start every executive review with a metric review. Tie strategy decisions back to specific metrics. Celebrate the teams that move the numbers. Make input metrics part of how your company thinks.

Final Thoughts: Small Changes, Transformational Results

Membership growth comes from small, consistent impacts that are measured, tested, and refined over time. The best membership companies don't just track outcomes—they understand what drives them. They create visibility, embed ownership, and treat metric improvement as a core operating discipline. And instead of trying to measure everything, they go deep on the few things that matter most.

The shift from outcome obsession to input ownership doesn't happen overnight. But when it takes root, it builds systems that compound: small wins lead to bigger wins, and over time, those wins add up to durable growth.

As Jeff Bezos famously said:

> "All overnight success takes about 10 years."

When accountability becomes part of your operating rhythm, metrics stop being measurements and start becoming levers. That's how membership businesses scale—by design.

The winners aren't the ones with the loudest launches; they're the ones with the steadiest cadence: a few input metrics that matter, clear owners, visible performance, and weekly iteration.

Do this well, and you'll build a membership business that doesn't just grow but grows stronger with every cycle of improvement.

Chapter 13

The Rituals of High-Performing Membership Teams

From Meetings to Momentum: Structuring Reviews That Power Growth

What gets measured gets improved. But measurement alone isn't enough. What separates thriving membership organizations from stagnating ones is how they review, interpret, and act on what the data is telling them. In fast-moving teams, business reviews become the operating system: the cadence that creates focus, surfaces tradeoffs, and turns insight into decisions. Done well, these reviews aren't "meetings." They're moments of clarity—showing what's working, exposing what's broken, and triggering the actions that drive sustainable membership growth.

Yet, far too often, business reviews devolve into tedious exercises that drain energy instead of creating it. They become bloated reporting sessions filled with endless slides, vague discussions, and no clear decisions. The wrong people are in the room, the right insights get buried in spreadsheets, and instead of leaving with action items, people leave wondering why they were there in the first place. The most effective membership organizations take a structured, tiered approach to business reviews. They recognize that different review cadences serve different purposes. For example, a weekly review should look vastly different from a quarterly review because the needs of the business at different intervals are fundamentally different.

In this final chapter before the conclusion, we'll dissect the architecture of effective business reviews, showing how to create a rhythm that drives growth rather than hinders it.

The Three-Tiered Business Review System

I've watched membership businesses die slowly, one unnoticed metric at a time.

The pattern is always the same: smart people, good products, but no rhythm. No structured way to spot problems early, debate what matters, or make decisions that stick. Instead, there are endless Slack threads, reactive fire drills, and a nagging sense that everyone's working hard but nothing's getting better.

Then someone implements a real review system—and everything changes. Not because meetings solve problems, but because the right meetings create a foundation that makes progress possible. They force clarity where there was confusion, ownership where there was drift, and action where there was endless discussion.

At the heart of every high-performing membership business I've worked with is a three-tiered review rhythm: the Weekly Business Review (WBR), the Monthly Business Review (MBR), and the Quarterly Business Review (QBR). Together, they create an operating cadence that drives consistent growth. Let me show you how each one works, and more importantly, what breaks when they don't.

The Weekly Business Review (WBR): Tactical Execution & Rapid Adjustments

The Weekly Business Review isn't just another meeting. It's your early warning system.

I learned this lesson early in my career when I was taught a simple principle: the people presenting should be the people who built the numbers. Not the most senior person in the room who can spin a story, but the analyst or product manager who actually knows what's in the data and can answer the hard questions without deflection.

This matters more than you might think. When executives run weekly reviews, they create their own narrative. When the people closest to the data run them, you get truth—uncomfortable truth, sometimes, but truth nonetheless.

Here's what a dysfunctional WBR looks like: it drags on for two hours, senior leaders dominate the airtime, and everyone leaves unclear on what to do next. The meeting becomes a performance instead of a diagnosis. Problems get smoothed over, root causes go unexplored, and by the time something shows up as undeniable, it's too late to fix it easily.

A well-run WBR is different. It's a 45-60 minute tactical checkpoint designed to track key input metrics, spot early warning signs, keep execution teams aligned, and surface wins, blockers, and next steps. The people closest to the data lead it. Analysts, product managers, and marketers present what moved and why. This structure builds ownership, clarity, and speed.

I once worked with a company that launched a new marketing channel that seemed to be crushing it. Traffic was up, sign-ups were surging, and the marketing team was celebrating. But in the WBR, when we broke the data apart by acquisition channel, an analyst noticed something: the cohorts from this new channel had terrible Month 2 retention. The members weren't sticking around.

This insight only surfaced because we had the discipline to review the data weekly and because the person running the numbers was the one explaining them. If we'd waited for the monthly review, we would have spent another three weeks pouring money into a channel that was delivering low-quality members.

Here's how to structure an effective WBR:

- **Weekly Metrics Scorecard (10 minutes):** Review your core metrics against weekly goals and the four-week average. What's moving? What's not? No lengthy explanations yet—just the facts.

- **Wins & Bright Spots (5 minutes):** What's going well, and what can we learn from it? Too often, reviews focus exclusively on problems. Highlighting successes creates momentum and reveals transferable insights. If one team figured out how to improve onboarding completion by 8%, that's worth understanding and potentially replicating.

- **Challenges & Obstacles (10 minutes):** What underperformed, and what's the root cause? This isn't about placing blame—it's about getting to the truth quickly. The analyst who spotted the retention problem in our marketing channel didn't just say "retention is down." They came prepared with hypotheses: Was it the targeting? The messaging? The member experience post-signup?

- **Experiments & Tests (10 minutes):** What are we learning from A/B tests or new initiatives? What will we ship or change next week based on what we learned? This section creates accountability for continuous improvement.

- **Action Plan (10 minutes):** What are the next steps, and who owns each one? Every meeting should conclude with clear ownership of follow-up items. If it's not in the log, it didn't happen.

Who should attend: 10-15 people maximum. The functional head (Head of Retention, Head of Acquisition), analysts who can explain the data, and cross-functional partners when relevant.

Format considerations: Some companies send information out 48 hours before the meeting. Others follow Amazon's approach and review the data silently at the start of the meeting. Some use presentations, others use narrative documents. There's no single right answer, but here's what matters: set clear expectations and hold people to them. If you use a pre-read, enforce one of two norms: everyone reads in advance, or the first 5-10 minutes are silent reading before discussion begins.

Pro tip: Maintain a running "Decisions and Actions Log" for each WBR. At the start of every meeting, review what was supposed to have happened since last week. Did it? If not, why not? This simple practice eliminates the most common failure mode of reviews: lots of talk, no follow-through.

The Monthly Business Review (MBR): Strategic Insights & Course Correction

If the WBR is your early warning system, the MBR is where you decide what to do about it.

The most common way MBRs fail is by becoming just bigger WBRs—more people, more data, same tactical focus. When that happens, you end up with senior executives listening to status updates for 90 minutes. Everyone leaves exhausted and nothing changes.

A good MBR is different. It's insight-driven, not data-heavy.

Here's what I mean: in a data-heavy MBR, attendees are doing math in real-time, trying to figure out what the numbers mean while someone clicks through slides. In an insight-driven MBR, the team has already done that work. The presentation leads with the answer: "Retention in our Premium tier dropped 4 points this month. Here's why it happened, here's what we're seeing in the cohort data, and here's what we're doing about it."

Going back to that marketing channel example: by the time we got to the MBR, we weren't still debating whether there was a problem. The WBR had established that. At the MBR, we addressed what we were doing about it. In the short term, we pulled budget from that channel. But we also talked about the longer-term fix: working with the marketing partner to share more data so we could target more effectively. The MBR is where we made that strategic call and aligned cross-functional teams on the path forward.

The Membership GM typically leads this meeting, and instead of looking at weekly fluctuations, the focus is on monthly trends. What's changing? Why? What do we need to do about it?

Each functional head should come prepared with a one-page summary of their area's performance, key insights (not just data points), and specific recommendations or decision requests. The goal isn't to present everything they know—it's to present what leadership needs to know and decide.

Here's how to structure an effective MBR:

- **Monthly Metrics Scorecard (15 minutes):** Review key monthly metrics against goals and the four-month average. This should be quick—everyone's already seen the numbers.

- **Breakdown by Business Area (20 minutes):** How is each vertical team performing? Each functional head reports on their area, but remember: insights, not status updates. "Acquisition is at 95% of goal" is a status update. "Acquisition is at 95% of goal because our iOS conversion rate dropped, and here's what we learned when we dug into the user experience" is an insight.

- **Experiments & Strategic Initiatives (20 minutes):** What tests have we run, what have we learned, and what's next? This creates accountability for innovation and continuous improvement. It also prevents the trap of endless experimentation without ever acting on what you've learned.

- **Major Risks & Roadblocks (15 minutes):** What's preventing growth, and what help is needed? This is where cross-functional issues get surfaced and addressed. Maybe the retention team needs engineering resources. Maybe the pricing team needs legal input on a new tier structure. The MBR is where those blockers get resolved.

- **Recommendations & Decisions Needed (10 minutes):** Where do we need leadership input? This ensures the meeting drives concrete action, not just discussion. Come with specific asks: "We want to invest $500K in this channel next quarter. Here's the business case. Decision needed by Friday."

Who should attend: The Membership GM, all functional heads, key analysts, and senior cross-functional partners.

Duration: 90 minutes is typical, though some companies extend to two hours if there's a major strategic topic that needs deeper discussion.

When done well, the MBR doesn't contradict weekly insights—it contextualizes them within the broader business strategy. It also acts as an escalation layer: WBR teams surface problems early, MBR leadership removes structural blockers.

The Quarterly Business Review (QBR): Executive-Level Strategy & Long-Term Vision

Unlike the WBR and MBR, which focus on what's happening now, the QBR looks ahead to the next six to twelve months.

This is the CEO's primary touchpoint with the membership team. This is where big bets get made. The discussion centers on whether the membership business is healthy, what major opportunities and risks are emerging, where to invest for long-term growth, and which strategic shifts deserve consideration.

The failure pattern in QBRs is predictable: executives multitask, half-listening while checking email. I've seen it more times than I'd like to admit, and it's always a warning sign. The team presents, but there's no real engagement— no sharp questions, no pushback, no new thinking. The meeting becomes ceremony instead of substance.

What makes a QBR matter is authenticity, openness, and ownership. The membership team walks in owning the results—the good and the bad—and brings clear thinking on what's happening, what's changing, and what they recommend doing next. The CEO and executive team bring fresh perspective, challenge assumptions, and ask the questions that only someone with distance from the day-to-day can ask.

To bring this to life, take the marketing channel example again. By the time we reached the QBR, we weren't debating whether to pull budget or tweak targeting. We were debating whether to prioritize a product build that would dynamically adjust onboarding based on acquisition source. The question for the CEO wasn't "Should we fix this channel?" It was "Is this important enough to the business that we should shift engineering resources toward it?"

That's where QBRs should live: at the level of tradeoffs, priorities, and decisions.

Here's how to structure an effective QBR:

- **State of the Membership Business (20 minutes):** Overall performance trends, competitive landscape, and market positioning. This is the big picture: Are we winning? Where are we vulnerable? What's changed in the market?
- **Deep Dives on Key Growth Levers (40 minutes):** Where are we seeing traction, and where are we not? This should include both successes to double down on and challenges that require strategic shifts. Come with business cases, not just problems.
- **Macro & Industry Trends (15 minutes):** External factors affecting the business—competitor moves, regulatory changes, shifting consumer behaviors. The membership team lives in the details; the QBR is where you zoom out and make sure you're not missing the forest for the trees.
- **Key Investments & Strategic Priorities (30 minutes):** Where are we placing bets for the coming quarter and beyond? This includes resource requests, major initiatives, and expected outcomes. Be specific about what you're asking for and what you expect to achieve.
- **Critical Roadblocks & Executive Decisions Needed (15 minutes):** What must leadership resolve to enable growth? This is the escalation point for issues that only the CEO can solve.

Who should attend: The CEO, the Membership GM and all functional heads, and other C-suite executives (CTO, CFO, etc.). Some companies keep a small invite list; others let the entire team listen in. What matters most is that afterward, everyone on the membership team understands what was discussed, the decisions made, and the direction of the program.

Duration: Two to three hours, and it requires substantial preparation. Don't go into a QBR without a tight narrative and clear asks.

Pro tip: End every QBR with a written summary titled "What changed because of this QBR?" If the answer is nothing, you're doing it wrong.

Pulling It All Together: The Compound Effect of Operating Rhythm

These reviews aren't just meetings. They're the heartbeat of your membership business. And the magic happens when all three layers work together.

This is the compound effect of operating rhythm. When you catch signals early in the WBR, you don't spend the MBR in crisis mode. When your MBRs are focused on strategy and course correction, your QBRs can actually focus on vision and long-term bets instead of rehashing issues that should have been solved weeks ago.

I've seen companies transform when they implement this system properly. Not because the meetings solve all their problems, but because the meetings create a foundation that makes solving problems possible.

Here's what that foundation looks like:

- **Weekly reviews keep you sharp and fast.** Problems get caught early, when they're easiest to fix.
- **Monthly reviews create focus and course-correct.** Leadership removes blockers and aligns the organization on what matters most.
- **Quarterly reviews drive long-term strategy and investment.** The executive team can actually think six to twelve months out because they're not constantly fighting tactical fires.

How to Implement This System

If your company has nothing right now, don't try to build all three at once. Start with a weekly review, even if it's just a few people looking at the key metrics together. Get into the habit of diving into the data. Get comfortable with the discipline of showing up every week, prepared, with answers.

Once you've built that muscle, add the monthly layer. Ask someone to prepare a presentation laying out the story of what's happening, why it's happening, and what's being done to improve things. Make it insight-driven from the start—no one should be doing math in real-time.

Then, when both of those rhythms are solid, add the quarterly review. By that point, you'll have months of data, clear trends, and a team that knows how to present with clarity and conviction.

Should every company do all three? Yes. Even if you're small, even if it feels like overkill, the structured approach creates a habit that will serve you as you scale. The discipline of weekly reviews, the strategic thinking of monthly reviews, and the long-term vision of quarterly reviews—that's the operating system that high-growth membership businesses run on.

The Foundation: Making Every Meeting Count

The three-tiered review system only works if you get the basics right. Before you implement WBRs, MBRs, and QBRs, audit your meeting culture. Too many organizations drown in status updates disguised as strategy sessions, discussions that should be emails, and "just in case" attendees who never speak. Here's the minimum bar every meeting must clear:

- **Clear ownership.** One person owns the agenda and drives to a decision. One person captures actions and owners. If no one leaves with a task, the meeting shouldn't have happened.

- **Ruthless curation.** If someone can't contribute or doesn't need to decide, they shouldn't be there. Meetings multiply through inertia, not intention. Start from zero and justify each recurring meeting based on value delivered, not tradition.
- **The right format.** Use dashboards for operational metrics (your WBR), decks for storytelling and context (your MBR), and narrative documents for high-stakes decisions (your QBR). Don't make teams waste energy on formatting when they should be thinking.

One final note for distributed teams: if even one person is remote, ideally everyone joins individually via video. Hybrid meetings fail when office attendees create insider dynamics that exclude remote participants. The review system works anywhere, but only if you design for equal participation from day one.

The Biggest Mistakes (and How to Avoid Them)

I've seen companies try to implement this system and fail. Here's what usually goes wrong:

Unclear expectations for the meeting. If people don't know whether they're supposed to pre-read or show up cold, if they don't know whether they're presenting or discussing, if they don't know what decisions are on the table—the meeting will be chaos. Set clear norms and enforce them.

Lack of preparation. These meetings must be data-driven. If the numbers aren't ready, if people are scrambling to pull reports during the meeting, you've already lost. Build the discipline of having materials ready 48 hours in advance.

No note-taker and no follow-up. This is the most common failure mode. Great discussion, good ideas, but nothing happens afterward because no one captured what was decided or who owns what. Assign a note-taker. Maintain a decisions log. Start every meeting by reviewing what was supposed to happen since last time.

Letting meetings become performance theater. When people start presenting to impress rather than presenting to inform, you've lost the plot. The goal is clarity and action, not applause. Create a culture where it's safe to surface problems, admit uncertainty, and ask for help.

Using the wrong layer for the wrong discussion. Don't debate three-year strategy in the WBR. Don't review weekly fluctuations in the QBR. Each layer has a purpose—use it accordingly.

The key is consistency and clarity. Use each layer of the system for what it's designed to do. And never let meetings become reporting for reporting's sake. Make them moments of clarity, alignment, and decision-making.

When you get this right, these meetings stop feeling like obligations and start feeling like the engine that drives everything else. They become the place where your team gets smarter, faster, and more aligned. They become the reason you spot opportunities before your competitors do and fix problems before they become crises.

That's the power of rhythm. And that's what separates membership businesses that drift from those that dominate.

Final Thoughts: Turning Conversations into Momentum

The best membership businesses don't just run meetings—they run systems that turn conversations into action and action into momentum.

Weekly Business Reviews keep your execution tight.

Monthly Reviews make sure you're solving the right problems and prioritizing the right bets.

Quarterly Reviews align everyone on where you're headed and what bold moves will get you there.

But the real magic is what happens in between. Because great reviews don't exist in isolation, they set the pace for your entire operating rhythm. They make sure every metric you track, every experiment you run, every decision you make pushes your business forward, faster.

If you do this well, your meetings won't feel like status updates. They'll feel like inflection points. Moments of clarity where silos fall away, decisions get made, and everyone walks out knowing exactly what happens next.

So, protect that discipline:

- Cut the noise. Kill the meetings that waste time.
- Keep the ones that create insight and action.
- Hold every participant accountable—if you're in the room, you're there to move the business.

Meetings are where strategy meets execution. Structure them right, and you'll never mistake motion for momentum again.

Do this consistently, and you won't just hold better meetings.

You'll build a membership business that hums with alignment, speed, and trust.

Conclusion:

From Flywheel to Force of Nature

Your Move

If there's a single thread running through this book, it's this: membership isn't a pricing tactic. It's a living system, an operating model that earns trust in small, compounding moments. You don't "launch" a great membership and walk away; you steward it.

Every chapter has pointed at the same truth from a different angle: when you align a clear promise, a clean path to first value, and a cadence of listening and improving, growth stops feeling like a treadmill and starts feeling like lift.

I've seen this from multiple seats: carrying a P&L, tuning funnels, building cross-functional teams, and standing in front of leaders who only care whether the inputs you've chosen drive the outcomes you've promised. The patterns don't change across industries as much as you might think. The labels shift: content, classes, credits, deliveries. But the human psychology underneath is remarkably consistent. People pay for whatever gives them time, agency, or identity back. Membership works when you consistently hand those back faster than alternatives.

What We Built Together (In Plain English)

A lens, not a list of hacks. You now have language for the difference between subscription (access) and membership (belonging). That mindset shift changes how you prioritize, price, and measure.

A map of the journey. The **Membership Flywheel™** gave you nine interlocking stages and showed how weak links anywhere create drag everywhere.

A way to tell if it's working. We reframed "data" from lagging outputs to leading inputs—owned, reviewed weekly, and tied to decisions.

A method for learning faster than rivals. We built competitive intelligence into a weekly habit (not a once-a-year exercise) so you can ethically borrow proven patterns and adapt them to your brand and economics.

A stance toward AI that's useful. We framed AI as a multiplier for personalization, analysis, and experimentation—not the strategy, but what makes good strategy compound faster.

Most importantly, we've hammered the idea that *the member experience is the product.* If it doesn't show up in the first week, it effectively doesn't exist. If your team can't measure it, it can't improve. If your members don't feel it, they won't pay for it.

Five Non-Negotiables to Take with You

1. **Acquisition ≠ growth.** You can buy signups; you can't buy habits. Acquire the right people with the right promise and your retention math starts working for you.

2. **Time-to-First-Value is the kingmaker.** Show unmistakable value in the first session and first week. If you don't, every other lever gets expensive.

3. **Behavior is your truth.** Surveys guide; behavior decides. Instrument real behaviors (uses, repeats, completions, depth) and let those signals set your roadmap.

4. **Builders beat presenters.** Reward the people who move a key behavior by 5–10% this quarter. Talk is cheap. Compounding isn't.

5. **Make leaving easy but coming back even easier.** Paradoxically, flexible, honorable exits increase trust—and winback. Trust is a moat. Contracts rarely are.

Turning Planning into Execution: Your 90-Day Practical Operating Plan

What to Do on Monday (Yes, Literally)

1. **Print the Membership Flywheel™ diagram.** Tape it to the wall in your team room. In the next team meeting, have every person mark the one stage they think is your biggest weakness right now. Wherever the dots cluster, that's your starting point.

2. **Start mapping your full member journey.** From the first touch to cancellation, create a visual representation using screenshots, recordings, or transcripts. Identify the top three friction points where intent dies.

3. **Create a review cycle.** Schedule Weekly/Monthly/Quarterly Business Reviews that ensure continued accountability and progress.

Days 1–30: Build clarity and strategic direction

Strategy. Meet with your team and deep dive on the following questions:

- **Value Prop & Segmentation:** Who are your core member segments, and which drive the most LTV? What is the "no-brainer" promise for each segment in one sentence?
- **Pricing & Offers:** How do you balance quantity of signups vs. quality of retained members? Does your offer and plan strategy change by cohort? What's your monthly vs. annual plan mix?

Action. Launch a weekly competitive walk. Each week, one person completes and records one competitor's join-to-cancel journey, then shares a quick debrief with the team. By Day 90, you'll have a library of patterns your rivals haven't noticed themselves.

Days 31–60: Create structure and start cadence of action

Strategy. Create the right team structure, being prepared to answer the following:

- **Accountability:** Who owns the Flywheel end-to-end at the executive level? Who owns each stage, and what decisions can they make without escalation?
- **Team & Culture:** Does every team member know the primary goals and the tradeoffs for the quarter? Do they know what success looks like for the business and for themselves individually?

Action. Launch a first-pass dashboard—even if it's manual. Lead with input metrics and named owners, then show output metrics with context underneath. Make it company-visible. Ship two friction fixes from your audit, measure the lift, and use the results to set next month's priorities.

Days 61–90: Codify the rhythm

Strategy. Run your first retention retrospective and convert the last 90 days into a decision log: what worked, what didn't, what to repeat, and what to stop. Assign owners and deadlines. Follow with a churn deep dive: top cancel reasons (by volume and revenue impact), churn split (voluntary vs. involuntary), churn by acquisition source, and a clear plan to reduce involuntary churn.

Action. Publish the member dashboard (even if partly manual) and set an automation roadmap. Launch a focused winback campaign anchored on "what's new" with an easy return path. Share cohort retention insights with marketing partners to improve acquisition quality.

From Plan to Power: Closing the Loop

If you actually run this 90-day plan—not just draft slides or nod in meetings, but *do the work*—you'll feel the business tilt in your favor.

Not because any one tactic is magic, but because focused inputs create focused outcomes. Clarity fuels execution. What gets measured gets improved—and what gets improved compounds.

Most companies will skim this and move on. Some will start strong and stall by Day 45. A rare few will finish all 90 days—and wish they'd started sooner.

I think back to that desert labyrinth—where every dead end turned out to be a turn. The path was always there. You just have to walk it.

You've got the map.
You have the language.
You know the first moves to make on Monday.

Now go build it.

Epilogue:
The People Behind the Flywheel

If there's one truth that ties it all together—one that turns good membership businesses into great ones—it's this: **People build the flywheel. Culture makes it spin.**

For years I thought "Culture eats strategy for breakfast" was a cliché. Then I spent two decades leading membership teams and saw it proven repeatedly.

You can have the best roadmap in the world, but if the team building it doesn't trust each other, challenge each other, and feel safe to share their best ideas, it won't matter.

So how do you get there?

I'm not a leadership expert, but I've worked at some of the most respected companies, under both incredible leaders and terrible managers. I took notes in every room—on what I'd copy and what I'd never repeat.

This is the list I'd use if I were building a team tomorrow:

1. Start with a Clear, Inspiring Vision—but Stay Flexible

Every great team needs direction. It starts with leadership that can articulate a bold, ambitious path forward—not just quarterly goals, but a larger purpose everyone can connect to.

This means obsessing about the strategy from the start but also being aware and present enough to pivot when needed. That's because great leaders don't confuse conviction with rigidity. They invite feedback, revisit decisions, and adjust when the data or team insight shows a better way. They always remember that flexibility isn't weakness, it's how you stay aligned with reality.

2. Surround the Vision with Doers

A great strategy means nothing without people who can bring it to life. The best membership teams are filled with people who run through walls to reach goals—but they also know which walls matter. It's not just about effort; it's about judgment. Balance your team with a range of mindsets: operators, creatives, analysts, skeptics. That diversity sharpens your decision-making and reduces blind spots. Execution thrives when doers are paired with challengers.

3. Hire for Potential, Not Just Pedigree

Membership is inherently cross-functional. It lives at the intersection of product, marketing, analytics, and service. That's why your team needs connectors. People who don't just execute tasks but *see how the system fits together*. Hire curious thinkers with a bias for action. Give them space, and they'll often outperform the polished experts. When you do hire, hire the best. There was a recruiting term at Amazon called "raising the bar". It means that every new hire, promotion, or project owner should be better than the average person currently in that role. It's a commitment to continuous improvement—not just maintaining quality but actively increasing it over time. Take that same mentality into every hire in your organization and you'll build a world-class team.

4. Make Trust the Default—Not the Reward

Challenging the status quo is *hard,* especially when it may be challenging someone more senior than yourself. The only way this happens is when the environment is safe enough to handle it. The strongest cultures normalize disagreement—not by softening it, but by making it safe. When trust is the default, people feel free to question ideas, poke holes in plans, and offer dissenting views without fear of being dismissed or penalized. Disagreements need to be solved directly, and managers need to get their hands dirty in fixing situations when they do arise.

5. Normalize Constructive Challenge

The best membership strategies don't come from echo chambers where everyone nods along with the most senior voice. They come from a culture where ideas are pressure-tested, even across employee levels. That tension—when rooted in respect—drives better decisions. Encourage your team to ask hard questions early. If the idea doesn't hold up inside the room, it won't hold up out in the wild with your members. Challenge isn't personal—it's how strong teams protect each other from launching weak initiatives.

6. Give Specific, Actionable Feedback—and Expect It Back

Feedback cultures make or break performance. Vague comments like "this could be better" help no one. Instead, give specific, actionable direction: "This analysis is missing key variables," or "Start with slide 14—that's your hook." At Amazon, this level of precision was standard—and sometimes harsh. At first, it was intimidating. Over time, I realized it was one of the most powerful growth accelerators I'd ever experienced. But remember: feedback is a two-way street. Build a structure that allows it to flow up, down, and sideways. Carve out time for peer reviews. Do structured 360s. And just as importantly: celebrate the wins. Feedback shouldn't just correct—it should reinforce what excellence looks like.

7. Practice Active Validation

This one's deceptively simple, but transformative. Before you critique or counter someone's idea, reflect it back to them first. *"What I'm hearing is…"* or *"So you're saying the risk is…"*

You don't have to agree—but validating someone's thinking signals that you're listening. And when people feel heard, they're far more willing to engage, iterate, and contribute. Some of your best insights will come from the quietest voices in the room—the engineer, the analyst, the customer support rep. Make sure you're building systems to hear them.

8. Celebrate Learning as Much as Winning

In membership, failure isn't failure—it's data. The test that didn't move retention may be more valuable than the one that did *if* it tells you what not to waste time on next. Encourage teams to document learnings—especially from failed experiments. When those lessons are available for the next hire or next sprint, they compound over time. That's how you build a *flywheel of learning*—where each turn makes the machine smarter, faster, and more precise.

9. Respect the Chain of Accountability

Creativity and collaboration matter. But every membership team needs clarity on who's making the call. You can't stay in brainstorm mode forever. Once decisions are made, alignment becomes your superpower. The best teams I've worked on drew a clear line between the ideation phase and the execution phase. Once a strategy is locked, everyone rallies around it—even if their idea didn't win. That's how you balance freedom of thought with focus of action.

Final Thoughts: The Human Element of Membership Success

At the end of the day, membership growth isn't just about data, strategy, or execution. It's about people—both the members you serve and the team creating the experience. And in a membership business, culture isn't a perk. It's the product. It's the operating system that determines how fast you move, how well you solve problems, how much value you create—and how long the best people stick around.

If you set up the right team, create space for fresh ideas, encourage open debate, and focus on real feedback, your membership business won't just grow, it will thrive in ways that transcend metrics and spreadsheets.

You now have the framework, the tools, and the mindset to build something exceptional. Adapt them to your context and remember: the most powerful force in your organization isn't your plan—it's the people working together in service of your members.

The playbook is your vehicle. Culture is the engine. And the road ahead is shaped by the members whose lives you transform.

The rest is yours to write.